Also available at all good book stores

9781785316272

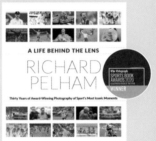

9781785315466

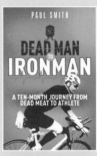

9781785316173

9781785316289

9781785316197

9781785316821

9781785317248

9781785315619

9781785314315

Drop in!
Billy Morgan

Drop in!
Billy Morgan
a snowboarding life

with Mark Turley

First published by Pitch Publishing, 2021

Pitch Publishing
A2 Yeoman Gate
Yeoman Way
Worthing
Sussex
BN13 3QZ
www.pitchpublishing.co.uk
info@pitchpublishing.co.uk

A CIP catalogue record is available for this book
from the British Library.

ISBN 978 1 78531 542 8

Typesetting and origination by Pitch Publishing
Printed and bound in India by Replika Press Pvt. Ltd.

Contents

Acknowledgements 7

Introduction. 9

Part One: Imposter Syndrome and How to Overcome It

1. Pyeongchang, South Korea, 24 February 2018 13
2. Art or Sport? 20
3. Going with the Flow 25

Part Two: A Kid from the Coast

4. Boys Like Billy 31
5. Mad Eddie and 'Risk'. 36
6. Square Pegs, Round Holes 44
7. Kickflips and Battling for Azeroth 49
8. All Change 59
9. Death Mesh. 66
10. A Taste of the Alps 76
11. The Morzine Scene 87
12. Ouch!. 95
13. Ridin' for the Man 103
14. Billy the Kid 112
15. A Team Game? 121

Part Three: Raising the Stakes

16. Snowboardin' USA 131
17. Fame and Hate 138
18. YOLO? 146
19. Big Win? Big Celebration 155
20. The Complexities of Success 160

21. Living with Injury 170

22. A Miracle Down Under. 177

Part Four: The Really, Really Big Stuff

23. The High Life 185

24. Huck It!. 192

25. A Gymnast on a Board 202

26. Redefining 'Possible' 212

27. How I Killed Style and Ruined Snowboarding 220

28. Post-Quad Life 227

29. Back on the Grind 232

30. Brains and Knees 239

31. Heart and Seoul. 250

32. Cometh the Hour 258

Part Five: And Then?

33. The Plan to Have No Plan 273

34. Where Will Snowboarding Go?. 278

Billy Morgan Career Highlights. 283

Acknowledgements

THIS IS one of those occasions where words are not really enough, but this is a book, so they will have to do.

First and foremost, I have to thank my family. My dad, Eddie, my mum, Joanne, my brother Ashley, my grandma, Shirley, and my grandad, Terry (RIP). They supported me from childhood, helping me to achieve things I wasn't even aiming for at the beginning. In truth, I was never a kid with a clear career path or much life focus, so I'm sure at times they worried about me and where I was heading. Despite that, they understood the raw materials I was made from and never tried to force me into a direction that didn't suit me.

My snowboarding career wouldn't have reached the levels it did or have been as relentlessly enjoyable without the input of many important people. Lack of space means I can't name them all, but the following key players were all incredibly important to me in different ways:

Hamish McKnight, my coach. Not only is Hamish an incredible snowboard (and life) mentor, but also a great friend. He supported me through some tough times and exceeded his role as a coach from start to finish.

Local legend, Steve Fox, was there from my early days on the dry slope. Without Steve I would have never been exposed to the

7

snowboard scene. He dedicated loads of time to taking me and other youngsters around the country for different activities. He did this for free and only wanted the 'stoke' in return.

Luke Paul showed me a new side of snowboarding. He introduced me to Morzine and a huge friendship circle. This meant I arrived in a new part of the world and was immediately comfortable.

Scott Penman is one of those people who makes others feel good. From when we first met way back at The Brits, we've been great friends. His charisma, alongside his incredible ability to make fun things even more fun, made my career so enjoyable. With guys like Scott around, things never got too serious.

Last but not least, GB assistant coach Jack Shackleton has to be mentioned. Being on the road most of the time can be tough for many reasons. Jack was always there for me through thick and thin and whatever I needed him for – someone to moan to, a shoulder to cry on, a drinking buddy. Thanks, Jack.

I also have to give a shout out to Mike Hurd, the manager of Southampton Alpine Centre where I started; my acro coaches, Pat and Mike Wakefield; my fantastic girlfriend, Samantha France; my agent and friend, Adam Phillips; and, of course, all the guys at Red Bull, who have done so much to support me.

My love and respect to you all.

Introduction

SUCCESS BRINGS different things to different people. My Olympic medal, which made me the first British male to win an Olympic medal on snow, means snowboarding, as a sport in the UK context, is now permanently attached to my name. In some ways I'm thought of as an ambassador or even a pioneer, which is crazy, as well as being a huge honour.

Now that my competitive career is over and I'm able to look back and reflect, the whole thing seems incredibly quick. It only feels like a couple of years elapsed between me riding ramps at the local dry slope and standing on the Olympic podium. Yet so much happened in the decade between those two points that the process becomes difficult to rationalise. On the one hand, I was just doing something I loved, having fun. On the other, like the rest of the UK crew, I spent a decade pushing limits and making radical gains.

Obviously, snowsports down the years have been dominated by a relatively select group of nations. It's a field in which natural factors such as climate and topography have a huge impact. Countries with lots of snow and mountains tend to be the ones that excel. That's just the way it is.

The fact that the UK has made such huge strides in recent years, with athletes such as myself, Jenny Jones, Woodsy Woods and others achieving success on the international stage is testament to the fantastic national strategy that has been developed. The UK has no right to be achieving any of this and no prior track record in doing so.

In that way, my successes are not mine alone. They belong to those who helped and cultivated me. And that makes them all the more sweet.

Part One

IMPOSTER SYNDROME AND HOW TO OVERCOME IT

'It's not what you are that holds you back, it's what you think you are not.'

– Dennis Waitley

1.

Pyeongchang, South Korea, 24 February 2018

THERE'S NOTHING like being up in the mountains … nothing. You breathe and everything evaporates, just dissolves away like salts in the bath. All around you, a panoramic vista of the purest, pure white. There's no white like it, anywhere, while the air teases your nostrils with precipitation, pine and wild herbs. That smell jolts me out of wherever my head was and plants me *bang* in the moment. After that, I'm on it.

Buzzing.

High on white.

Sounds beautiful, right? That's the true winter sports vibe, what the purists live for. Long days absorbed in immersive, rich environments of natural beauty, time and routine disappearing. But here's the reality crash: in truth, professional competitions are mostly nothing like that romantic ideal, especially big competitions and especially my main event, known as 'big air'. Big air just needs a ramp and some snow, which could be artificial, or even brought in from somewhere. That means wherever you can construct a ramp, you can have a comp. I've done my thing before crowds in London, Los Angeles, Beijing and many other places where there are no mountains (or natural snow) for miles.

The South Korean Winter Olympic venue was set in the Taebaek mountain range, but inside a fishbowl stadium, with the snowboard big air and the ski jump competitions facing one another from either end. When you were up there, getting yourself together, it wasn't white and alpine and immersive. Not at all. It was concrete and cables and car parks. People rushed here and there with clipboards.

That part of South Korea, known as Gangwon Province, has an average of two feet of snow a year, so all the stuff in the snowsports arena was fake. The big day was actually a warmish one too, mild enough for me to wear only a T-shirt and a hoodie as I waited. Petrol fumes lingered in the air, mixed with the rainy, sludgy scent of snowmelt and the murmur of a few thousand voices. I sat inside the gazebo the organisers set up as a waiting area, took a few deep breaths and tried to get into the right headspace.

Near me sat Seb Toutant in Canadian red, with his highly rated countryman Max Parrot. Seb's cool, all smiles, but Max is harder to read, a serious pro. He keeps himself to himself. Kyle Mack was on the other side, chatting with his coach. Mack's a rarity, an American who manages to be genuine and one of the cool kids. That's not an easy combination to pull off. Near him was Michael Schärer from Switzerland and the Kiwi, Carlos Knight, a young, technical and stylish rider with infectious enthusiasm, having the absolute time of his life. Then there was the regular slew of Swiss and Scandinavians, pure naturals, the type who look like they were born on a mountain and never left. All the best riders in the world, basically.

Yeah, I remember thinking. *This line-up is stacked. The action's gonna be savage.* And then it properly hit me, like really, really hit me. *Shit, this is the Olympic final.*

We were all trying to act casual, despite the calculation and self-talk occurring inside. Snowboarders are like that, a cultural thing. *Whatever dude ...* But people misread it, that attitude. What we do can never be half-hearted. Each of us has an acute understanding of what can happen.

Pretty soon I knew I would take my turn, careen downhill then take off from a 49-metre ramp arching up at an angle of 40 degrees. It's common to achieve speeds of up to 50–60mph while doing so. Most people don't experience that outside of their car.

Sometimes, depending on weather, you stand at the top of the run and can't even see the bottom. You're flying blind, hurtling down into fog with nothing other than adrenaline, cortisone and whatever else your endocrine system can muster. *It's okay,* your inner voice says. *Don't sweat it. You'll see the ramp when you get there.*

Fortune favours the brave, right?

Right?

After that, 'whoosh', you're airborne for two or three seconds, which is the weirdest combination of total presence and complete absence you can imagine. You're so in the moment that the moment disappears. All there is at that time is you, the sky and the ground below. It's peace and danger and excitement and calmness – everything and nothing. Ski jumpers, sky divers and the rest will know this feeling too, but it's the closest thing to being born or dying you can experience. It's like staring the universe in the eye. If I could choose one moment and make it last forever, that would be it. Total focus. Total absorption.

The sky is my zen place.

The difference for us – me and other big air athletes – is that we don't glide and go for distance or wait for the right moment to ping off a parachute. While jumping we perform as intricate and difficult a combination of tricks as we can manage. We twist, turn, switch, roll, somersault, flip, rotate and grab, before attempting to land on a deceptively hard surface. Most think snow is fluffy and soft. But up in the mountains it freezes, gets compacted. You may as well be jumping on to concrete. Get it wrong, which we all do often, and you can review your performance in hospital rather than in the bar.

That's our spectre at the window. The ghost that haunts us. The chance of serious, life-changing injury hangs over every event like a thundercloud. We can never escape it. It's part of the deal we make with fate and, while I want to win, I really don't want my mates (competitors) to get hurt. By all means fall, screw it up, get a terrible score, but please don't go and wreck yourself.

Please.

In the outside world, away from our snowsports bubble, boxing, martial arts, gridiron or rugby injuries get a ton of media hype. Those guys take massive hits on a regular basis, but while, in recent years, combat or heavy contact sports have sought means to become safer, investigating dangers and how to limit them, the reverse is true for us. Snowboarding's development is all about pushing boundaries. Everyone wants broken records, new marks, raised bars.

Bigger, higher, riskier; recent years have seen boarders brain-damaged, suffer major organ trauma and smash bones like matchsticks. Outsiders think of us as goofy kids with baggy trousers and backwards caps, but that's only a type of shield. We're too cool to admit it – *we're young, this is fun* – but we need total, insane focus to make this work. 'Progression' – that's what it's all about for us.

Up above me, the American phenomenon Redmond Gerard went to make his run. The kid was just 17 and took gold in the slopestyle event two weeks before. What on earth do you do with the rest of your life when you win the Olympics at 17? I guess he'll either be president or in rehab by 35.

16

Red's jump was decent, a backside triple cork, but he looked a bit off-kilter as he came down to land. For a moment he looked like he might stack it, but just about held his feet. It was a little sketchy and he put a hand down to keep himself up, which is good for injury prevention but not for getting points. That's a big no-no as far as judges are concerned. From there he had two more runs to put things right. And I knew it would be my turn soon.

As I waited, I had a constant internal dialogue going on, building inside my guts, a bubbling soup of doubt and dread.

What if I really mess this up?

What if I make myself look stupid?

What if I can't do it?

I didn't articulate my fears. You don't speak terror out loud, not if you've got any sense. That might manifest them into reality, but I dwelled on this stuff, every sharp aspect. I really tried not to, to keep it out of my head, but sometimes it even kept me awake at night.

'Billy Morgan, two to drop!' The official's words cut through my inner voice like a guillotine. I had to move.

My team-mate, Rowan Coultas, stood with me. 'Yeah boy!' He bumped my fist with his.

Hamish was there too, my coach. 'Go on Bill,' he said softly. 'Get it.'

We shuffled over, out of the gazebo and into a sort of queuing system. Hamish and Rowan followed me up for moral support. I always needed someone there, if only to distract me from what I was about to do. If on my own, I could overthink things. It's important to have some banter on at the top.

We reached the summit. There were a couple of South Korean kids operating the lift and a screen to watch the ongoing action. I always preferred not to watch, so hung out with Hamish and Rowan, burning time.

I could see the rider ahead of me, in front of the curtain, awaiting his turn. Once you walk through that curtain, you're gone for a while. It's you and the sky.

The signal came for the guy in front.

'Billy Morgan, one to drop.'

We shuffled further up the mountain and another rider filled in the space behind. A conveyor belt, one by one, like we're walking the plank. The curtain sat in front of me. The stage door. I got my nod from the official and passed through.

It's strange when you go out on to that platform. The guy in front of me was mid-jump, so although I emerged into a huge, public arena, with a circle of cheering fans, flags and whistles way below, I felt alone. All eyes and cameras were on the jump in progress. No one was looking at me. I may as well have been standing in the dark.

I put my gloves on, adjusted the cuffs on the bottom of my hoodie. My sleeves always need to go over my gloves, or I don't feel right. I made sure the tension on the bindings that hold my feet to the board was right, another pre-jump ritual. I knew I had about 60 seconds to fill before my drop, so I kept checking – boots, laces, gloves – everything, over and over. To anyone watching it would have looked like OCD, but I knew that if I stood up, with nothing to do, looked down the hill at the ramp and the supporters, then fear would kick in. Overpowering, insurmountable fear.

My equipment was fine, I knew that, but fiddling with it gave me something to do.

'Billy Morgan, drop in!'

I stood.

Hamish and Rowan piped up.

'Send it, Billy!'

'Nail it!'

Back in the gazebo, I knew the other boys were watching. It was me against them after all, although we were also in it together. Later, I knew, we would all get smashed, drinking and laughing until all this was a crazy blur.

But right then, I had to go and fly.

2.

Art or Sport?

CONSCIOUSNESS AND human nature are mysterious things. But whatever they are and wherever they come from, the human spirit is playful. I say that because, throughout history, humans always engaged with the world functionally but also light-heartedly. We work and we play. That's how we are. That's actually pretty poignant if you think about it.

Nature provided us with struggle and purpose, but also with *fun*. We're never happier than when we have fun and never freer than when out among nature. There's got to be something in that, hasn't there?

Somehow though, these things we start spontaneously, for fun and pleasure, become ever more codified, even artificial as they grow in popularity. Maybe that says something about human consciousness too? We have a fundamental need to impose order on chaos.

Snowboarding, the sport in which I made my name, is quite a new one. The Pyeongchang Olympics of 2018 were just the sixth Winter Games to feature it. And in a demonstration of the many different ways humans can have fun, six very different snowboarding events were included:

- Slalom and Giant Slalom, which are just like their skiing counterparts. A sort of downhill time trial in which competitors complete the course as fast as possible while weaving through marker flags.

- Snowboard Cross (sometimes called Boardercross) features between four and six guys on the slope, traversing obstacles such as jumps, raised barriers, rollers and drops, all against each other to get to the end. It's a bit like the motorbike sport of motocross, but with a race element, which increases danger due to the risk of collision.

- Halfpipe, in which guys ride along a semi-circular ditch dug into the mountain with walls up to 7m high, performing tricks while going from side to side and in the air above the pipe. (Similar to the skateboarding event of the same name.) It's scored by judges.

- Slopestyle competitors ride a course usually comprised of three rails and three jumps, performing tricks as they go. They're also awarded a score by judges at the end.

- Big air is my favourite and the easiest to explain. The name pretty much says it all. A big ramp, a big jump, some aerial stunts and a landing. Again, it's scored by judges.

This variety gives an idea of snowboarding's evolution. Originally called 'snurfing', after a guy called Sherman Poppen glued two skis together to 'surf the snow', it began to take off in the USA in the 60s. Following Poppen's example, a skateboarder by the name of Tom Sims suffered a fit of youthful recklessness, tacked some carpet on top of a piece of wood and ragged down a mountain on it. Around the same time, a former competitive skier called Jake Burton began experimenting with his own snowboard designs.

Within a decade both had gone into business and become the first real manufacturers of snowboard equipment. Sims and Burton snowboards remain two of the biggest and most respected snowboard companies to this day.

These beginnings, from these three individuals, meant snowboarding was born with heavy surfing and skateboarding influences, although it took place in such different terrain. For the next 20 years or so it remained a minority pursuit, mainly in the States. Devotees just turned up on slopes with their boards and did what they felt like. Some sped downhill, others enjoyed jumping off banked snow. Others performed tricks and stunts. Let a thousand flowers bloom.

This caused friction with enthusiasts of the more established mountain sport of skiing, who viewed the youthful newcomers with suspicion. I never understood that vibe. To me, it's all the same thing. One sport has two planks on their feet, the other, one. Why get twisted about it? But back in the 70s through to the 90s, a skiing vs snowboarding ideological battle was waged, perceived to be middle-aged stiffs on one side against weed-smoking, dropout teens on the other.

'They don't respect the slopes! They don't behave appropriately! They're a danger to themselves and others!'

'Yo, chill dude, calm yourself!'

Snowboarding even ended up being banned in several resorts. This all meant, from its very early days, snowboarding's self-image went miles beyond the narrow confines of 'sport'. It was a sort of counter-cultural movement, a way of thinking and a lifestyle choice rather than a competitive discipline. A lot of 80s magazines referred to it as 'the new rock 'n' roll'. For many boarders, with their long hair and grungy music, that pretty much summed it up.

For this reason, even now a purist hardcore exists who think it should never have been regulated. The way they see it, rules, contests and prize money detract from snowboarding's true ethos. The ethos of freedom. The ethos of rebellion.

There's undoubtedly something deeply spiritual about riding the frozen wilderness, far from the rest of the world. It can be a pretty fierce trip. A different environment gives a different perspective and sometimes, especially after a stay of more than a few days, it can be hard to return to 'normality', whatever that means. Ask anyone who has done a four-month winter season then had to go home to a provincial British town to find a job. It's one of the most savage culture shocks there is. That's why there has always existed a subset of winter sports devotees who choose not to return, finding ways to follow their passion full-time, becoming 'ski bums' in the eyes of wider society. All that white can become addictive.

Snowboarding crossed the Atlantic to the UK in the 80s. Soon after, across the USA, Europe and elsewhere, competitions began popping up. The ISF (International Snowboard Federation) was formed in 1990. As the popularity of extreme sports grew in general, the annual 'X Games' began in 1995, showcasing skateboarding, BMX riding, rollerblading and other, more niche events. The first winter version was held in '97 and, of course, snowboarding played a big part. In 98, snowboarding debuted in the Winter Olympics in Japan.

By the turn of the millennium, popularity was booming and, much to the displeasure of alpine snobs everywhere, snowboarding overtook skiing to become an enormous, global industry and the dominant mountain sport. They say that all revolutions are either doomed to fail or become the establishment they once despised. Well, those snarky kids with piercings and hoodies conquered a world they entered as interlopers. And some of them, it has to be said, are now extremely wealthy because of it.

Eventually, in the most pointed of ironies, skiing even ended up mimicking snowboarding. Inspired by the boarding scene, freestyle, trick-based skiing is now as popular as its downhill sibling. Winter sport will eat itself.

For me, personally, I entered the picture in about 2009 and have ridden for the last decade as a competitive snowboarder. I've pushed the sport's limits, won events, earned prize money and turned professional. I've had corporate sponsors such as Visa, Samsung and BMW.

Through all of that I consider myself truly fortunate, but not for material reasons. I'm lucky because my passion has become my living. I don't need to endure the culture shock and go back to reality. Snowboarding *is* my reality.

So, purists, artists and cool kids can turn up their noses if they like, but success doesn't mean I don't love to shred. No way. I'm all about the love.

I just can't afford to live on love alone.

3.

Going with the Flow

I SHUFFLED over to the top of the drop. The air hit me. The crowd looked up. I felt their eyes. There was some cheering, a few whistles being blown. My spine tingled and I felt that intense sense of purpose that an imminent big-air attempt always creates.

Everything faded into the periphery – the stadium, the crowd, the sky, the past, the future, everything. The world closed around me into a kind of personal tunnel. A series of calculations whipped through my subconscious. I wasn't computing, – it was all instinctive – but wind strength, ramp speed, resultant angular momentum, energy conservation, heart rate and flight curve flickered behind my eyes in a handclap.

This is physics as well as sport. Complicated physics, performed by a human projectile and calibrated in the blink of an eye.

Constructed on a huge piece of scaffolding, the drop constitutes the point where you launch yourself into your run. The speed at which you begin is crucial, as you gather further momentum riding down the ramp before take-off. Many a promising jump was doomed to end in pain before it even got airborne because the rider misjudged the initial drop.

'From the United Kingdom, Billy Morgan,' the tannoy announced. The crowd hushed. Suddenly I could hear my own breath.

The standard competition format is to elect two tricks, which have to differ by direction of spin. Essentially one needs to be clockwise and the other anti-clockwise. You get three runs and you're scored on your best two runs of the three from tricks that don't spin in the same direction.

That allows you one wipeout if you nail the other two. This being the final, I knew I might need to get adventurous later on, but for my first run I was going with a backside triple cork, my go-to move. I had done so many I could land it nine times out of ten. It would give me a platform to build on.

The backside 1440 triple cork essentially involves heading into the jump back first, then performing a kind of triple backflip with an extra 360 degrees of rotation. It's an advanced manoeuvre because you have to go off axis, then go upside down three times (your head needs to go below your knees for it to count). Landings can be tricky as you come down facing the wrong way. I needed to do a big one, with a hand movement known as a nosegrab. That would give me the most amount of points possible for that particular trick, but it had become quite a routine thing for me.

This is chill, I'm thinking. *No problems.*

Usually, a moment comes when I'm just about to go, when all the inner dialogue switches off and a strange calmness hits. I waited for that moment. I needed it.

The jump they set up in South Korea was a real thing of beauty, 19 metres to the knuckle, 25 to the sweet spot. There wasn't quite enough space in the landing area to pull off the really big stuff, like a quadruple, but I knew there was bound to be some maniac that tried it. Not me. Not then.

Come on, I thought to myself. *Enough.*

I got my wish. They gave the nod and I started my run, but in my eagerness I set off a little too fast.

Shit!

Once in the air, I realised I was higher than I should be. I was aiming to see the knuckle, the start of the landing point. I was rotating round and round, and after the second cork, the knuckle went by. After the last cork, I knew I was still too big. I had got a problem. I was going high.

Very high. Too high.

Then I was coming down, fast. It was a huge jump, no question about that. I could tell by how quickly the ground hurtled towards me. I was heading towards the end of the landing area and there's big points for that.

Right to the end, come on!

The ground accelerated in that weird way it always seems to in the last few metres before impact and I hit it hard.

Very hard. Too hard.

Initially, I managed to hold it. The impact on my quads, glutes and back muscles was heavy, sending a shockwave up my spine. To absorb that kind of impact, you need to be in the right position, but I was a bit 'backseat' (leaning over my back foot). Could I hold on to it through the transition? I did a kind of wheelie out of the compression, with the nose of my board up in the air, but lost balance. That's the way it goes. You can cheat gravity for a while, but not forever.

I was down. My most dependable trick, in the Olympic final, and I was down.

'Oooohhh,' went the crowd.

For a few moments I skidded along the snow on my arse.

No! How?

I didn't really want to get up. I just wanted to vanish. Once my momentum petered out, I stood, put my hands on my head and went over to the waiting area by the scoreboard. I didn't really want to, but it's protocol, a bit of theatre for the cameras. They flashed up my score and I made a gesture of exasperation for the TV viewers. We were live on BBC, after all. Then I headed back up.

All that was going through my head was negativity. *This is the Olympics and I'm letting my country down.* My second trick was much less reliable and I needed both the other two runs to have a chance of landing it well.

I knew there were millions watching at home. I didn't want to make a fool of myself. People from the crowd called my name, shouted questions as I passed, held out hands for contact, but I was in no mood to listen or respond. Instead, I sought out Hamish, the top man. At times like that he's like a frigging druid or soothsayer and I needed some of that wry Scottish wisdom. He was waiting by the bottom of the lift, scratching his chin, eyes narrow.

'It's okay,' he said, calmly. 'Just go again.' I nodded. 'We go back to basics.' His accent soothed anxieties, like a single malt. The guy's never panicked, never anxious.

'Just forget that happened,' he said. 'It's jump one again. You go back.'

'Right yeah,' I replied. I felt a bit better already.

He almost smiled. Hamish never properly smiles, but sometimes it looks like he's about to. That was one of those moments.

'Yeah,' he said, as we began to head back up the mountain. 'We go back to the start.'

Part Two

A KID FROM THE COAST

'The challenge of maturity is to recover
the seriousness of a child at play.'

– Friedrich Nietzsche

4.

Boys Like Billy

SCIENCE WILL tell you people are products of two things: genetics and environment. Everything else is just luck. Or some sort of magic. I grew up with the sound of the docks in my ears and wind in my hair, in a municipality of a quarter of a million people, called Southampton, on the south-west coast of England. It's a university town with a busy port, best known for being the departure point of the RMS *Titanic* in 1912. Proximity to the sea means local sporting reputation comes from water sports such as sailing or rowing, although it also has a football (soccer) team that has spent most of recent history flitting between the top two divisions of the English league.

Britain, and especially the southernmost part of it, isn't a country renowned for extremes of climate. Like its people, it's generally mild, grey and wet. Average summer temperatures in Southampton hover around 22°C, while the winter months drop to 8° or 9°. Real snowfall is rare. Most years see none at all, and when it does come, it's usually little more than a dusting. Enough to turn roofs white and inspire mild excitement but not enough to interact with. As a small child this meant the concept of 'snowsports' held zero relevance to me. I'm not even sure I knew what the term meant.

Growing up by the coast meant home life had strong nautical influences and my dad, Eddie, was a marine engineer in the Royal Navy. After leaving the forces he continued working in the private sector, repairing parts and engines for merchant or industrial vessels. Dad is one of those guys for whom his work was more than a day job. It was the core of him, his very being.

The old man's fascination with functionality and maintenance gripped me from a young age. His concerns were never very aesthetic. He didn't care how things looked, he just wanted them to work and continue working.

'Mad Eddie', as his mates called him, applied this view to everything we had in the house. If something broke down, we never threw it away and bought a new one. That's wasteful. That's consumerism. He damn well fixed it. As a toddler it was usual for me to walk from room to room and find Dad on his hands and knees surrounded by saws and screwdrivers. Our garage was like a mini engineering works, full of tools, springs and ball bearings. Often, I would go in there and find him using a soldering iron or an angle grinder or something.

'What are you doing, Dad?'

'Mending the boiler/washing machine/fuse box. Come here and hold this for me.'

As far as I was concerned it was normal, but people who visited found it comical. The fridge had a brass pull handle because the actual handle fell off. There would often be sections missing from walls and floors where Dad was adjusting wiring or pipework. There was a toilet roll dispenser on the kitchen wall for some reason and a wooden platform he constructed under the roof to carry out tile or gutter maintenance.

Centrally mounted on the front of the house, facing the road, was a large, municipal clock. Dad pinched it from a local railway station that shut down and went to ruin. From the street it gave our home the appearance of some sort of civic building.

The best bit was the downstairs loo, which flushed via a home-made system of buckets and siphons, collecting waste water from the shower then carrying it in pipes around the outside of the house to a reservoir in the garden. My childhood home could easily have been the location for a movie about a crackpot inventor.

'Repair, reuse, recycle,' Dad would say, deadly serious.

'Yes, Dad.'

'There's far too much waste and inefficiency in this world.'

'Yes, Dad.'

Then he would get on one of his motorcycles and burn off down the road on a mission.

Dad always enjoyed a drink and was known locally as a bit of a character too. When I was still a small child, he went out one evening, got his groove on and jumped out of a first-floor pub window. It's the sort of incident that might well have gone unrecorded but for the fact that there was a spiked fence on the pavement below. Dad, being Dad, impaled himself and dangled there, howling in agony until a couple of mates ran out and gingerly lifted him off. When the ambulance arrived, they confirmed that the spike skewered one of his buttocks. There was hospital time and stitches after that. Even today he still has the scar.

My mum, Joanne, spoke about it all with an air of resignation and bafflement. 'What on earth was he doing?'

Our grandma and grandad lived in the house next door but one, and we often spent time there too. Our grandad, Terry, another former military sailor and engineer, was great with kids and made learning fun, building things out of plasticine to help hold our attention. As a family, we were all very tight.

Taking after Mad Eddie, my brother Ashley (two years my senior) and I were vigorous boys from a young age. As soon as I could walk, we would chase each other upstairs or around the garden, bouncing on beds and sofas, the sort of kids who existed in only one of two modes. We were either asleep or moving.

In an attempt to channel all that natural energy, Mum took me to an activity session called Tumble Tots when I was three. Set up in a local church hall, there were small, coloured frames to climb and hang from, balance beams, slides and soft blocks to jump off, all arranged in a little circuit. It's a well-known organisation, which lots of kids in the UK will have experienced in their early lives. The idea was to encourage very young children to explore and use their bodies in a safe environment.

Everyone's different, I guess, and while some toddlers had to be helped around, holding hands with their parent as they went, I felt completely and strangely at home there from the first time I went. As soon as Mum removed my shoes and set me free, I flew around the equipment, totally absorbed in my own enjoyment. No one had to tell me what to do or how to do it. The half-hour session would vanish in a heartbeat and, more often than not, I had to be dragged away reluctantly at the end.

Mum had been taking me for two years or so when the supervisor, a middle-aged lady with a permanent smile, asked to speak to her.

'Mrs Morgan,' she said. 'You know that conversation we had a couple of years back about Ashley?'

Mum smiled. She knew what was coming. Ashley had started at Tumble Tots too, but quickly outgrew it and moved on to gymnastics.

'Already?' Mum asked.

The lady nodded. 'It's not about age,' she said. 'Boys like Billy really need something more structured.'

That stuck in my head. *Boys like Billy.*

Within a couple of weeks, I found myself following in Ashley's footsteps by enrolling at the Southampton Gymnastics Club. It was housed in a large sports hall and the first time I went I stood in the doorway and marvelled at the giant equipment scattered around the room – springboards, vaulting horses, balance beams, horizontal bars. It all looked so big, so mysterious, like stumbling into a new and alien world.

In some ways, I suppose that's what it was. Everything is alien until it becomes normal. But for me, gymnastics became much more than a once-a-week activity or a chance to blow off steam. It was a signpost, pointing my way forward.

5.

Mad Eddie and 'Risk'

GYMNASTICS SESSIONS took place in a building called The Deanery near the centre of town. Inside was an old-fashioned gym hall, similar to a typical school gym from the mid-20th century. It was a decent-sized space, with wooden bars and beams that could be folded back against the wall. Next door to that was a smaller room for the younger ones to train and I was initially placed in there.

My coach was a man called Ken Bell, an old chap with a walking stick and John Lennon glasses. Although he frequently smiled, he also gave off an aura of seriousness. We were there to learn and not to mess about. Unlike primary school, which I had started by then, where some teachers struggled to manage their classes, everyone at gymnastics did exactly as they were told.

The club ran a 'kitty-kat' badge system, which meant progress was clearly structured. We would be taught a group of exercises for a period of time, tested on them and earn a badge if we completed them satisfactorily. To begin with, it was basic stuff, similar to that which all children get taught in primary school PE.

'Okay, forward roll! Good! Well done, Billy. But once you've finished remember to stand up straight.'

'Tuck jumps now! Knees nice and high!'

The first badge I got was for performing a forward roll, a backward roll and a 360, which essentially meant jumping and executing a complete full-body rotation in the air. Obviously, as a six-year-old, I had no idea, but that sort of move would go on to play a very important part in my life. Every time I got a badge, I got a little buzz, and soon, as buzzes so often do, it became addictive. I began to crave new exercises, new physical challenges, new things to learn.

Soon I was doing cartwheels and then Arab springs, a complete revolution of the body achieved by lunging headfirst from an upright position, then bouncing off your hands. They look great, especially when videoed and watched back. You start doing things like that and think, *yeah man, I'm getting good at this!*

Once you got to that sort of level, which I reached quite fast, it was only a short step to performing backflips from a standing position, considered something of a yardstick. In order to pull off a successful backflip, you had to jump high enough, tuck tight enough and give yourself the right rip going backwards to do a full 360-degree rotation and land back on your feet. There were a few weeks of getting it wrong, of landing on my face in the foam, but by the age of about seven or so, I nailed that too. It got to the point where I could pull off backflips casually, whenever I felt like it. I could be walking across the playground at school and someone could say, 'Give us a backflip', and I would throw one out, virtually without breaking stride.

For two years, from the age of six until eight, I trained in floor gymnastics, competed in little competitions and even won a few medals and trophies. By then Ashley had moved into the other room and was training specifically in men's acrobatic gymnastics, known as 'acro', a different, more spectacular discipline, conducted in a team.

Acro has a very long history, pretty much as long as gymnastics itself, dating as far back as the Ancient Egyptian period. Despite that, it's the least known of the major gymnastic disciplines, isn't an Olympic sport and only became officially recognised by the International Gymnastics Federation in 1999.

Ashley worked with three other guys and performed as a 'top', meaning he was the smallest, lightest gymnast, the one who appeared at the peak of human pyramids, stood on others' shoulders and generally got thrown around by the bigger guys. After training one day, when we had finished packing away equipment, Ken took me to one side.

'How do you fancy following in your brother's footsteps and giving the acro squad a go?' he asked. 'We reckon you're ideal for it.'

I was thrilled to be asked, partly because I wanted to prove that I could do everything Ashley could. So, while still a very slight, young boy, I moved into the big room where gymnasts as old as 25 were preparing for national competitions. Immediately, things got much more serious.

Sessions in there were run by Pat and Mike Wakefield, an old, married couple who had been around the scene for decades. Pat had big, white permed hair and Mike sported a decent belly, but both would be there in their red club tracksuits, watching and conferring about everything. There was absolutely nothing those two didn't know about gymnastics.

Like Ken, they also seemed to have that natural ability, probably honed through experience, to be friendly and welcoming, but at the same time extremely disciplined. Every session would start with big smiles and a little joke, but I was coming to acro to work.

Recognising my natural exuberance, along with the fact that I was still very young, after my first few sessions they put a special black mat in the corner of the room for me. If I was over-energised, running around or not following instructions, I would have to stand on it and face the wall. It didn't take too long for me to get the message.

Sessions began with a warm-up, often a jog around the hall and then some simple exercises to get going. After that we would practise specific elements of our routines. Then every session finished with a good 15 minutes of static stretching. That part got pretty intense as you needed to ensure particular areas of your wrists or back were able to support your bodyweight, often in quite strange positions. As a result, stretching time would usually culminate in partner stretching, involving someone else sitting on a part of your body, pushing your tendons and ligaments to the limit, while you grimaced in pain. I hated it, but after the torture was over, it was finally time to relax.

I was placed into two groupings: a men's four and a men's pair. In both, I was automatically assigned as the 'top', like Ashley. As I was still relatively small in stature, it would be my role to be thrown into the air and caught by others, or if there was a group balance of some kind, I would be the uppermost figure of the team.

On the other side of the room, Ashley still adopted the same role in two other groups, which helped to enhance our natural sibling rivalry. He always seemed a step or two ahead of me – at least it felt that way from my perspective – which gave me an incentive to learn as fast as possible. Coaches noticed that energy between us and encouraged it. To them, it was simply another tool they could use to get the best from us.

My early gymnastics experience showed me that I loved learning and mastering new things. The coach would explain something, or I would see it demonstrated by one of the older kids, even Ashley, and I would then practise it relentlessly. No one had to force me to practise. In fact, I didn't even think of it as practising. I was enjoying myself. I was having *fun*.

As the two of us grew, our jostling for position intensified at home, too. Age advantage meant Ashley was always stronger and could beat the shit out of me more or less when he felt like it, so I had to be inventive in my approach. He had such a terrible temper and it became a game to wind him up, then watch him explode, like poking a tethered bear with a stick. I loved him, in the unspoken but heartfelt way kids always love their family members, but we still clashed. He was such a serious guy, even as a youngster, as if everything was some kind of transaction. *If I do X and Y, then later I'll get Z.* He spoke often of his plans for the future. I didn't think that way at all. To me, the future didn't really exist. It was just a story.

Whenever I pranked Ashley, which was often, the danger of getting caught and suffering the consequences was real. I had to face that reality more than a few times, ending up bruised and breathless with my face pinned to the floor, but somehow that element made it exciting and enjoyable. It made me want to keep doing it. If there had been no risk, it would have been boring.

All the while, Dad inculcated this same characteristic very strongly in both of us. I don't know whether it was a deliberate thing or was just his natural approach to parenting, but Mad Eddie constantly subjected us to danger. He taught us to use knives, build things with our hands, use fire safely, all that sort of thing. He constructed a zip wire in the garden between the house and a tree and had us whizzing back and forth, several metres off the ground. One time he came home with a bunch of fireworks, which we attached to cuddly toys before gleefully firing them up into the air. While we were both still primary school kids, we would go out on day trips to the woods or the countryside. Dad would invariably construct something to climb on, or a high rope swing that flew out over a river.

'Go on!' he would say.

Ashley would go first, his extra age and size giving him bravado. Then it was over to me.

'Go on, Bill!' Dad would repeat.

'Err ...'

'GO ON!'

I had no choice and became accustomed to putting myself in situations where there appeared to be a genuine chance of injury, but through that I also developed a greater understanding of what I was physically and psychologically capable of. On one occasion the whole family had been up to the Lake District for a holiday and on the way back, cruising down an A road somewhere, we passed a huge, old-fashioned water mill at the edge of a field.

'Shit!' Dad cried. 'Did you see that?' We all looked at each other with bemusement. 'We need to go and check that out. It looks amazing!'

Mum wasn't keen, as usual, but Dad pulled off the road and found somewhere to park. 'Come on!' he shouted.

Before we knew what was happening, we were all trudging back across the grass to investigate this great contraption that so fascinated him. Mum stood back, arms crossed, with deep, deep concern on her face. She knew Eddie Morgan and his foibles only too well.

It didn't take Dad long to discover that you could get inside the main iron wheel, which was absolutely massive, probably about six metres across, and run, like a hamster, to make it turn.

'Come on, now,' Mum pleaded. 'This is getting silly. You've had a bit of fun. Let's go back to the car.'

But we were riding the wave with Dad by then, learning, to our growing excitement, that if you ran for long enough and built up enough momentum, you could get the wheel spinning, grab hold of one of the spokes and the thing would carry you right up into the air, like some sort of demented, daredevil Ferris wheel.

Mum was horrified. 'What do you all think you are doing?' she scolded. 'Come on.'

We were all too wrapped up in what we were doing to listen. With her warnings ignored, Mum refused to take any more part in the madness and went back to the car.

Ashley did it first, and I remember watching, as he peaked on the curve right at the top of the wheel, eight metres up, and thinking, *If he falls off now, he might actually die. Like, really die.*

It was a long drop, and if the angles worked against you, you faced a strong possibility of falling into the churning machinery and getting tangled in the great iron spokes of the rotating mechanism. You would be like meat in a mincing machine. Rather than a stretcher, the ambulance crew would probably carry you away in a couple of buckets.

I don't know whether Ashley considered any of this or not, but he yelled with excitement as the thing took him up, while the look of exhilaration on his face as he hit the apex was something to behold. Then he was over the worst of it, returning to the ground and it was obvious all would be okay. When he reached the bottom, Ashley jumped off, wide-eyed, cheeks flushed, hot with adrenaline, and Dad motioned to me. I swallowed some spit and shifted from foot to foot.

'Ummm …' I wanted to do it, but I was scared.

Despite Ashley's success, it was a pretty insane stunt for a kid so young. There were boys my age still learning to ride bikes. But Dad did his usual thing and refused to take no for an answer.

At first, I was absolutely petrified, convinced my hands would sweat so much I would lose my grip, or sheer nerves would weaken me, but as the wheel carried me up and I watched the ground shrink, as the breath came short in my lungs and the hairs on the back of my neck stood up, I knew there was no way I would let go. It was like I was glued to the bar. As I passed through the highest point, I found myself upside down, looking down on the ground where my family stood.

Soon I was on the descent, and as the wheel brought me steadily back to earth, I felt elated, surging and sparking as Ashley had been. It was like a yin-yang; the fear you felt before, increased the rush of joy after. We headed back to the car buzzing with energy, full of zest and vigour, to find Mum utterly exasperated. 'Can we just please go home now?'

That sort of thing was normal for us. Other kids would have backed out, allowed nerves to get the better of them, considered the pros and cons and walked away. Some would even call such safety-first, timid behaviour 'common sense'. But we never had that option. Common sense wasn't in our vocabulary because our dad was Mad Eddie Morgan.

6.

Square Pegs, Round Holes

MY PROGRESSION in acro was quick, and within a short space of time I moved on from the basics to training more complicated manoeuvres on the foam blocks. We were taught to throw ourselves backwards on to them, so you could feel yourself going over and get used to where your hands go. Once you developed a feel for tumbling and how to control it, you could move to the mats. That way you could attempt things, knowing, if they went wrong, there were two or three pairs of hands waiting to catch you.

Pat and Mike had a bell in the room, and whenever someone was about to do something new and unaided for the first time, they would ring it. It was a signal for others to watch you perform and cheer you on, then give you a clap if you nailed it. That created such a positive, encouraging atmosphere and it made you want to keep learning. When they rang the bell for you, you felt like you were going places.

I worked as the 'top' in a men's four with some older lads – Ollie Rix, Matt Fly and a big unit called Matt Gregory. The three of them had been doing acro for several years already, which made my life a little easier. Essentially, I had to learn some cool flips and spins, then rely on them to catch me on the way down.

The first time Pat and Mike rang the bell for me, it was to perform a double backflip to platform. That essentially involved the three of them throwing me up in the air, me going through 720 degrees of rotation, then landing back on their hands. We pulled it off and got some nice recognition from the rest of the club. I was ten years old and that was the first time in my life I went upside down twice in the air during a manoeuvre, a really significant moment. I was elated.

Meanwhile, outside of the acro club, my growing abilities proved both a blessing and a curse. No one else could do the things the Morgan boys could do and at Tanners Brook primary school we became known as the mad kids who backflipped at will and jumped out of trees without a second thought. That gave us notoriety and a bit of kudos, of course, but also a form of isolation. Not that we were friendless – Ashley and I both had groups of mates – but school is such a tribal, herd-like situation. When you have something about you that makes you different, you're marked forever. In the eyes of the masses, Billy and Ashley Morgan were freaks. Entertaining, funny, slightly mental freaks, but freaks, nonetheless.

In the classroom I was never a naughty kid, in the sense of gobbing off at teachers or being purposely disruptive, but I found it so difficult to sit still for long periods of time. As a result, I did get into mischief. I was constantly admonished for being on the wrong side of the room or up on my feet. Once I was sent home early because I used some scissors to cut a girl called Amy Varney's hair off in art class. She got putty stuck in her pigtails and I valiantly offered to help. Sadly, it seemed my solution wasn't the one she hoped for. Her mum came around to our house that evening and had a massive go at mine.

'Boys will be boys,' Mum said. What else could she do?

Mum had it about right, though. As far as I was concerned, my misdemeanours weren't down to nastiness. I wasn't trying to upset anyone or cause harm, although plenty of teachers didn't understand it. I think the truth was I just wasn't suited to that situation. Asking a kid like me to sit quietly, read and write things down for hours was like asking the class geek to jump backwards off the top of a climbing frame. That was my thing and this was theirs. Square pegs, round holes.

Throughout my younger school years, it became clear that my intensive gymnastic training boosted everything physical that I tried. My suppleness, flexibility, core and leg strength were way above average for someone of my age, which made perfect sense, as while I was in the gym nearly every evening after school, most of my classmates were at home playing computer games or watching TV.

This made school sports sessions easy. I didn't necessarily win every running race or event, but I was good at everything, across the board. I was especially good at anything that involved launching myself into the air in some form. Long jump and high jump, for example, were events I won comfortably, without even having to try that hard.

School learning was complemented by Dad, who continued his own brand of informal education at home, teaching us to ride motorbikes when we were both way too young for that sort of thing in the eyes of wider society. He found a Suzuki FZ50 in a skip somewhere in Southampton, brought it home and fixed it. Ashley and I would take turns to burn around the garden on it. Over the next few years this process was repeated several times.

We had a Honda CB100 as our first geared motorbike, which was much too big for me to ride unaided. My feet couldn't reach the ground from the saddle, meaning Dad had to run alongside to help me get going. After I had ridden around for a while, I had to circle back to wherever Dad was, so he could help me down, or I would fall off and be unable to pick the bike back up.

Ashley and I both loved that bike so much and we thrashed the life out of it over the course of a few years. The electrics were hanging off and the thing was on its last legs, so Dad drove us down to Warsash where he worked at the Maritime Centre. He pulled the bike out of the back of the van, turned it over for one last time and told Ashley to send it into the drink. It was like something from a movie, as Ash revved up, then rode it down the pier and off the end, flying in an arc through the three-metre drop and into the sea. He came up after a few seconds with a big grin on his face, as our beloved Honda sank to a watery grave. Not long after that, Dad got hold of a Kawasaki KLX250.

Dad's engineering abilities meant he was able to pick up machines other people discarded as useless, make a few tweaks and adjustments and get them running. Of course, we never rode on public roads as we were far too young, but motorcycling became as much a part of our DNA as gymnastics.

Next to Southampton central station lay a patch of waste ground and we would wheel the bikes up there then buzz about on them. Sometimes Dad took us to Hut Hill by Chandler's Ford, a lovely area with a variety of terrain: woods, rocky areas, streams and fields. It was perfect for ragging about and was frequently used as a course for local moto trials clubs. Ashley ended up taking trial biking quite seriously and even entered a few competitions. In some ways it was my first experience of what I would now call a 'freesport'.

Rollerblading became a hobby too, during the same period. I skated with a few friends from school and particularly a guy called Joe Munden, then I began inline skating from the age of ten, at a place called Mayflower Park down by the quay in Southampton. Mum used to take me there, then sit and wait for me to finish. Gymnastics had given me a love of finding out what I could do with my body and it felt natural to me to try new things.

That's something I think about often. The way Dad brought me up, alongside all those hours flipping into foam pits with Pat and Mike, showed me a way to live, a way of looking at my time on earth. It was a way based on exploration of physical limits and of seeking, rather than avoiding, risk. The rewards on the other side – the feeling of achievement, the buzz of breaking boundaries, a feeling that I've later learned to refer to as 'stoke' or 'being stoked' – always outweighed the fear.

By the age of 11, as I prepared to head into secondary school, my acro club buddies and I fantasised about the lifestyles we could pursue with our skills. Beyond gymnastics competitions, in which we were already participating regularly and doing well, there was the possibility of stunt work for film or TV, even joining the circus! Working in the stunt shows at the Legoland theme park was a popular choice for many ex-acrobats. The future, adulthood, all still seemed so vast and unknowable, but at least that stuff made some kind of sense to me. Conversely, the idea of doing what most people did – getting GCSEs, maybe some A levels, going to college and working in an office – never entered my head.

I didn't know what I wanted to do, but even as a pre-teen I knew I needed to be engaged and energised. I needed to have fun, to feel stoked. If what was on offer was unexciting, I would withdraw from it. I would simply drop out.

7.

Kickflips and Battling for Azeroth

BELLEMOOR SCHOOL for Boys; the name sounds like something from a black-and-white movie now, as if there were teachers with mortarboards, Latin lessons and a stern, red-cheeked matron. In 2008 they changed it to Upper Shirley High and made it co-educational, but I attended as part of one of the last cohorts of the old system.

Pretty much bang in the centre of Southampton, Bellemoor looked like your typical British comp, with boxy buildings designed around cubes and rectangles in the modernist style. It was surrounded on three sides by rows of terraced houses, with an industrial estate down the west flank. As secondary schools tend to, it seemed huge to my 11-year-old self and at first was a little overwhelming. Suddenly, I was surrounded by 700 or so other kids, the vast majority of whom outsized me, were fully tuned in to the unwritten rules of the schoolyard and ready to pounce on any evidence of individuality or difference.

Being an all-male environment, the place could have quite a hostile atmosphere. Older boys picking on smaller ones, teasing them, tripping them up as they crossed the playground, shoulder-barging them into corridor walls – all these things were everyday occurrences. You couldn't get away with a quirky haircut or big ears or anything that made you stand out from the crowd. I get the impression that schools try to stamp down on that sort of thing now and even classify it as bullying, but at Bellemoor in 1999 it was just how things were. It was the culture. You dealt with it any way you could, and all of us, as new boys, developed our own coping mechanisms.

Ashley was already there, a couple of years above me and in full-on, super-intense Ashley Morgan mode. He had been spending lots of time with our grandad. Even at the tender age of 13 or so, Ashley knew he wanted to follow Grandad's and Dad's example and join the military. He had his sights set on the Air Training Corps, to be a helicopter pilot, so he methodically set about doing everything necessary to make that happen. His school uniform was perfect. He was punctual to lessons and completed work to the best of his ability. He was never rude to teachers yet held his own with the bullies. He knew how to have fun and could be a great laugh, but he picked his moments for it carefully. Ashley worked hard and played hard. Always upright, everything correct, as if in his mind he was in the forces already.

Ashley joined the air cadets and even started a savings account. 'I'm just preparing for the future,' he would say. Who does that as a teenager?

Dad and Grandad cultivated that. They used to give us both little jobs to do. Our pocket money was always earned, never given. We would empty the bins or rake leaves in the garden. The Morgan family wanted to instil us with a work ethic, to teach us that you don't get something for nothing. Later on, we both had paper rounds to earn extra cash.

Ashley also dedicated himself to doing well at school, a perspective I never shared. He had a full desk set up in his bedroom, with pens and equipment placed neatly in pots. He would spend an hour or two every evening in there, beavering away, stuck into his books.

At home, this simply created even further opportunities for me to bait him. My mate Jake Whitlock and I figured out that we could climb into the loft over the landing and pull the ladder up, so he couldn't get up there. Safe from his rage, we could then lean through the opening and swing a rope with a heavy knot on the end against his door repeatedly, *bang-bang-bang*, to disturb him while he was working. We played a game of guessing how many bangs it would take to make him flip his lid.

'I'm saying five.'

'No, he looked pretty aggro already. I'm going three.'

Inevitably, as the thudding against his door continued, Ashley would roar with anger, come crashing out and there would follow a mad, high few seconds where we would pull up the rope as fast as possible, lower the loft hatch, then sit there listening to him absolutely losing his shit, crying with laughter. Often, he would run into my room and smash it up in retaliation. One time he was so annoyed he pulled the mattress off my bed and threw it out of the window into the garden.

When not tormenting him for entertainment, I sometimes used to watch Ashley go about his business and puzzle over him. *What the hell is he on?* I would think. Was it really possible we shared a significant percentage of genes? I never got on that serious, methodical and practical vibe at all. Although aspects of our characters were similar, our inner motivations, what drove us on, were so different and, as a result, we didn't get on particularly well.

To begin with, for me the secondary school curriculum was deadly, excruciatingly boring. Oxbow lakes, the Battle of Hastings, *pour aller à la gare s'il vous plaît*, sonnets and haikus? Come on! I had a feeling like I should care, that somehow, because so many people said so, it was all incredibly important and I should worry about achieving. So, I tried, but just couldn't bring myself to take much of an interest. The only subject I saw any point in was maths, as it came hand in hand with building things and engineering. I could see how maths had some sort of real-world application. Other than that, the majority of our work just seemed pointless, an exercise in memory and not much else. I enjoyed school from a social point of view, but my marks in most lessons were uniformly average. As far as someone like Ashley was concerned, or probably most of the teachers, I completely lacked ambition.

As Year 7, the first year of secondary school, got underway, Dad had a nasty motorbike accident, which required a couple of months of hospital time and a few major operations. He was riding his Kawasaki KLX450, which he was using to commute to work in Warsash. A young girl pulled out in front of him in a Nissan Micra and he stacked it into the side of her car. The handlebars twisted to the left on impact. That stopped him flying off down the road but sent him crashing on to the bonnet and crushed his leg. He was in such bad shape that after the ambulance crews took him away, medical staff returned to the scene of the accident to retrieve as many bone fragments as they could. Doctors estimated his left leg had shattered into at least 80 pieces. The other leg was broken too, as was one arm, both hips, multiple ribs, his wrists and his skull. He lost a great deal of blood and was in hospital for three months. He had to have skin grafts.

Recovery was slow. It left him with a limp, robbed him of some of his vitality and left Mum with the full responsibility of Ash and I, while also caring for Dad. When they first released him from hospital, just before Christmas, he had to walk with a Zimmer frame and sleep on a bed in the living room to avoid the stairs. For the first time in my life, I began to be aware that in his late forties Dad was showing signs of slowing down, of getting older. It was sobering. Mad Eddie wasn't some immortal natural force who would continue his freewheeling life forever.

'Peg leg, peg leg!' I still hear that ringing in my ears. 'Oi Morgan, your dad's a fucking peg leg!'

It became the go-to jibe for anyone wanting to upset me. Ashley brushed it off, remaining stoic, but not me. Perhaps the fact I found it genuinely upsetting created a vicious circle. Once they know they've got something on you, they keep at it.

'Oi, peg leg, give you a pound if you backflip off the art block!'

As far as I was concerned, that kind of stuff was a no-brainer. 'Alright, you're on.'

Usually a little crowd would gather, shouting insults and obscenities as I shimmied up the side of the building. I would wait until a few of them had thrown money on the floor.

'Come on, Morgan, jump!'

Looking down from the asphalt roof, I would grin at all those sneering faces and staring eyes, grin for England. What else could I do? More often than not I think they were hoping I would fall and smash my head open, just for a giggle, something unusual, a story to tell, but I never did.

Knees high, a nice, tight tuck, then I would flip through the air. There would be a beautiful moment of silence as I launched myself and, just for a second, all the schoolyard bullshit would be replaced by genuine anticipation, mouths open, eyes agog. That always meant something, that moment. It showed the power of it all. Anything that could make a crowd of 13-year-olds stand in stunned silence had to have something significant behind it.

I would land and kneel to pick up my takings, then go about my business with pockets full. A nice, tangible reward to go with the spiritual. It also gave me something to banter back with.

'The joke's on you, dickheads! I've used your money to buy a new pair of forks for my bike!'

Following the example of Ashley's financial acumen, I started selling sweets in the playground, too. Stocking up at the cash and carry then punting them out. Some teachers even became regular customers and by Year 8 I had a few hundred quid set aside, which I used to buy myself a new mountain bike, my latest out-of-school hobby. Before long, Ashley and I both got little jobs. We worked at On the Tiles, a tile shop down by the docks, to earn extra money. We had been brought up to work and that's what we did.

Through a shared interest in mountain biking, I became close with a boy called John Budden and we would frequently hang out together in our spare time, heading up to Lordswood to rag around on our bikes with another couple of kids called Josh Rowe and Ben Stevens. Sometimes we would be up there all day, digging, building jumps, dragging wooden pallets up there to construct obstacles and little courses. Often Ashley would rock up with a couple of his friends too.

I began going back to John's house to hang out, especially when the weather was bad, and found that, when at home, my new best mate, his dad and brother were obsessive about computer games. They each had their own PC in the house and would play for hours at weekends, either against one another or in teams. The first time I saw it, I found it weird. The games they were playing didn't look like the standard shoot-em-up or driving games I was used to.

'What's this?' I asked, as they carefully guided characters around lakes, hills and buildings.

'They're called MMORPGs,' John explained. 'Massive multiplayer online role-playing games.'

And I would sit and watch as he took his goblin hunter to raid the Silverpine forest, or whatever. John was also in with a little crew of kids at school who enjoyed playing other kinds of fantasy games – Dan Hitchcock, Dave Freeman, Joe Ross and Paul Sheath. They were bang into World of Warcraft, Warhammer, RuneScape, that kind of thing. According to the never verbalised but always understood social hierarchy of school life, these weren't the cool kids at all. Far from it. Glasses and greasy hair proliferated and many were seen as geeks by the wider community, which was viewed as the lowest echelon of the teenage pecking order, but I didn't care about any of that. I was immediately absorbed by the gaming.

In Warcraft you had to build up your 'honour' by doing things in the game. Through that you could then develop to the point where you took on some of the bigger challenges. The level of commitment appealed to me. These weren't the sort of games you picked up for 20 minutes then put down; they were almost a lifestyle choice that required you to invest time and energy. Not only did you have to learn how to play, but you had to develop your character's attributes and abilities while figuring out a long-term strategy. Sometimes you would have to undertake a task in order to unlock something else later on. It was the evolution of it all, the long-term strategy, the progression that hooked me.

The whole thing turned into a regular friendship group. We would meet up at weekends and play online. Some of the others even painted figures and moved on to the tabletop boardgame stuff, cross-referencing everything in thick rule books.

'Hmm, rolling a four when the wind speed is at six knots means your arrows lose velocity and the Orc Lord advances east.'

I never really went that far, but it wasn't unusual for us to convene on a Sunday and have an eight-hour game on the computers. Conversely, it was also around this time that skateboarding first invaded my consciousness. Loads of Southampton kids skated and I got my first board at the age of 13, in 2002. Boarding enthusiasts seemed to be divided into the townies, with their regular clothes and football-lad attitude, and the grungers, who went for it properly with all the baggy clobber and freaky hair. I immediately attached myself to the latter category, seeing myself as a full-on 'gribbly' skateboarder, although I still had the short and sensible, military buzz cut my dad did with his clippers at home.

There was actually an interesting link between skating and gaming. Some sort of weird youth-culture crossover. A few of the Warcraft crew were also into skateboards and the music of the two scenes was the same – bands such as Linkin Park, Korn, Papa Roach, Slipknot, Blink 182 and Alien Ant Farm. From the outside there probably doesn't appear to be much to connect obsessing over wizards and jumping down flights of stairs on a wheeled plank, but it all made perfect sense to us.

Board time would be spent cruising the streets until we found some stairs to 'gap' and ledges to 'grind'. Whatever I was doing, geeking out with the Warcraft boys or shredding with the skaters, it was the absorption I felt the most, the fact that when I got really into it, everything else, including the passage of time, faded into the background.

As usual, my acro groundings meant I picked up skate basics quickly. My balance and enjoyment of learning pushed me along, although practice time was too limited for me to really get on top of it. With gymnastics still taking up most evenings and weekends, skateboarding just slotted in alongside the biking, motorbiking, inline skating, gaming and other random crap I did when I could. My technique was never great but that didn't matter to me. I just enjoyed trying tricks that most kids found scary. If someone jumped a four set of steps, I would go out and find a five set and fly down it, just for the buzz.

I think it's fair to say that at that age, too, I didn't think of any of these things I was doing as being 'sports'. I wasn't trying to be better than other people or thinking about competition. My 13-year-old self was a purist in the truest sense of the word. All that mattered was fun.

A lot of the kids who hung out at Hoglands skatepark were bang into the scene, wore the clothes and bought magazines or DVDs. They talked about top riders such as Tas Pappas, Tony Hawk, Bam Margera or the icon, Danny Way. They followed competitions at the X Games and could reel off lists of gold medallists, but none of that ever caught my imagination. Skateboarding, to me, was just about getting out on my board and doing it.

It was freedom. It was friendship. And it was creativity.

One sunny day at Hoglands, the place was full of skaters of different ages busting their moves. A little mixed-race kid turned up, fully padded, in shiny new gear. He shyly slid in by the corner of the skatepark and began to tentatively push himself along the flat bank, obviously very new to it all and unsteady on his board. In skater lingo, these little kids, newcomers who couldn't skate, were called 'groms'.

He was clearly nervous and didn't seem to know anyone there. I was sitting on the top of the quarterpipe and listened in as a group of older kids, cool lads with earrings and branded caps, stopped next to him. One of them grinned. He towered over the newcomer.

'New board?' he asked.

The innocent youngster's face lit up. 'Yeah!' He proudly showed the older kids his brand-new Element skateboard, turning it over so they could see the tracks, spacers and wheels.

'That's rad, man,' one said.

'Awesome!' said another.

'Keep practising dude!'

Each took it in turns to pay the little guy a compliment or offer encouragement, touching fists or slapping his back, before they all rode off. He went back to his own riding with a big smile.

That scene really stuck in my mind. There, at the skatepark, the grom's differences didn't matter. He was small, he was mixed race and he was a novice but, above all, he was a skater. He loved the shred and that meant he was one of us. End of story. It was the polar opposite to the attitude at school. And for me, that summed up skate culture.

8.

All Change

BY THE time I was 13½, acro virtually became a full-time gig. That was the serious 'sport' in my life. Ashley and I were going to different gyms. He was at The Deanery and I was going to Redbridge, which were on different sides of Southampton. Dad had a white Harley-Davidson at the time and used to give us lifts to training on it. He would take one of us and Mum would take the other in her car. One time he started showing off, tried to burn out of the car park and binned me off the back by accident. *Mad Eddie*. Standard.

By that point, training took up every weekday from 6–8pm and Fridays from 6–10pm. Saturdays were another four-hour bash, from 1–5pm. However you cut and diced it, it was a big, big commitment for our parents and a huge investment of time and energy for us. It got to the point that when I closed my eyes to go to sleep at night, I still saw buckets of chalk and smelled the uniquely pungent funk of other people's feet.

Training was very competition-focused by then. Every day my four worked on a combined routine involving balance and dynamic work. My partners became a massive part of my life. It's probably difficult for people who have never experienced it to understand, but an acro team is a very intimate relationship. Like an army platoon on active duty, it's a literal human support system whereby you're relying on others to prevent you from getting hurt. Especially as a top, I was all too aware of this. I needed those guys below me to be on their game. If they weren't, I would be smashing my face on the floor on a regular basis. We didn't always get on brilliantly on a personal level, but that was an important part of it too. Sometimes you have to work hard to achieve a common goal, even with someone you may have just argued with.

At the end of the Saturday session, Pat and Mike would let us all into the swimming pool next to the sports hall for an hour, where we all went crazy, hucking tricks, double backflipping into the water and letting rip. With a couple of metres of water to break your fall, you could let your body take you in different directions and at different angles without fear of injury, launching yourself into the unknown, or 'hucking it' as we call it; all part of the experimentation needed to improve. It might have looked like we were just messing around, but that was essential stuff. Those coaches knew what they were doing.

The Tuesday and Sunday squad sessions at The Deanery remained a far more professional set-up, with a viewing gallery. Even there, the last 15 minutes were mess-around time in which we held impromptu handstand walk or backflip contests. As soon as that time began we changed from competitors back to silly teenagers, meaning that balance between work and fun was maintained and the boundary between them blurred.

Once a month we headed to King's Lynn in Norfolk for competitions, where we had a fair bit of success. The two Matts, Ollie and I were British champions twice in our age category.

Then, when he reached 16, Ashley quit acro because he became too big, physically, to continue as a top. He switched to high-board diving and it did feel a bit like the end of an era. For eight years the Morgan brothers had trained in the same sport but now I would be going alone. Maybe for the first time I began to wonder whether there might be life outside of acro for me too, although at that stage I had no conception of what.

When you drop a stone in a pond, it makes ripples. Maybe it was some kind of energy-flow thing, like chi or karma or the universe pointing me in a certain direction, but in the months after Ashley quit acro and I began having doubts myself, everything seemed to go into flux.

My partner, Ollie Rix, broke his ankle and left. He went off to university to study computer science or something. There followed a period where we tried to replace him with different people and it didn't work. While this dilemma was being grappled with, Matt Fly and Matt Gregory announced they were starting new college courses and would be leaving too. My men's four had become a men's one. This meant the decision was taken out of my hands, and my acro team, with whom I had trained and competed for eight years, was broken up. I went to see Pat and Mike.

'Thanks for everything guys, but I'm going to call it a day.'

'Yeah, we thought you might be saying that. It's understandable. We wish you only good things, Billy. Good luck out there. Good luck on your journey,' Mike said.

'Cheers,' I smiled. Those two had been so good to me.

In many ways, leaving full-time gymnastics was actually a relief. It had become such a dominant part of my life that I felt this great sense of freedom. Freedom can be dangerous though. And when you haven't had any for a long time it can even be intoxicating.

I still had friends who did gymnastics and I continued acro as a hobby, going to adult nights once a week. Those sessions were basically just a raucous free-for-all in the large gym, where anyone could turn up and use the equipment. As well as lapsed acrobats like me, attendees included local free-runners, breakdancers and anyone else who fancied chucking themselves around. There was a real feeling of exploration. We would set up equipment in new ways and try things you would never be allowed to do in a formal gymnastics environment.

James Kingston, who is now a well-known free climber, was often there and earned himself the nickname 'Cunning Fox'. He would jump up on the ceiling beams, then spend hours flipping and balancing on to things most would find hard to stand on, ten metres off the ground, looking down and smirking. There was something a bit unhinged about it. The guy really buzzed off heights. Since then, he's gone on to make quite a name for himself with his daredevil YouTube videos and Instagram pics. He's even made appearances on *This Morning* on ITV.

Of course, less gymnastics meant I had much more time to skate, mountain bike and generally mess about. I suppose life took on a character more typical for a teenage boy. I was mostly happy, mostly ebullient and mostly all over the place. I developed tons of interests, some superficial and fleeting, some more lasting, the majority of them physical. Sometimes I would head out in the evening with a group of friends and run around in the town, climbing up buildings, swinging from balconies, jumping from roof to roof, then scampering off if police turned up. People would call it parkour now and put videos of it on the internet, but as far as we were concerned, we were just larking around.

Another favourite of ours was to hang out in the disused ice cream factory down by our local park. It was only about 300 metres from my house and had been derelict for years. Local homeless people used it for shelter, giving it a strange, musty smell. Most of the windows were broken and plants and moss popped up through the floor randomly. It had the feeling of an industrial space being slowly reclaimed by nature. We built a rope swing inside and used to head down there for mess-around sessions.

At school everyone found their own little rut, whatever they could do to distract themselves from the routine and the minor, daily indignities of it all. It was purely about survival for most of us. Isn't it like that for everyone? We did whatever we could to get through it as psychologically unscathed as possible, then got on with our lives.

But free time wasn't something I had much experience of. Like a lot of teenage boys, I didn't always fill it the best way.

Just after quitting acro, my friend Junior, who lived down the road, turned up at my door with a funny look on his face.

'Can I come in?'

'Course, yeah.'

We went up to my bedroom and he pulled a little plastic bag out of his pocket.

'I just found this on the road,' he said.

'Straight up?' I asked.

'Yeah, is it what I think it is?'

I took it off him, opened it up and smelled it.

'Yeah, I've been around kids smoking this at the skatepark.'

'Shall we hit it?' he asked.

Loads of kids smoked around Southampton, especially ones on the skating, freesports-type scene. It went with the clothes and the music. I guess more than that, it went with the attitude. *Whatever, dude.*

Junior and I went down to the shed at the bottom of the garden and ended up making a bong with a plastic bottle and a Bic biro. I had the genius idea of putting some frozen peas in with the water to make it as cold as possible. We had a few puffs each and started giggling like toddlers.

'Man, I wish I had a giraffe,' Junior said. 'It could feed me peaches and stuff.'

'Yeah ...'

'And keep a lookout. Giraffes can see for fucking miles.'

We looked at each other and laughed for what felt like hours.

Slowly but surely, weed became virtually a daily habit. I enjoyed the buzz, although it made me feel dizzy and even a bit sick. Getting high chilled me out and slowed me down, which was a nice contrast to my usual state of frantic hyperactivity. But I found that the more I smoked the less active it made me, which I didn't like. There were times I would get stoned and then not feel like skating or anything afterwards. This was really unusual for me. Dad often found me smoking at home, too. He didn't chastise me because that wasn't his style, but he sounded a little concerned.

'You're smoking on your own now. It's become a habit.'

It was a scene thing as much as anything else. Most of the kids I hung around with began smoking too, especially the skater crew. We all got into it. Most friendship groups have rituals that bind them together and getting wasted became one of our most important ones. One evening, while up to no good, we found a disused prefab office at Southampton docks. It was around the back of the tile shop near where Ash and I worked. We broke in and claimed it as our smoking HQ.

It was a small space, but it was ours. Legally it wasn't, of course, but that was just a technicality. As far as we were concerned, no one else was using it and it was fair game. We put a lock on the door and covered it in posters – rap stars, bikini babes, giant marijuana leaf motifs. Between us it became known simply as 'the hut', a phrase guaranteed to cause nodding heads and knowing smiles.

'Going down the hut tonight?'

'Definitely bro!'

The car dealership next door had security lights, but we figured out where they were triggered and picked out a path to get in without setting them off. The whole thing had that element of secrecy and danger needed to make something really fun, another little adventure, a covert operation. *Us against the world, yo!*

There was a business desk in there and we filled its drawers with weed paraphernalia – rolling mats, grinders, different size Rizla papers. If those four walls had ears! During our time of hanging out in the hut we must have talked enough stoned crap to fill a surrealist encyclopaedia. Yet, despite all the fun, I had this feeling that something was missing.

9.

Death Mesh

AS THESE thoughts began to circulate in my mind, strangely enough it was school that provided a turning point. In Year 10, Bellemoor ran an elective PE system whereby students had to pick activities from a list. I had never been especially keen on standard school sports, team games such as football, cricket and rugby. They were all too normal and macho and conformist for a little flippity-dippity freak like me.

'What do you reckon?' I asked John at lunchtime. We sat together on a bench beside the playground and perused the options.

'Hockey?' he asked.

'Nah. It's just football with sticks.'

'Cross-country?'

'Hell, no!'

Eventually we decided, along with another couple of pals called Ben and Jake Whitlock (known to all as the ginger twins, for obvious reasons), and another kid called Will Morris, nicknamed 'Fish' for some reason, to put our names down for skiing, the only vaguely interesting option on offer. One of the great benefits of going to Bellemoor was that our school was just a five-minute drive from the Southampton Outdoor Sports Centre. This was one of those things you don't fully appreciate as a kid, but few towns are as lucky to have such an impressive space. In addition to areas for more mainstream sports, the centre ran the only dry ski slope in the region. Our next six weeks of PE would take place there.

At first, as we lined up at the bottom of the slope for initial instructions, I listened avidly, but the health and safety stuff really dragged on. The lessons were like so much of school PE, way too pedestrian for my tastes. I wanted to get up on the skis, bomb around, fall over a lot and learn by trial and error, but nearly the whole first lesson was taken up with an explanation of the equipment, how to get the skis on and how to use the slope without endangering others, before they let us slide down a short distance right at the end.

'That was a bit shit,' John said afterwards. I nodded, but over the weeks that followed, they gradually allowed us more ski time. By the last couple of lessons, my little group of mates had got quite good, or so we thought. I enjoyed the fact I could control the amount of danger I experienced. I decided how high to go up the slope, which dictated how fast I went. We soon got to the point where we were able to ski down the whole slope, change direction and stop on our own. I enjoyed the feeling of gathering momentum, the wind on my face. It was a buzz.

By the time the six-week block was ending, we were sad at the thought of finishing and had conversations about coming back to ski in our own time. Then came another of those moments that seemed so inconsequential then but hugely important now. At the end of our final lesson, the four of us were getting changed by the entrance to the slope's shop/café when a few older kids passed us on the way in, holding snowboards. The first kid had a black board in a glossy finish with some kind of skull motif on it. It caught my eye straight away. These kids weren't straight-edger skiing types. They looked like skateboarders, with long hair and piercings, walking the walk and talking the talk. They didn't notice us and bustled straight through, engaged in intense conversation. But we noticed them. We really noticed them. We hovered around for a few minutes, watching as they got ready. Something kept us there.

The first of them went up the slope, rode down, threw a couple of 'ollies' (a fundamental trick known to all skateboarders and snowboarders, essentially a little jump), swerved to a stop at the bottom of the slope, then gestured at his mates and stood on the end of his board to pick it up. He hadn't done anything particularly special but had a nice, flowy style, all loose and unflustered like he could just float off on the wind. It looked so damn effortless and *cool*. John, Ben, Jake and I headed out in a sort of contemplative silence and started down the path that led away from the slope.

'That was dope, wasn't it?' John said, at last. All of us had obviously been thinking the same thing.

Over the next few weeks, we moved to badminton, the next activity on the PE rota, and stopped going to the ski slope, but John kept bringing it up. He watched a programme on late-night TV that showcased American snowboarders pulling off 'gnarly' stunts. By then we had all become well versed in the lingo through skateboarding. He talked about it endlessly. The whole thing seemed to have taken a hold of him.

In the end, about three weeks after our PE sessions finished, he convinced all of us to go. The problem, of course, was that none of us had a clue what we were doing. In reality we needed private lessons to teach us the fundamentals, but they were £45 an hour, way beyond our budget. General, public sessions, on the other hand, were just £7.50, but to be allowed to do that, you had to be vaguely competent to satisfy health and safety regulations.

Another mate of ours, Matt Norman, whose physiology earned him the highly imaginative nickname 'Longneck', had been on skiing holidays a few times with his family. He briefed us in the bushes outside.

'Don't worry too much about what happens on the board,' he said. 'The truth is people stack it all the time. Most riders out there will be beginners. But the real tell is whether you can get on the lift or not. At this place, that's a biggie. It's right outside the office so the staff will see how you manage it.'

We all nodded. The lift was a drag lift, meaning a pole came around on the mechanism, you had to grab it with your right hand, put it between your legs and allow it to drag you up the hill. It's not a chairlift, so you don't sit on it. If you tried to do that, which seems the natural thing to do, it would just sag down on to the ground. Many absolute beginners needed a few attempts to mount it successfully.

The other problem, Matt said, was that if we dismounted the lift at the first stop, anyone watching would know we were scared. In order to pull this off successfully we all agreed that the first time we had to act super casual, nail the lift, then let that bad boy pull us all the way up to the top.

We queued up nervously and borrowed some snowboards from the store. You had to fill in a form and all of us ticked the box that said we had prior experience. The guy behind the counter seemed a little sceptical.

'You've all ridden before, right?' he asked.

'Oh yeah, yeah, loads, course we have, yeah.'

We strapped our boards on at the bottom of the slope, known as the runout, and exchanged glances.

'It's cool,' Matt said. 'It's gonna be just like skateboarding.'

We nodded. Smart enough. That seemed like common sense. The snowboard was bigger than a standard skateboard but of vaguely similar shape, while the necessary stance seemed identical, although a skateboard isn't attached to your feet. We headed for the lift.

'Once you start moving,' Matt explained, 'keep your weight central and a bit of weight on your back leg. That will stop it pulling you over forwards.'

Surprisingly, I managed the lift well at the first attempt. That meant I was there. At the top. There was only one way to go.

I shifted my weight through my knees and waist a little. How hard could this be?

'One, two, three ... go!'

My first impression of snowboarding was that it was really hard to gather any momentum. On skis, gravity did all the work. If you lacked control, you would fly down the hill. On a snowboard, it was something approaching the opposite. On my first run, before I had even picked up a little bit of speed, I fell over.

Wow, I thought, as I dusted myself off, *this sucks. I would rather ski.*

After another two or three attempts, it began to flow for me, though. I learned to start moving sideways and that you could pick up or lose speed that way. I later discovered that they call that 'the falling leaf' – that you go down on the heel edge facing forwards, going left to right and rocking side to side as you go. Suddenly, it all made sense. I was 'surfing'.

I also quickly learned that any similarities to skateboarding were very superficial. On a skateboard, you turn by tilting the board and letting the trucks guide you around, but on a snowboard there are no trucks. You actually turn by a combination of weight shifting and pressure, then sliding sideways. You need to try to keep your weight centred, rather than using it for forward momentum. The hill will take you down naturally. You're not pushing yourself along a flat surface.

Without teachers saying what we could and couldn't do, the whole group of us spent a blurry couple of hours on the slope, often falling, always laughing. Unlike in the skatepark, there were no tricks or stunts. It was enough of an effort to get from the top to the bottom while retaining balance. We kept it simple, kept turns to a minimum, rode in straight lines but enjoyed ourselves hugely.

So, we went again a few days later and spent a whole afternoon falling over ourselves and each other. A couple of days later we were back, and again, and again. Through some sort of teenage magic we went from first-timers to ski-slope regulars almost instantly. Suddenly, this was 'our thing' that we did. For a few months, a bunch of us would turn up as often as possible, pay for an hour, then ride for about three until the staff noticed and we got thrown out. My skateboard and mountain bike sat in the house gathering dust.

We picked up the basics quickly and soon became acquainted with an unhappy feature of our new hobby, the regularity of injuries. Obviously, while learning you tend to fall over a lot but, to compound that, landing awkwardly on the dry slope surface was absolutely brutal. Like most other dry slopes of the period, the one in Southampton was made of a material called Dendix, composed of plastic bristles, with diamond-shaped spaces between them. It looked like an upturned scrubbing brush. Sometimes, on heavily worn sections, bits of metal or plastic from the base would stick up through the bristles, too. Any skin contact resulted in instant burns and chafing, but even with gloves on, it was so easy to snap bones. You lost your balance, put out a hand, and fingers got stuck in the holes as the rest of your body hurtled forward. *Ouch.* We devised a tactic of wearing socks on our hands instead of gloves to keep our fingers together.

Within a couple of months, all of us had suffered. Minor hospital trips within our group became part of the routine, reaching the point that we gave the surface a nickname: 'Death Mesh', or the even more melodramatic 'Diamonds of Doom'.

Despite these downsides we all got hooked. Enthusiasm is a great educational asset, and once we had mastered the simple stuff, we started attending ramp nights run by a 40-year-old, perma-smiling dude with pierced eyebrows, called Steve Fox. He was a snowboard instructor at the slope and would put equipment out, mostly rails and jumps, so everyone could freestyle around for a few hours.

As had become my habit by then, I threw myself into these evenings with total commitment and found I was soon able to perform some more challenging manoeuvres. My first was an Indy grab, a jump off a ramp in which you hold the board with one hand, mid-air. I had long dreamed of doing one on a skateboard but was far from good enough, so was buzzing for a couple of days after I pulled it off.

Often, groups of older, more experienced boarders would turn up too, which also introduced me to something else, something as important as the snowboarding itself: the culture. These guys could 'shred' some real bad-boy stuff, jumps that required loads of airtime and confidence. Seeing them immediately gave us something to aspire to. On one occasion, we were leaving and this older kid threw a backflip off the 'kicker' (a snowboarding word for ramp). It just looked so cool.

'No way! Did you see that shit?' I commented.

'That was banging, mate!' John replied.

But adolescent boys can be fickle animals, and as the months went by, the mates I started with began to drift away. Even, in the end, John as well. They went back to skating and biking and found other new interests to obsess over for a few months before tiring of those too. Snowboarding was just a phase for them, which like all phases eventually lost its appeal and became something peripheral rather than central to their lives. They found other passions to get hyped about, but for some reason, not me.

It's not always easy to say why you fall in love with something or why it grabs you by the balls, but snowboarding, even in the unglamorous surroundings of the dry slope, had absolutely conquered me. I couldn't stop. I wouldn't stop. As a result, I found myself heading down to the slope for my first ramp night alone. It was a strange feeling, turning up there without the boys. Having never been one of the cool or popular kids around school, I did feel a little awkward without the safety net of my little gang.

At the time, I was practising a move called a backside boardslide on the rails, basically an ollie in which you jump up and slide along, with your board perpendicular to the rail. It sounds incredibly simple when you describe it but can be challenging for beginners, particularly in coordinating around the waist. To make it to the end of the rail you need your legs perpendicular, like your board, but your shoulders parallel. It's one of those weird, counter-intuitive things that you have to make yourself learn. It doesn't come instinctively.

I had a few goes, with mixed results, then went to sit on the sidelines to drink some water.

'Hey Billy,' a voice said from above and behind me. 'You're starting to look good on those rails, mate.'

I looked up to see Steve Fox there, a broad smile on his face, as usual. It was the first time we had spoken one to one. 'Where're your mates tonight, buddy?'

'I'm here by myself,' I shrugged.

'Oh, it's like that is it?' Steve gestured for me to get up. 'Last man standing, eh? Come on.'

I followed Steve around the slope and he introduced me to some of the other regular riders – cool, older kids – whose faces

I knew but had never spoken to, in particular Luke Paul, who I immediately recognised as the guy who chucked the backflip, and Steve Fellows. These were guys who had been abroad and boarded on actual snow. Luke was pretty much top boy around there and even had sponsorship deals with Trespass, an outerwear company, and Atomic, the board manufacturer. To me that made him some kind of guru. The guy was virtually a professional! Steve, on the other hand, was incredibly reckless. He was a good snowboarder and miles better than me but was one of those guys who would try anything. The more time I spent at the slope I soon realised that approach, known as YOLO (you only live once), had its drawbacks. Steve injured himself constantly.

Despite their greater experience and vastly superior technique, Steve, Luke and the others were welcoming and non-judgemental. I suppose, in many ways, being separated from the security blanket of my schoolfriends was my first true taste of the snowboarding scene. I quickly noticed how it shared similarities with the easy, inclusive skateboarding attitude I always liked so much. From there, I began to feel involved, a part of something greater than myself. And that's a truly powerful thing for a teenage boy.

John, Jake and Ben still showed up occasionally, but because I was at the slope more often, a gap in our abilities grew quickly. The cool, older guys we began by looking up to became my friends and all of us formed into a loose group, united by the dry slope and a common passion for freestyle snowboarding. We would get out on the kickers whenever we could and huck moves for as long as possible.

I often watched Luke chucking backflips off the kicker, a move I was so familiar with from my years of gymnastics, although trying it with a board and a ramp would be something new for me. I watched the way he positioned his body, where he held his weight. It was different because of the sideways stance on a snowboard. Sooner or later, I told myself, I would be doing them too. I practised like mad. People saw my dedication and responded to it.

Mike Hurd, who ran the dry slope, saw something in me and offered me free access, which was a huge help and allowed me to progress more rapidly. Then, after I had only been snowboarding for about six months, Steve decided to organise us into a team, or a 'posse' as he called it. He came up with the name 'Ill-Eagle Boarders', which we all liked, so I got on the internet and found an image of an eagle and designed a logo. Steve had T-shirts and stickers done and suddenly that was it, I was part of an actual snowboard crew.

Foxy, as we called him (following the tried and trusted British method of nickname creation – if in doubt, stick a 'y' on the end of a surname), owned a car. It was an enormous barge-like thing, a people carrier with three rows of seats. About eight or nine of us would pile in with our gear on the roof rack and he would drive us around to meets and competitions.

It must have been a strange time for my mum.

'So, what are you doing tonight, darling?'

'I'm going to Suffolk with this dude and a bunch of snowboarders.'

'Suffolk? Really? That's very far away you know?'

'Is it?'

My first meet was at Wycombe Summit dry slope, an hour and a half away. We turned up with our Ill-Eagle gear on, gave it loads and I surprised everyone, including myself, by winning a prize for a 360 (a full-body rotation) off a ramp. I won a pair of Zeal goggles that night, my first-ever snowboarding prize. I wore them all the way home.

10.

A Taste of the Alps

FOR THE next couple of years, the Ill-Eagle crew continued doing their thing. We cruised around the country in Steve Fox's car, rocking up at nights here and there, making noise.

'Come on,' Steve said, one evening in 2004, 'there's a big jam on at Tamworth this Friday.'

'Tamworth? Where's that?'

'In the Midlands,' he said, grinning, 'near Birmingham. They've got a snowdome there, a proper slope, about 170 metres long.'

'Cool!'

Making the step up from Dendix to actual snow was always exciting, even if it was just the British, indoor variety. It almost felt like a little holiday. Traffic was kind that afternoon and we shot up the motorway, arriving an hour or so before they were ready to let us in. It was a warmish evening and none of us felt like sitting inside the car. Luke pointed out of the window.

'Do you reckon you could backflip off that wall?' he asked. To me, that sounded like a challenge. He had barely finished speaking before I flung the doors open and jumped out. As it turned out, I could backflip off the wall. Not only that, either. With a couple of the other kids in tow, I began an impromptu parkour session outside the venue. We just freestyled our way around whatever was there, jumping from one stair rail to another, walking on our hands downstairs, backflipping off bus shelters. Bit by bit, a small crowd and then a larger one gathered. Soon we had maybe 100 stoked people clapping and cheering as we flipped about.

At last, they let us in. A rush of cold air hit my face, while snow covered the indoor slope. It wasn't snow as you see it on postcards. It was greyish and thinly distributed in places, but still an improvement on death mesh. The place smelled a bit like a swimming pool, which was weird, but the actual run itself was longer than ours at home. To my inexperienced self it felt like being on a real mountain.

They set up all kinds of mad little contests. Who could ollie the highest, who could go the biggest off the quarterpipe, all that sort of thing. Our crew absolutely sent it and had someone on almost every podium. Later at the same event, Luke and I shotgunned the jump line, doing backflips and frontflips all the way to the bottom. The audience was absolutely stoked.

Afterwards, the *Tamworth Herald* gave us a fantastic writeup, saying, 'The Ill-Eagle Boarders from Southampton came and provided great delight to the waiting crowds with a display of parkour. In the snowdome they were equally impressive.' Steve read it to us at the dry slope, with a huge smile. Our name, it seemed, was spreading. Mad as it sounded, this bunch of seaside kids had a growing snowsport reputation, albeit at the lower end of the scene. It was exciting. It felt like this thing of ours was developing. It was something cool.

Central to all of that, of course, was Foxy. An incredible guy, important to everyone, but especially me. Steve was one of those people who went way beyond what was necessary. Yes, he was an instructor at the dry slope, but this wasn't just about work for him. He gave so much of his free time, too. He wanted us to feel good, to pay it forward and help youngsters reach their potential.

In the car he would blast loud music and make dodgy jokes. He gave the impression of having a bit of a Peter Pan complex, heading into middle age but at the same time unable to let go of his old, renegade self. He even fostered kids whose lives had gone off the rails and used snowboarding as a tool to focus them.

Through Steve's energy and dedication, the Ill-Eagle crew took my introduction to snowboarding countrywide. I got to know boarders from everywhere and even developed a little name for myself, known as a kid who would attempt and even sometimes pull off some pretty gnarly tricks.

'You've got balls,' people would say, when they saw me throwing myself into tricks they were afraid to attempt. In one sense, they were right. My long-standing relationship with risk meant I was probably less afraid of injury than your average punter. But there was more to it than that. My gymnastic training had given me aerial awareness that other snowboard beginners took years to develop. Spurred on by Luke and Steve, I was one of very few kids at ramp nights who could throw backflips off the kicker.

It even got to the point, while I was still only 15 or so, that I sometimes received comments dissecting my form. Older guys standing around watching me and scratching their chins.

'Amazing energy, but your arms!' someone would say.

'What about them?'

'They're all over the place, dude.'

That sort of comment ended up following me for years. Essentially, I could do the trick and land it, but for the aficionados, the stylists, the purists, the YouTube critics and the technicians, it didn't look very good. It occurred to me straight away that this was something else out of the Mad Eddie manual of life.

Dad was all about making things work, appearances were of secondary importance, and I was taking that Morgan ethos into snowboarding.

The truth was that as a pure snowboard rider negotiating my way down a hill, I was bang average. There was very little to distinguish me from any other teenage hobbyist. Even my turning skills were basic, but my focus wasn't on that stuff. What I did was point myself at the nearest obstacle, hurtle towards it, then fly off it. That was my thing. It was clear that I was becoming a 'park rider', as it was known, not a racer.

I rode incessantly. The work ethic Dad and Grandad instilled in me made sure of that. No one had to tell me to practise, and I was all about the board and the slope. That was it. I was never a kid who read magazines or watched videos online. I just wanted to be out there, doing my thing. I didn't get turned on by showing off, but if I landed a trick that I had found impossible a month previously, I got a massive buzz.

In the background of all of this, as snowboarding took a growing role in my life, the everyday strain between Mum and Dad got worse at home. As they aged, they seemed ever more like two magnets whose natural energies repelled each other. It didn't help that we kept getting burgled, either.

Attracted by Dad's motorbikes and tools, we suffered break-in after break-in during the space of a year. Dad reported them to the police, but nothing was ever done and the situation became frustrating. Every time you opened the front door, you would step inside warily, wondering whether it had happened again.

Dad, being Dad, refused to accept victim status and took action, constructing a booby trap with a shotgun cartridge, a blasting cap and weird little device he made out of wood. It was connected to a trip wire and Dad always maintained the idea was only that anyone entering the garage would trigger it, be frightened by the resultant blast and abandon their robbery. He wasn't trying to kill anyone. But being a sort of crazy perfectionist with his DIY jobs, Dad couldn't leave his new invention alone and spent hours each evening tinkering with it. One Tuesday night he was sitting in the conservatory by the garden, experimenting with different types of ammunition, and the thing exploded in his lap, sending a shower of hot lead into his belly.

Howling in agony, Dad managed to phone himself an ambulance, but, of course, as soon as the crew arrived and saw what was going on, they involved the police, too. Dad had to undergo surgery to remove 20 pellets from his abdomen, then ended up in Crown Court on a firearms charge. It was big news in Southampton and the story made the front page of our local newspaper, the *Southern Daily Echo*. Mum, as usual, was mortified. At least the burglaries stopped.

Not long after that incident, the inevitable happened (or at least it seems inevitable looking back on it) and Mum and Dad split up. They were such different people and I think Mum just had enough. The failed booby trap was her tipping point and she moved out. It was an amicable break-up. Ash and I were given the choice of where to live and we both decided to stay, hoping it would bring Mum back, but it didn't. Fortunately, her new flat was only a minute's walk from Dad's place.

Their separation was upsetting at first but didn't devastate me in the way it probably would have done five or six years earlier. I think by my mid-teens I already understood that they were individuals with their own paths to follow. They didn't give the impression of validating each other, and for most of my life they just co-existed, but nonetheless it did affect me. I often found myself in a more thoughtful mood than usual.

At the time, Foxy had another of the Ill-Eagle Boarders, a kid called Dominic Ball, staying at his house. Dominic was from

Bournemouth, 35 miles away, and stayed at Steve's place so he could get to training more easily. Dom was a great kid and quite similar to me in that he always wanted to try the biggest tricks he could, so I spoke to Steve at the dry slope and asked whether I could come and crash at his place for the weekend too. It would be a way to escape the weirdness at home and let rip for a couple of days instead.

The sort of guy that Foxy was, he was never likely to refuse, so that evening I threw some spare underwear in a bag and headed down to his place in Gosport, which was a great release. Dominic and I ended up bouncing off the walls for a couple of days. Steve had some old dry slope mats in his garage, so we got them out and laid them on the roof of the house, then spent hour after hour boarding off the roof, backflipping, ripping 360s and landing in the garden. God knows what the neighbours must have thought.

I had such a great time that the weekend turned into two weeks. When I finally went back home, it didn't seem so weird that Mum wasn't there.

During my stay at his place, Steve mentioned he was planning a holiday for family and friends to Les Deux Alpes in Mont-de-Lans, France, something he organised every year. As my snowboarding was improving, he felt it would be beneficial for me to come. Steve spoke to Dad on the phone, as Dad had been skiing a couple of times at the ski centre and knew Steve, so he agreed to come with us. For the next few months, I existed in a state of high anticipation. Even though I enjoyed all our nights and afternoons at the dry slope and our trips around the country with the crew, I didn't yet really think of myself as a snowboarder. How could I be? How could a kid from Southampton who never rode on snow be a snowboarder? I was a Dendixboarder, or at best a kid who had ridden on artificial snow in snowdomes.

So, out of this weird period of my life, in which so much seemed to be changing, came my first visit to the Alps and my first sample of mountain time. I had a sense from the beginning that it was going to be special, and on the drive to the resort in a minibus, as we approached the foothills of the mountain, with the peaks and glacier rising up in the distance, it felt like entering a movie set. Everything was bathed in blue and white. I couldn't stop staring.

'Is that where we're going?' I asked.

'That's it, buddy,' Steve replied.

Les Deux Alpes is one of the few all-year-round ski destinations in Europe and, as well as regular piste skiing, boasted an amazing snowpark. Very popular with Brits, there were loads of UK boarders as well as freestyle skiers there and plenty of people I could learn from. Although no one from our group was my age, on the first day in the snowpark I met a French kid who I bonded with, although we had no common language. I could only say bonjour and au revoir, and his level of English wasn't much better, but there's a lot of commonality in snowboarding.

'Tu fait le switch backside neuf cent?'

He was a few years older than me and could chuck some incredible moves out of the halfpipe. He took me under his wing and I followed him around for a bit. The snowpark was spread over the top of the glacier and contained six separate kickers, a whole area full of tabletops, another of boxes and rails and yet another with two pipes. For a kid like me, whose prior experience was of death mesh, it was mind-blowing. The mountains have that particular mountain smell. The air is so clear. The riding's faster, everything's bigger. You're not just stuck to where the plastic is, you can go wherever you want.

While in Les Deux Alpes, I did my first legitimate jump of about ten metres and got such a buzz. I must have lapped it a hundred times, just straight air. Then on the last day I got Dad to pitch up on the knuckle with a camera and I threw a backflip. It felt unbelievable, not like backflips on the dry slope, which were over so quickly. I was in the air for ages, watching the world spin around. I landed and had never been so stoked.

Every waking moment of mine was spent in the park. I rode from one section to another, almost as if I was doing a slopestyle course, using all the equipment I could, then catching the lift back to the top and starting again.

Two full weeks of riding on snow every day had quite an impact. It triggered something inside, and when I came back and rode at the dry slope, it felt like my game went up a notch. Other people saw it, too. Something was definitely happening.

Les Deux Alpes hadn't just been my first experience of riding on snow, but also my first foreign holiday. Perhaps that was also all part of the process that was occurring. The more my snowboarding journey went on, the larger my world became.

My time shredding around with the Ill-Eagle Boarders took me beyond my childhood arena in Southampton and introduced me to so many other parts of the UK. Journeys to competitions allowed for a lot of exploration. Usually, we would pile into Steve's car, banter about, stop on the way somewhere and skate in a car park or something, then arrive at a venue, ride and huck tricks for a couple of hours, before piling back in the van and going home. Bristol, Liverpool, Norwich, Cornwall – we travelled to every corner of the country. It was great fun, and truly mind-expanding.

Of course, we all had our own motivations, but from my perspective, I desperately needed all of that. Without it, my possibilities were limited. Predictably, I walked out of Bellemoor at 16, with only a handful of GCSEs at grade C and D. Of all possible futures ahead of me, I clearly wouldn't be reading law at Cambridge. One to cross off the list.

I enrolled at a place called Taunton's College, on a BTEC Public Services course, just because I thought I should. The qualification was intended for people going into the army, police or fire brigade, but it really, really bored me and I was a thoroughly unmotivated student. I packed it in after a year.

Dad saw that I needed direction and got me a job with a builder friend of his called Mick Judge. Mick was a great guy, a typical beefy-looking builder type, but very intelligent and reflective. I learned so much working with Mick. He taught me loads about construction work, but more than that, our long chats here and there in the van also taught me about myself.

'If your job's something you enjoy, you'll never work a day in your life.' That was one of Mick's favourite lines.

What I really enjoyed, of course, was going snowboarding, but like a lot of people who have something unconventional they think they're meant to do, this gave me a problem. The one thing I loved didn't pay any money. How could I solve that? I decided to have a chat with Mike Hurd.

'I'll give you a job at the dry slope,' Mike said. 'It'll be perfect for you. You'll get to hang around here even more than you do now!'

That's how the next phase in my snowboard development began. Being an employee meant I had a set of keys and could access the place whenever I wanted. That presented the possibility of out-of-hours riding.

I quickly became part of the furniture at the dry slope, using all the knowledge and experience I picked up from Dad and Mick. Just like Mad Eddie, I was good with my hands. I built jumps out of pieces of wood I found for ramp nights. I performed a lot of maintenance on the ski lift. That thing needed daily care just to keep it rolling. Maybe my favourite duty was running the 'ringo' sessions for kids. It was basically a mess-about hour when children rode down the slope on rubber rings. I supervised, but, of course, I also joined in and had a great time throwing myself about.

Slowly, over the weeks, I started to become close to a girl who worked there too. Sarah Hillen had been on my radar for a little while and sometimes came to dry slope contests with me and the other Ill-Eagle Boarders, but I was pretty shy with girls and had no 'game' at all. Sarah was brunette and cute and got inside my head, but I had no real idea whether she liked me too.

Then, in that awkward way that teenagers operate, we started finding excuses to be around each other. Sometimes we forgot our work, getting entangled in conversations about anything and everything, an unusual thing for a quiet soul like me. One day I was about to head down into the woods by the side of the dry slope to build a tabletop jump. I saw her coming.

'Hi, Sarah.'

'Hi.'

'Umm … can you give me a hand?'

I held up the tools I was carrying to show that I had a task to perform. She nodded. 'Sure.'

So that's how it all happened. We were alone in the trees with light rain filtering through the branches. She was holding a plank of wood still for me and by accident I put my hand on top of hers. Everything seemed to stop for a few seconds. There was a weird heat and electricity between our skins, my heart raced, and we ended up kissing. I hadn't planned it at all. From that moment on, I had a girlfriend.

That was cool and gave me something else to do, another aspect of life. It was a fun relationship and more than anything else was built around our mutual enjoyment of snowboarding and other freesports. Sometimes we would go down to the beach and bodyboard together or go for bike rides in the woods. We were very movement oriented, which suited me. We were never a typical teenage couple that went out to eat together or met for dates in the cinema.

A couple of months after Sarah and I got together, Steve organised one of his regular freestyle contests at the slope. There were the usual jumps and rails out, everyone rode for half an hour or so, then a panel of judges chose eight people to go into the final. As usual, I arrived looking a mess, in a motocross T-shirt, but threw backflips for fun and had one of those nights where everything I tried came off. In the final I had zero nerves. The judges declared me the winner and gave me some snow boots as a prize.

Afterwards, Luke Paul came to speak to me and Sarah. He had a bit of a light in his eyes.

'Billy,' he said, 'you're looking decent out there, mate! You know what you need?'

I shook my head. 'What?'

'You need to do a winter season. It would be amazing for you.' I had always respected his opinion. 'I'm heading out to Morzine this winter. Fancy it?'

Morzine, I thought. *Where the hell is that?* It was something I hadn't seriously considered before. But spending a winter somewhere with mountains and sky and nothing to do but snowboard, away from all the distractions of home, seemed like a sweet, sweet idea. Sarah was immediately into it, too. We didn't even discuss it. It was on.

Sarah immediately began the process of sorting everything out, going online to find apartments, breaking down the necessary payments, all that stuff. We read together about Morzine on the internet and our excitement grew.

11.

The Morzine Scene

THERE ARE certain places around the world that are Meccas for the ski and snowboard communities. Often areas where there's year-round snow and rideable conditions on- and off-season. Since the ski popularity boom from the mid-20th century, some of these have turned into ski- and snowboard-specific towns, meaning their economies are solely snowsport-focused. Even if the villages they grew from may have first been built as farming or herding settlements, now residents all work in the industry: hotel workers, restaurant staff, bartenders, ski guides, instructors, maintenance crew. If you ask around, you'll find that everyone living permanently in these places is employed, directly or indirectly, in snowsports.

Chamonix, Hintertux, Tignes, Lake Tahoe in the USA and many more; places where you can go at any time and lose yourself in all the white. Avoriaz, where Morzine is located, by the Swiss border in the French Alps, has no snow in the summer and is quite a low resort, but back when Luke first mentioned it to me in 2007, it was the undisputed top spot for the British snowboarding crew. If you were young, you wanted to shred and you had a few quid in your pocket, it was the place to be.

But that was the big problem. I was young – *tick* – and I wanted to shred – *tick* – but I didn't have a few quid in my pocket. Two out of three is a nice start, but the one missing was the foundation stone. A full winter season in Morzine, including food and accommodation, even done on the cheap would cost at least £3,000. At the time, my wage at the dry ski slope was £7 per hour. Raising finance would be a struggle.

So, I knuckled down and started saving every penny of my earnings. Sarah did the same and we set targets for how much we would put away by particular dates. I was very fortunate that Dad recognised the focus I was showing and offered to support me.

'You're really up for this season lark, aren't you?' he asked one day in the kitchen.

'Yeah, I'm buzzing for it. My riding's come such a long way. I just want to see what it's all about.'

He took a moment to stir his tea, then said, 'I'll tell you what I'll do. If you can save half the money, I'll match you and you can pay me back later.'

'Really?'

'Really.'

That conversation changed everything. Getting to £3k would have been touch and go, but I knew I could get to £1.5k. That was the side of Mad Eddie Morgan that some people didn't see. Sure, he was a bit eccentric and had his wild moments, but he was also a father who cared deeply for and understood his kids. Dad saw how important this was, and from that day onwards, I knew that Morzine was on.

Nonetheless, when the deadline arrived to pay and I sent a French holiday firm £3k for our accommodation, it absolutely blew my mind. We hadn't been there yet. We hadn't seen the flat and didn't even know that it actually existed; £3k was by far the most money I had in my life and I just sent it overseas on a promise.

With the money in a French hotelier's account and Sarah in tow, I flew out in December. Our apartment did exist, which was reassuring; a tiny studio flat on the main high street about 600m from the centre of Morzine. It consisted of half a basement, with a window at ground level. There was just room enough for a bed, a shower cubicle and a cooker. But we were there. That was all that mattered. For us, it was perfect.

The village itself presented a classic Alpine scene with wooden buildings and balconies, all covered with snow, of course, like a Christmas card or something from an episode of *Heidi*. The town rang with the sound of vehicles running on chains, and snowcats. There was even a little train to ferry people around, known, of course, as 'le petit train'. Everywhere you looked, people carried skis and snowboards. The air had that smell, the mountain smell. It made everything feel so authentic, a very different vibe to Southampton.

Luke Paul had already been there for a couple of days. I texted him to let him know we had arrived and he turned up at our door within a couple of hours. He told us about the Morzine scene, how all the park riders headed up to the Avoriaz area, then hit the infamous Cavern bar at night. Morzine ran free buses for skiers and snowboarders, which drove right through the town up to where you could pick up the gondola to the slopes. Everything there was geared to get you up into the mountains as quickly and easily as possible. It was all about that.

All about the mountains.

All about the white.

For our first night, Luke suggested we head to a local bar, called Robinsons, whose speciality was some sort of double strength ale called Mützig.

'Be careful dude, it'll wreck ya!'

We walked down there and Luke introduced us to a bunch of people in the bar, most notably another sponsored rider called Ben Knox. Conversation was entirely about what would be happening the next day.

'So, look, we meet at 9.30 and then head up to that part of the slope we were at yesterday. There's been a fresh dump and one of the cliffs is gonna be on.'

'Cool, I'll let Cooper know …' And so on. It intrigued me, and although I didn't talk much, I loved how focused everyone seemed to be on their riding. These guys hadn't just come out to the Alps to drink and mess about, although it may have looked like that to anyone who didn't know them.

Sarah and I walked back to the apartment through the town around midnight, tipsy and happy. I could tell that Morzine was going to be special.

The next morning, I got up early and sorted out my gear. After a quick bowl of cereal, Sarah and I walked up through the town towards the lift, crunching through snow that had frozen overnight. I had never been so excited in my life.

We met Luke at the bottom of the lift and headed up. From the lift stop we then rode over to another lift. After disembarking from that we rode to the Avoriaz area, an amazing clifftop ski and snowboard experience, with 51 runs and 130km of rideable slopes. The variety was incredible – powder runs, good fast lines, snowparks. The top elevation there is 2.5km above sea level and vehicles are banned around Avoriaz, giving the air an ever crisper, mountain feel. Luke took us around and showed us a few spots. His knowledge of the resort was invaluable.

For the next couple of weeks, I followed Luke around and he introduced me to lots of people: guys such as JJ Jones, Tommy Bowers, Lucas Bramall and Scott McMorris, funny and charismatic riders, guys who were great value in front of a camera.

This was a new angle for me. Up to now, my snowboarding had been about hucking tricks at the dry slope and entering little competitions. I hadn't done any filming before, not in any serious way. In Morzine, nearly everyone was recording footage and putting it online.

Ah, I started to think, *so this is what it's about.*

I loved exploring the mountain, its different slopes, its conifer trees. Sometimes I even spotted a stray antelope or a marmot. Every now and then, if I stopped and looked up, I might see a golden eagle circling the sky.

That amazing natural space, so different to the industrialised, mechanised world I came from, became my new home. There were no petrol fumes up there, just air. All my life I had smelled petrol. Petrol and the sea. Not the sea of sandy shores and dolphins though, not the nature documentary sea, but an oily sea, choked by container ships and trawlers. In Morzine everything felt fresh. So beautiful and pure and clean. It does something to your head, all that.

It changes you.

It changed me.

I began to see too, how snowboarding worked in reality, for people who made it an important part or maybe *the* most important part of their life. Every morning people would come together in the snowpark and see who was around. Kids would get chatting and decide what to do. Some would stay in the park and huck tricks, others would go touring around. Some might have discovered some special feature nearby they wanted to experiment with.

'We're going to go and shoot this gnarly cliff, see what happens, who wants to come?'

It was like each day could be anything at all. The possibilities were endless, with everything focused on the mountain.

For three months, I learned to mould my life around those mountains. Riding was my primary need. Everything else came second, everything. Just outside our apartment door was a boiler room where we could dry our clothes after washing them in the sink, meaning we avoided the expense of the launderette. We used our one window as a fridge, buying cheap brie or milk from a local supermarket then keeping it on the window ledge to stay fresh. Food was simply a matter of getting as full as we could, as cheaply as possible. Cheese baguettes from a shop called Sherpa, evening dinners cooked in the room, consisting of chilli con carne or spaghetti bolognese. Big piles of carbohydrates, with whatever protein was on special offer in the shops. All that mattered was fuelling myself for the next day's shredding.

Out on the slopes, kids teamed up into crews with their cameras, putting together little films they could fling out on YouTube. With the right tricks, some decent camera work, or maybe some luck, it was possible to get tens or even hundreds of thousands of views. The global scene was that big.

Luke told me how, at the end of the season, the Cavern bar ran a competition called the 24/7. Every crew could enter a snowboarding film and judges would declare a winner. The idea wasn't just to do hard tricks, he said, but to do something quirky, off-key or funny. I knew I would have to get involved.

Every day I rode with different people. Two or three guys one day, a different two or three the next. And although we were just having fun, every day I acquired new skills. You could learn from everyone. One guy might be great at frontflips, another at basic board technique. Maybe his friend was a sick rail rider.

There was no objective to this, no overall plan. I had no specific or concrete aims (as usual), but day by day I became more proficient. Our videos started looking cooler. They were nowhere near the level of people we aspired to, of course, the Red Bull productions with guys such as Travis Rice. We knew we were miles away from elite level, but we also knew that didn't matter. For all of us, the thrill was in personal progression, in putting a trick we had just learned into a video. Last week I couldn't do a decent front board, now I can. I found a crew of people who thought just like I did. That made me feel good.

No, scratch that. That made me feel awesome.

By January, after a solid month of daily riding, I could throw double backflips off the kicker on a regular basis. This began to draw attention. I was still learning so much, still a beginner in so many ways, but as before, my background helped me stand out. In 2007, no one else in Avoriaz could do that. It was weird, but people began to whisper my name. I would pick things up, in my peripheral vision or hearing.

'Yo, there's that double backflip kid.'

'Where?'

'Over there!'

Towards the end of that first season, I started chucking rodeos too. They're a more complicated manoeuvre, essentially a backflip with an added backside 180 towards the end. They soon became my trademarks. At the end of a day's riding, I would head down to the bar and find myself on the receiving end of some nice comments as soon as I walked in.

'I heard you back-rodeoed the big line today, Billy.'

It was a weird feeling. Not unpleasant, but weird. People were talking about me and my riding. It made me nervous, and I never knew how to respond, so I would just smile and say, 'Cheers.'

One afternoon in February, near the end of that first winter, I was doing some filming. I began by throwing straight airs, then mixing it up. A few backflips and I felt good, so I chucked a double backie, then a rodeo, on adjacent jumps, one after the other in quick succession. A little crowd of onlookers whooped and aahed their appreciation. Luke was there to give me some knuckles.

'Awesome dude. You're smashing it.'

From behind Luke, another guy approached, a slightly older guy with a short beard. He looked maybe 35 or so. 'Billy Morgan?' he asked.

A jolt of anxiety juddered through me. For some reason, I instinctively thought this guy was some sort of official and I was about to be scolded or fined for an indiscretion.

'Yeah,' I responded warily.

'Can I have a word?'

Oh God, I thought. *Here we go.* I followed him away from the crowd, worrying that the situation felt very conspiratorial. If he wasn't going to arrest me, what was he going to do, ask me out for dinner? Offer me a job with MI5? I actually started to get nervous about what he would say.

'I'm Neil,' he told me, leaning in, 'and I work for a hat company called Ignite Beanies. We love your style out there, Billy, really. You're doing it! Would you be interested in receiving some sponsorship?'

Just for a moment, I swear I saw a halo around his head. Suddenly, everything made sense, like life is a long, old equation and I began to see a solution. To say I was stoked is an understatement. I wasn't just Billy from Southampton any more. No.

I was a sponsored snowboarder.

12.

Ouch!

THE DEAL with Ignite wasn't anything life-changing but meant a lot. There was no real money involved, but the free hats I received in exchange for online promo felt like validation. This wasn't just aimless messing about in the snow. Yes, it was fun, but there was real-world value in it too. It was even worth money to some people. It *could* lead somewhere.

The winter finished with the 24/7 party at the Cavern, followed by a big barbecue out on the hill. The highlight of the end-of-season celebrations was a British vs French freestyle comp called 'The Battle of Waterloo'. There were two teams of eight riders each and I was genuinely thrilled to be selected for the British team. More or less the whole town was going to watch and I viewed it as a privilege to compete. I performed well and loved the craic. As a competition, it was a step up from my old Ill-Eagle meets. Morzine was just an unbelievable time, full stop, and while I was caught up in it, it seemed it would never end.

But it did.

By the time April hit and we headed back to England, it felt like a lot had changed. Four months of solid snowboarding raised my game immeasurably, but more than that, I had tasted another life. My experience of the Alpine lifestyle meant I would never be able to settle for staying in Southampton year-round and working for the weekend. The eagles, pine trees and marmots in my memory wouldn't let me. There was more for me out there.

Not that I necessarily saw snowboarding as a 'career', not yet, but with the failed experiment of college behind me and nothing else in life I particularly wanted to do, snowboarding was now *my thing*.

Bus, plane and then train brought me back to Southampton. It still smelled the same, and while part of me was definitely pleased to be back, another part still had its head in the Alps. With bag and kit on my back and in a poignant frame of mind, I arrived back at Dad's front door in late afternoon, to find it had been left open. Strange shoes were scattered all over the doorstep. Music pulsed from somewhere.

Oh shit, I thought to myself. *What's going on here?* I was in no mood for a party.

As if to welcome me back, a large firework whistled over the roof of the house. Rather than zooming straight up into the air, the thing maintained a low, missile-like trajectory, as if it had been modified. (A favourite Eddie Morgan trick was to cut the stick off the bottom of fireworks, so their flight path was flatter.) It arched neatly over the house and exploded on the kerb behind me, about a metre away from a parked car. In the distance I could hear Dad's voice.

'That weren't quite right,' he said. 'Hang on, I'll try another.'

I walked through the house and found him, predictably, drinking in the garden, having a barbecue with a few mates.

'Son!' He came running over to hug me, but I was exhausted by all the end-of-season events and the journey.

Fuck this, I thought. 'Hey Dad, just wanted to say hello. I'm staying at Mum's tonight.'

'Yeah! So good to see you son!'

I left him to it and went to the relative refuge of Mum's.

After that, life quickly picked up just as it had been previously. Dad asked what I was thinking to do long term, whether there were any jobs I was keen on, but he did it in a laid-back way. Pressure was never Dad's style.

'You can't just be on a jolly forever, you know,' he said.

'I know, Dad,' I replied.

But that was as far as it went. I was still only 18, after all. Ashley was already in the Royal Navy by then and had gained a promotion to Petty Officer, but I had learned to stop comparing myself to him years before.

I went back to working at the dry slope and very swiftly all the other nonsense that comprised my life in Southampton kicked back in. Free-running, skateboarding, motorbiking and a bit of getting wasted. It was great to see the guys again. The ginger twins and John, Junior, Lewis, Matt and Fish. Fish had got well into snowboarding while I was away and was keen to hear all about Morzine. I told him about the riding there, how smooth and fresh it was, how it felt like a different world. He saw my excitement and a light went on in his eyes.

During evenings and weekends hanging out, he often brought it up. He would get me to tell him about different parts of the snowpark in Avoriaz, how big the jumps were, the other features.

One night a few of us were at my place, having a drink. He put his beer down and looked at me. 'Are you going back this winter,' he asked.

'Definitely,' I replied.

'Then I'm coming too.'

Fish made plans with Junior and Lewis to join me. It would be a squash in that little apartment with Sarah there as well, but we reckoned for a week it was well worth the craic.

With my focus on working and saving money, my summer plans were slightly disrupted when a friend of mine called Dayne Mulford bought a pit bike, a small motocross machine. We took it up to a little track in Chandler's Ford with Ashley, while he was on leave. Ash had just bought a new car, a bright green Ford Focus RS, which he was super proud of.

The three of us took turns on the motorbike and ragged around, but on my last go I came around a berm too fast and upended over the top of the slope. I went over the handlebars and landed heavily. It was nothing major, a bog-standard motorbike crash. I was a little shaken but had a helmet on so didn't think much of it. As I stood up, I was very aware of searing pain in my elbow and began walking back to Dane and Ash.

'Are you alright?' Dane asked. I saw his eyes travel down to my crotch area. As I rubbed my sore elbow, I looked down at my legs and gasped. My shorts were completely soaked in blood.

Panicking, I looked inside my pants to see a flap of skin hanging off my scrotum. The wound was so bad, the white of one of my testicles actually showed through the tear. I quickly pulled the skin back over it and cupped it with both hands. Fortunately, Dane was in training to be a paramedic at the time.

'How bad is it?' I asked him.

He frowned. 'It's not bad, but you need to go to A&E as fast as possible.'

'Fuck the ambulance,' Ashley said. 'I'm taking him now.'

We piled into Ash's RS and I immediately went into shock, turned white and started shaking. Ashley drove back into town like an absolute renegade, foot down all the way, jumping red lights, crazy overtaking, the works. I reckon it was pretty much a dream for him, as he had an excuse to race his new car without repercussions.

On arrival we ran into A&E and I went straight past the queue into a doctor's room and dropped my pants. They brought a bed out for me without hesitation and drugged me to calm me down. I waited there, in limbo, until they operated, and Ashley came in to see me.

He had a packet of biscuits he had bought from a vending machine.

'Okay?' he asked.

'Yeah. They're gonna stitch me up.'

'Good … let's have a look then.'

I pulled my shorts down to show him the injury. For some reason Ashley exploded with laughter and spat several chunks of biscuit straight into the wound.

'Shit!' he said. 'Don't worry about it!' And I laid there for an uncomfortable 20 seconds while my brother picked bits of Jaffa Cake out of my ball sack.

While resting and allowing the stitches to heal, I managed to use my summer at home for something more positive, by picking up another sponsorship arrangement. A meeting of minds with a guy called Andy Sherman-Mills resulted in him becoming my first agent. He ran a ski and snowboard shop called Route One and had a good business brain.

'I reckon I can help you,' he said. 'Let's see what we can do together. I'm sure we can make a few things happen.' That sounded good to me. Andy would go on to represent me for the next five years.

Something else, less poetic and profound, that had changed as a result of my first winter away was my relationship with alcohol. All those nights down at the Cavern, getting smashed on schnapps, Jägermeister or just the local beers with the snowboarding crew, had given me a new taste for booze. During Ashley's spells at home on leave, this meant something new – we had a common interest other than extreme sports. Suddenly the Morgan brothers were drinking buddies!

We began heading out on these crazy nights out together, a sort of union of his friends and mine. Twenty of us would descend on the town, crawl the pubs, then end up in nightclubs like Oceana, a vast warehouse of a place on three floors. In Southampton there are considerably more nightclubs than would normally be found in a town of that size, catering for all the students from the university.

A few drinks in and Ashley and I would start throwing backflips on the dancefloor. I always liked to make sure it was in time with the music. I would be boogying away, cutting shapes, wait for the drop. 'Yes, Mr DJ!' Then – *bam* – chuck one over. We had backflips engrained in us from such a young age that it didn't matter what condition we were in. I could be out of my mind, half unconscious on a sofa at the back of the club, and someone could come over, peel me up and say, 'Come on Billy, do a backflip!'

Tongue lolling, about to be sick through my nose, it didn't matter. Muscle memory is an incredible thing. I could throw it, land it perfectly, then collapse back down. Bouncers began to get annoyed about it. It seemed backflips contravened some sort of health and safety rule and I started to get a reputation. As we queued to get in, some huge steroid monster in a bow tie would tap me on the shoulder: 'No backflips tonight please, Billy.'

Other kids got thrown out of clubs for fighting or drugs. Not us. The Morgan boys got thrown out for acrobatics. Sometimes on those nights out, we saw kids from school here and there. The cool kids, the ones who used to be a little bit unkind. They had all stayed around the town and got themselves jobs. Some had put on a little weight. One or two looked as if they were charging straight into middle age already. Anyway, they still thought we were freaks. To them I would always be 'backflip Billy' and I was cool with that, as was Ashley. We owned it.

After one particularly heavy night of revelry we came out of a city-centre dive, absolutely steaming, and the two of us backflipped all the way up Southampton High Street. We both broke our record of 18 consecutive flips, as people stopped and stared. Some filmed it, until we collapsed in a heap, laughing outside Co-op.

As summer rolled into autumn and I began to firm up my plans, Mike Hurd from the ski slope told me he had set up a little partnership with a ski and snowboard store called Filarinskis. I had been working overtime, skipping leave, trying to earn as much money as I could, so I had a lot of accrued holiday. Steve said if I wanted I could use my unused holiday as credit in the shop, which was one of the best feelings ever. I went in there and chose myself some cool, multicoloured snowboarding gear, without having to pay for it.

I went home and modelled it in the mirror. 'Yeah, bwoy!' It was a vision in blue, purple and yellow. Dad opened the door behind me and raised an eyebrow. 'What do you reckon?' I asked, turning proudly, spreading my arms. 'Didn't even have to pay for it.'

'You look like a packet of liquorice allsorts,' he replied. 'Bertie Bassett.'

Throughout that whole off-season, apart from when I was healing, I continued boarding regularly at the dry slope. We started heading out to Calshot too, which also had a plastic slope inside a sort of aircraft hangar. There was a great scene there with a university snowboard club hanging out. Fish was always keen to join me, as were a few of the other guys. Although I did find the adjustment weird, there was never a question of me waiting for the next winter to ride again. I heard of some people who refused to go back to artificial surfaces after their first season away. That wasn't an option for me. I needed all of it too much.

Of course, riding on the artificial surfaces meant modifying what I did. There was no question of hucking a double backflip at a dry slope, for example. The ramps weren't big enough and there would be a chance of doing yourself serious damage, but I never concerned myself with that. It wasn't a question of going backwards or stagnating. As long as I kept riding, I was happy.

13.

Ridin' for the Man

WHEN I returned to Morzine in December, with Sarah, it was a strange feeling. In some ways it felt like going home. Once we disembarked from the airport bus and walked up that main road again, saw le petit train and all the wooden balconies, it returned almost instantly. The smell, the white, what power it had!

Just like the previous year, Luke Paul and Ben Knox were out there, but this time I was returning more as an equal to them. I was sponsored too, although not quite at their level. People remembered me from the previous year. I was Billy Morgan, the kid who does doubles. The rodeo kid.

Fish, Junior and Lewis arrived for their week's holiday. Fish and Junior had spent some time practising prior to their arrival, but Lewis was way too much of a stoner and managed to break his collarbone immediately. The first morning I took them up on the lift and we set off, but Lewis struggled to keep up, skidded on some ice and came off. He rode for about 150m and that was it, then spent the rest of the week in our little studio flat playing Xbox.

I took Fish around and showed him the ropes. He was as enchanted by it all as I had been. We spent a lot of time at The Stash, a sort of eco snowpark they built in Avoriaz, entirely out of wood and other biodegradable materials. The idea was to be able to ride jumps and rails and all the rest of it, but to do so in as natural an environment as possible.

There was a halfpipe in Avoriaz too, which Fish enjoyed, but I would only bomb through there for a bit of fun. Despite its status, it never interested me as much as some of the other features. At the time, halfpipe was still the only snowboarding event recognised by the Olympic committee and seen as the main snowboarding discipline. If you wanted to be big time in 2008, you had to *shred* pipe. The American legend Shaun White had recently emerged and was sweeping the board in all competitions, following his Olympic gold in Turin in 2006. The Winter X Games on the other hand, although more niche, had been showcasing a variety of snowboard events, including slopestyle and big air since the 90s.

Because I was self-taught and started boarding so late, the harsh truth was that I wasn't technically good enough to ride halfpipe. I could throw myself around on it for a laugh and do a few tricks, but my turning and overall board control were nowhere near what they needed to be. With pipe, your edge control needs to be good enough to deal with the harsh compression in the transitions, while doing your tricks. If you can't, then you'll either land on the deck or in the flat bottom, neither of which is a good day out.

Halfpipe is one of those things that outsiders watch and go 'oooh' and 'ahhh', enjoying all the flying around, without appreciating what an incredible amount of skill is involved. Technically, that stuff is so, so difficult. When you see a guy like Shaun White doing his thing, you have to fully respect the mastery being shown. The dude is a ninja.

From my point of view, I was clearly a park rider and what I liked best were jumps and rails. Because of my acrobatic background, big jumps suited me the best. I don't think at this point I was actually aware of big air as being a thing. I just knew I liked to go high and send it. That was my strong point.

Starting my second season with a high baseline meant that with the rapid improvement brought by mountain riding, it felt as if an evolution was coming. I was one of the first to arrive on the hill in the morning and the last one to leave in the evening, clocking huge amounts of practice time. Combined with my childhood time as an acrobat, it meant I was heading towards that magical figure of 10,000 hours of practice.

There were probably about 15 to 20 good riders in Avoriaz in those days, and in 2008–09 I was carving out a reputation as one of the better ones. That meant conversations around me changed and became increasingly about potential next steps. Not that I was looking for anything myself. I was happy just to be out there, doing my stuff, but people kept mentioning certain things. In particular, there were regular whispers about the British team, two words guaranteed to put a sneer on the face of any snowboarding purist.

'The team' was one of those things that lurked in the background of the Morzine consciousness, a phantom at the window, like Freddy Krueger. There was this amazing Alpine panorama, like a movie set, a fantasy world within a world, and we were all within it. A bunch of kids messing about, expressing ourselves, shredding and going wild in the evenings, but there was also this dark force lurking in the shadows – a force that wanted to pull you out of that fantasy world and into another, a force that wanted to make everything grey and professional and serious, to measure what you did in points, to regulate you, to put you in a uniform.

The British freestyle ski and snowboard set-up was run by a Scot called Hamish McKnight, a furtive, almost mythical figure. Rumour had it that he appeared out of nowhere, waving a spreadsheet and talking about marginal gains if you looked in the mirror and said his name three times.

At that point, the team, as a concept, was quite new and had been convened with the aim of training British riders for elite competition. Hell, the Yanks, Canadians, Swiss and the rest had official teams, so why shouldn't we? That's how I saw it. Up to then, Brits had just done their own thing in places such as Morzine, then turned up at comps unprepared. The early British competitors, the pioneers, were self-funded and self-trained. What a huge disadvantage that gave them against their rivals. *What's the point in carrying on like that?* I thought. *If you're going to do it, do it properly. Go hard or go home.*

But the vibe in Morzine was heavily against it. Even people I knew and respected spoke in very negative terms about it. Ben Knox had spent a short time on the team himself but left when he found out how it worked.

'Fuck the British team, bro! You have to pay three grand for that shit. Imagine what you could do with £3k? They get their claws in you, then you're just riding for the man.'

'You have to pay for it?'

'Yeah. And what do you get for your money? A coach, some competitions? You can get all that here and it's much cheaper. You don't need that shit!'

In truth, I wasn't someone who had strong views either way in this debate. So many people got passionate about it, but although I loved getting out on the mountain, riding, landing tricks and shooting little films, the idea of competitions didn't offend my sensibilities. I didn't see why people found them so upsetting. Why were they being so precious? On a personal level, I enjoyed the many little comps Foxy took us to, with the Ill-Eagle crew, while the Battle of Waterloo had been one of the most enjoyable days of my life. If it created even more fun, what was wrong with competition?

One guy in the Cavern, some beery philosopher with a nose ring, proclaimed that snowboarding was like yoga: 'You don't put the best up against each other and score them, do you? They don't put yoga in the fucking Olympics! It's spiritual! You just appreciate the form!'

I nodded, because I'm not the type to start unnecessary beef, but that analogy didn't work for me. My background in acro showed me how a physical artform could also be a competitive event. Acro was also about self-expression and fun and enjoyment but needed major doses of discipline and determination too. That was the trade-off, and in the necessity to make that trade-off was where the greatest improvement was made.

At the time I had no idea, but these drunken debates in Morzine mirrored what was going on in the snowboarding world, not just in the Alps, but everywhere. Since the success of the Winter X Games and the creation of icons such as Shaun White, the big brands were turning their eyes away from YouTube and Vimeo and towards competitions. The elusive cache of professional status, with its accompanying dollars, was no longer just for cool, handsome young boarders who could look 'steezy' in a promo, but for finalists, medallists and winners. This was changing how snowboarding saw itself. The old guard didn't like it, of course, but I came along right in the middle of that process.

At the same time, I had an internal feeling of continued development. More attention, more offers of involvement, like this, was building up for me. I just didn't and couldn't know what it was building up into. If during these early days one of the big companies had come along and offered me a living to ride for them and make videos, I may have gone down that route. But I wasn't at that stage. My riding was too loose for that.

As the season got underway and my YouTube channel picked up views, I gained another couple of sponsors in quite quick time.

Luke hooked me up with Atomic snowboards, a great brand. I was also approached by a woman called Sue Garlick who I had known for a while. Sue attended many dry slope events back home in the UK but lived in Morzine and represented Westbeach outerwear. Sue did everything she could do to help me. She really invested her time and helped to come up with a plan.

'This could lead somewhere for you,' she told me, 'but you have to steer it in the right direction.'

Sue became a kind of mentor throughout my Morzine days and her advice was absolutely invaluable. Through her intervention, I also suddenly gained free clothes, a huge boost. Along with my board deal, it put me in a great place. A decent snowboard cost £250 and I was likely to go through two a season, so Atomic saved me £500 a year by themselves.

I think, reflecting on the whole thing, the idea of the artist, devoting his life to stoke and flow, with no ties to anything but his board, is lovely and romantic, but also a bit of a myth. Before the big comps came along and sucked everyone in, the only full-time snowboarders were guys who got sponsored by major corporations or, I guess, kids with rich parents to cover their expenses. But that first group, the original snowboard pros, who felt they had a monopoly of the ethos, were also 'riding for the man', in truth. Ultimately, they just became pieces of human marketing to promote their sponsors' brands. So, I think that's why, as an 18-year-old kid, I saw no real difference between the two sides of the dispute. All I knew was that I wanted to keep snowboarding. Whatever that meant and whatever form that took was fine.

It was in light of all of this, that towards the end of my second winter in Morzine, I made the decision to enter the British championships in Laax, Switzerland. They took place in April and meant I could finish my winter season then head there to see how I got on.

As before, the season ended with the vid night at the Cavern and I caused a stir at the barbecue afterwards by stuffing fireworks down my trousers and setting them off. Proper Eddie Morgan business. Everyone thought that was insane. I could hear people screaming 'fucking hell, he's lost it!' and 'Billy's batshit crazy!' as they ran off. The truth is I knew exactly what I was doing. Dad taught me how to handle little explosives from when I was very small. The angle is key. As long as you put them in correctly, you don't come to any harm. It was one of my party pieces.

I managed to catch a lift from a carful of guys heading to Laax and found that when I arrived for my first Brits, my developing reputation had tagged along with me. People saw me as reckless, both on the slopes and off. Big tricks and big fun. Wild child Billy Morgan. I guess I enjoyed the image to some degree and could see why people thought that, but it wasn't entirely accurate.

Yes, I liked a drink but who didn't in the snowboarding world? When people saw me out on the hill hucking tricks, they just thought I had massive balls and didn't care if I got hurt. But that's nonsense. Everyone cares if they get hurt unless they're suicidal and I definitely wasn't that. I suppose the kernel of truth lies with Mad Eddie and his relationship with risk, but there was so much more to it. There was reason and experience and almost a form of studiousness. I understood this stuff, injecting enough risk to make it fun, but not so much as to make it foolhardy.

In exactly the same way, when I acted an idiot and stuck fireworks down my pants, I knew exactly what I was doing. There are ways of doing these things that remove a chunk of the danger. That's what people didn't understand. I enjoyed doing stuff where it was possible to get injured because jeopardy creates a buzz, but it was calculated. I never expected to get injured.

Much like Morzine, the scene in Laax was all about freestyle snowboarding and partying. While Morzine was very Brit-centric,

Laax was pan-European. The event was essentially a week-long festival in which anyone could enter and ride alongside some of the country's best, as long as they stumped up the €20 entry fee. I got myself a place in the big air competition, as I thought it was the one I would enjoy the most, and I soaked up the atmosphere.

The set-up was impressive, with an absolutely enormous halfpipe, known as a superpipe. Seven metres high, 200 metres long and 22 metres wide, it was commonly referred to as 'the stunt ditch'. In fact, the thing was so huge that the run-in for big air was down the side of it. We actually dropped in down the wall of the halfpipe.

I knew that all the UK team coaches would be there and kept an eye out for the mysterious Hamish McKnight. As the competition got underway, I spotted him sitting halfway up the lift. He had sunglasses on. Beneath the smoky glass his face barely moved at all. He gave the impression that he was studying and scrutinising everything, like some sort of professor.

The star of the big air show was a kid from Bradford called Jamie Nicholls. Comparing myself to him gave me a real inferiority complex. He was so young, just 16, four years younger than me and so, so good. *Shit*, I thought. *How can I compete with that?*

Jamie had mega style and was good at all aspects. He was the benchmark for my progression. He had sponsors, was known in the USA and was such a natural. I knew, in my guts, that I couldn't ride like that. He had a serious face, scary focus and a super-professional attitude. He didn't drink at all and had been on the team almost from childhood.

I finished with a standard double backflip, which brought a cheer from the crowd along with a bit of excited babbling from the MC and earned me sixth place. I was pleased with that, in my first big competition. For whatever it was worth at that time, I was officially the sixth-best big air snowboarder in the

UK. That felt like decent progress from my starting point four years earlier.

When I got back to Southampton, I went around to Mum's flat for a catch-up and a cup of tea. Dad appeared too and the conversation turned to what I had been up to for the last couple of years. She was happy, but concerned, as Mums so often are.

'What are you going to do about work?' Dad asked.

I didn't know what to say and made a sort of non-committal gesture.

'He's doing what he loves doing,' Mum said.

'So that's it, is it?' Dad asked. 'You're dropping out, then?'

I thought about Morzine, the mountains, the air, riding every day. I thought about all that *fun*, what it meant.

'No Dad,' I said, 'I'm dropping in.'

14.

Billy the Kid

BY THE time of my third season in Morzine, in December 2009, there was more of a feeling of urgency. Something needed to happen. For the previous two years my existence had revolved around working summer and autumn at the dry slope, then spending winters boarding in the Alps. It was a cool little routine, but how long can you keep going like that? I was 20 years old, no longer a teen. How could I continue to justify this lifestyle to myself and others?

I became ever more aware of what other people were doing. All my old Southampton friends were on courses or apprenticeships, starting work. Some of them had serious jobs in the financial sector or business. Snowboarding was my passion, and my inner voice told me I should do it, but the longer you pursue a passion without earning a living, the more you start to question it. That's human nature.

I loved snowboarding. I loved everything about it. I wanted it to be my focus, but it felt like I was reaching a point where I would have to decide what to do, and I knew there was a strong possibility I would have to look at a career. In that case, riding would be relegated in my priorities and become a hobby.

Sarah and I planned to head out to France together again, because it had become a habit. In truth, we weren't clicking that well any more.

'So, I've planned this winter in Morzine,' she said one evening.

'Cool.'

I needed someone to plan for me as I never had a logistical mind but could feel that our relationship was petering out. We had been together three years and for kids of our age that was a hell of a long time. No other couples we knew had been so committed. We started to grow apart in various ways and there was a distance between us where none had existed before. We weren't on the same path.

In my third winter, I spent a lot of time at the Westbeach house in Morzine. The other guys on the team got a place together with some of their mates, but Sarah was on a different vibe altogether, hanging out with Luke Paul's girlfriend and her other friends. The Westbeach connection kicked my riding on again and I spent countless days shredding with Andy Nudds and Matt McWhirter, two very experienced and stylish riders who had made a big name for themselves on the video scene. I still rode a lot with some of the older crew, but the Westbeach guys pushed me in different ways, which boosted all of my riding.

Nuddsy (also known as 'the Terminator' because he was such a machine) was super tall for a snowboarder, had come from the famous dry slope scene up in Halifax and was renowned for his front side spins, off his toes. McWhirter, 'the squirter', was much shorter and 'steezier'. He loved nothing more than doing cool tricks on the rails. My innate desire to push myself, to go big and high, combined well with them and we made a tight little trio.

Inspired by those two, I began thinking about a quite high-end trick, known as a 'backside double cork 1080', comprising two full flips and one full spin. The 1080 part, as is standard in snowboard terminology, describes the total amount of aerial rotation because each flip or spin consists of 360 degrees. At the time, this was considered an elite-level trick, requiring a lot of core and leg strength to initiate and control. In the winter of 2009–10, there were probably only about 20 guys in the world doing them, most of whom were big names I had seen in videos and mags.

I built on it steadily, whoever I was shredding with, then one day I turned to Luke and said, 'Shall I just rip a cork backside 5, like hard, then just hold on and go over twice?'

'Yeah,' Luke replied, nodding sagely. 'As long as you stay tight and get it round, you'll be safe.'

I gave it 'hoon', and although my landing was a bit sketchy, I held it. I could hear Ben shouting from a nearby ridge. Over the next few weeks, the trick became steadily more and more solid.

The backside 10 became my first truly *big* trick. It was a kind of rite of passage in my progression, the point where I moved on from 'huck 'n' chuck' tricks that most people could try, to doing something genuinely gnarly. If you attempt a backside double 1080 and it goes wrong, you might very well end up in a body bag.

Towards the end of that winter, the inevitable happened. Sarah and I had a big argument and she went home. We hadn't been spending that much time together anyway, and it was for the best. Of course, there was sadness there, but I was too into my riding to stew on it. I had just a few weeks of white left and wanted to make the most of them.

The end of that season saw heavy snow down in the village and one of the popular seasonaire accommodations called The Marmots built some rails, jumps and features in their garden, like a mini snowpark. The idea was to have a backyard jam right there, in the village. A big crowd turned out, with a few media folk, too.

Usually, snowboard writers and photographers are riders themselves – guys who have found another way to make their passion their job, by creating content about it. That day, a photographer called James North was there. He was already developing a reputation as one of the most interesting chroniclers of the scene and he got a super-cool shot of me jumping over a stream, doing a little grab. The Morzine local newspaper, known as 'Sno', picked up the snap and featured it on their front page, with the headline 'Billy the Kid', my first bit of print. For a week or so afterwards, I would walk around the town and see people reading it or go into a bar and find someone had left a copy on the table. It was strange and also a little exciting to see my image circulated so publicly.

During the last few days in Morzine, I teamed up with a cool videographer called William Nangle to make an end-of-season edit at the Arare park in Avoriaz. I started a little excitedly and tried a double backflip, probably a bit too early in the day. I messed up the take-off, so the only way to land it safely was to go with it. I ended up going a bit backside at the end and landed switch. Rather than a double backie, I had accidentally done my first 'double rodeo' instead.

Nangle ran over to me with an ecstatic look on his face: 'What the fuck man! Did you mean to do that?'

'Dude, I thought I was gonna die.'

'Well, I got it and it looks sick!'

This was another genuinely *legit* trick and a fantastic way to begin. (A double rodeo is a backside spin, with two backflips, that's initiated off the heels.) Later, in the same afternoon, I stomped a really solid backside 1080, too. To that point it was the best I had done.

I also found with tricks like that, the double rodeo and the back 1080, once you did them, you broke through a sort of mental barrier. Before there were questions and doubts, but once you proved to yourself that you were able to do them, they became easier. Not that I could necessarily land them every time, but the more I did them, my body seemed to remember what to do. After a while, all the little adjustments and manoeuvres became instinctive.

I felt so uniquely focused and it was an amazing day, where everything went perfectly. The resultant video was top notch, thanks to William's production values. It even had credits and a hip-hop soundtrack. When it went up online, people were pumped, which was truly exciting for me. Viewers were especially enthused to see those types of tricks being performed by a British rider. It got nearly 50,000 plays and a flurry of admiring comments in no time.

'Your hustling is epic!'

'Billy, you're getting tooooo good. When are we gonna see you on TV?'

For my part, it was the first time I admitted to myself I was beginning to look like a pro. Not that I was on a level with real elite guys yet, but I was heading in that direction. Watching the video back gave me a sense of pride in my own achievements, something I hadn't allowed myself to feel too often in my life.

Even Luke was excited by it, and as we watched the vid together over a few beers in my Morzine flat, you could sense a slight shift in our relationship. Only a few years before, he had been my idol, but now the stuff I was doing was the next level up. I was beginning to ascend beyond the level of the casual seasonaire. Bit by bit, I was moving towards international class. At this time, Luke was recovering from a broken back and began a chalet rental company that started to do very well. This meant he had no longer been riding on a daily basis, as I had.

As the video ended, there was something else in his eyes, something other than enjoyment. I think he knew. Just like me and Sarah, me and Luke were parting too. Luke had come to that crossroads, read the signs and taken a turning, but I was still on the highway.

Of course, all this was just an accumulation of feelings inside. I hadn't 'made it' yet, whatever 'making it' means. I still rarely had more than a few pounds or euros to my name and as yet was unknown beyond the Morzine circle but, within that, the public perception was that I was a guy who was fully yoloYOLO. I liked that and played up to it. Over the years I even cultivated it, but people who saw my videos didn't necessarily appreciate what had happened before. All the practice, the hours of endless repetition that I did of my own accord, made these things happen. Hour after hour, day after day, sometimes week after week of doing the same thing over and over until I perfected it.

YOLO? Not really. I was obsessed.

Once again, we headed out to Mayrhofen after the season came to a close. I entered a video into the prestigious Oakley Jib Vid comp with Andy Nudds. Between us we came up with a sort of Narnia magic wardrobe theme, where we emerged straight from a cupboard on to the mountain and started shredding. We loved doing it and they gave us sixth place for that. It seemed, just then, that sixth was a recurring theme in my life.

While I packed my bags, with the last day or two at my apartment left to run and my mind on Laax again for The Brits, some older guys invited me out on a little trip into the backcountry. The crew was led by James Stentiford, who later became the Quicksilver team manager. Known as 'the Silverback', Stentiford had been a legend of European snowboarding since the 90s and was undergoing a kind of transition. With his professional career behind him, James had lost interest in snowparks, jumps and rails, preferring to get away from anything artificial. His lifelong passion for snowboarding led him to seek out the wilderness, using his immense board skills to explore the natural world.

As well as James, Nelson Pratt, Scott McMorris, Mike Austin, Johno Verity and Gary Greenshields were there, all UK legends of the sport. The riding was awesome and a bit transcendent, far from man-made features and manicured pistes. No marker poles or equipment, no facilities, not even really any other people, just nature. It was incredibly powerful and I gained so much respect for James, but I guess at the time we were at opposite stages of our snowboarding journeys. He had found his niche. I still had to carve mine.

Going to the backcountry was like getting high and it took me a few days to come down from it, but as soon as I did, it was off to Switzerland for the intensity of The Brits again. Luke came out to support me and we chatted through my options on the journey. The backside double cork, if I could pull it off under pressure, would give me a great chance of finishing higher than the sixth I placed in 2009.

I chucked a double rodeo on one of my first tricks and landed it. Buzzing with adrenaline, I made my way back up to the drop and saw Hamish McKnight again, in exactly the same place he had been the year before, as if he had never moved. This year he wasn't wearing glasses, revealing piercing, steely brown eyes, narrowed in concentration. He didn't look the most approachable guy, but I was still pumped and fizzing from my jump.

'Hey, mate!' I called out, surprising myself. He looked around. 'What am I doing wrong on this trick?'

His expression didn't change. He spoke very calmly. It was almost a bit eerie. 'You're doing well,' he said. 'But you need to look at your take-off. Stay on top of your board more. Drive through the back foot.'

Something about him made me feel like the words carried extra emphasis and I thought about them, like properly.

'Thanks,' I said, heading back up to the top in contemplative mood.

Before my next jump I rolled the advice over and over in my mind. No one had ever spoken to me like that about snowboarding before. In my early days, Foxy had given me a few tips and I learned a hell of a lot by riding with guys such as Luke, Ben, Nuddsy and McWhirter, but the ability to break a jump down into elements of specific technique and verbalise them was completely new to me. To some extent, it blew my mind.

With Hamish's words bouncing back and forth inside my skull, I completed my next two jumps, smashing the backside 1080 on my last run.

There followed the obligatory period of waiting, huddled around with friends in the audience, before they began announcing the results over the tannoy. As is standard in these things, they do them in reverse order, and by the time they reached the bronze medal position, my name still hadn't been called.

Result, I thought. *I'm on the podium.*

'And in third place this year, Jamie Nicholls!'

There was a noticeable gasp from the crowd. 'Oooh!'

I caught Jamie's eye through the sea of bodies. He kind of shrugged and seemed to take it well.

'And in second place, Scott Penman!' the tannoy announced. Suddenly, all around me was mayhem. Luke and the other guys by my side cheered wildly. It took me a moment to twig. *They've announced everyone except me, and there's only first place to go … Oh shit!*

'And in first place, ladies and gentlemen, your Brits big air winner 2010, from Southampton, Billy Morgan!'

They gave me a cheque for £400 and the most surreal feeling I had experienced in my life. I was the British champion. It took me some time to accept that I had actually beaten Jamie. What a statement that was to make to myself. On the podium, with cameras popping and video rolling, he was all smiles. He shook my hand and congratulated me.

'Great jump,' was all he said, although his eyes remained flat. I could tell it pained him a bit inside, which I could fully understand, but it was to Jamie's credit that there was nothing in his manner or attitude I would have called 'salty'.

Needless to say, I took my prize money straight to the bar and was halfway through my second beer when Hamish came and found me, shouldering his way through the revellers. 'Really good work out there,' he said.

'Thanks.'

'So, when are you gonna join the British team? We're heading out to Breckenridge, Colorado in December. You should come.'

'I don't have three grand,' was all I could think of to say.

Hamish's eyes sparkled a little bit. He half-smiled. 'We can work something out,' he said.

15.

A Team Game?

FROM THAT point on, I kept in touch with Hamish McKnight. Despite all the whispers, rumours and misconceptions, he would go on to become one of my closest and most important friends, as well as my coach. The guy was very much the stereotypical 'onion' personality. Once you peeled off the outer layers, you kept discovering new ones. His serious and quiet demeanour masked the fact that he was a genuine freesports nut.

That's probably not saying it strongly enough, in fact. 'Nut' suggests something light-hearted and kooky. I guess I was more of a nut. Hamish was driven and fanatical. He lived, breathed and ate snowboarding. He was insanely focused on his mission. That impressed the hell out of me. I had no mission. I still felt I was winging it, doing my thing and seeing what happened. Hamish had all manner of plans and schemes.

Lots of snowboarding purists talk about doing things for love, or art, or stoke, but a lot of people who talk that way don't mean it. It's just a bunch of words to say when they're high. But this stuff was pretty much all Hamish had ever done. He was consumed by it.

He had grown up in Edinburgh, Scotland and like the rest of us started skateboarding as a young kid. Unlike the rest of us, he got pretty damn good at it. He discovered snowboarding at 14, just as I had, but, being the natural he was, became proficient very quickly. By the time he left school at 16, in 1998, he already had brands and sponsors. Imagine that.

This was before the competition era kicked in. The Winter X Games only began in 97 and snowboarding was yet to reach the Olympics. The scene was all about videos and promo, yet as a teenager Hamish was already a fully fledged professional. He didn't have to compete because it was unnecessary to compete to make a living in those days. His riding career was essentially about delivering advertising for the brands who sponsored him. Is that 'art', or is that 'ridin' for the man'? You tell me.

While I was still doing acro or falling on my arse during my first sessions at the dry slope, Hamish was being sent up mountains with photographers and film crews. His picture was regularly in industry magazines such as *Snowboard UK*, not that I ever read them, and he lived the pro snowboarder lifestyle, travelling here and there, shredding and partying for the best part of ten years. For the latter half of that, being the reflective, thinking man that he is, he started to get more into the technical side. What makes a good jump or a good ride? What are its component parts? How can we make it better? How could we take someone with that level of proficiency over there and make them into someone with a much higher level? Which steps would need to be taken to achieve that? He sketched out ideas on his laptop, along with designs for ramps and training equipment. It was written in the stars that he would end up in coaching.

In 2007, when I was still a backflipping novice and doing my first season in Morzine, Snowsport GB (as it was then called) asked Hamish to manage their freestyle team. At that time, freestyle meant halfpipe, as that was the only freestyle discipline in the Olympics. The British authorities were very Olympics focused. To them, nothing else mattered. So, the idea of the original invitation was that Hamish would simply become the coach for these halfpipe riders, but Hamish didn't like the sound of that, for one simple reason. British halfpipers found it very difficult to compete at the highest level on the world stage. The mechanics required for successful halfpipe riding weren't easily developed in the UK, due to our environment and facilities.

He mulled it over and agreed, but only if the team could become a combined halfpipe, slopestyle and big air set-up, open to both snowboarders and skiers, which in those days was revolutionary. No other country in the world managed these disciplines together, probably a hangover from the old skiing vs boarding war of the 80s and 90s. Would there be conflict? Punch-ups and rows? Hamish was resolute. He was sure it would work.

He also insisted on taking the emphasis away from halfpipe, by including slopestyle and big air within the training regimen. In fact, they would become the team's main focus. It's easy to understate this, but it was an extremely bold move at the time, bearing in mind that neither event had received Olympic recognition.

The businesspeople asked what his aim was. Was he just setting up a team to compete in niche freesports events? Why would we fund that? Surely the target was to promote crossover success for British snowsport, wasn't it? The sort of success that could be shown on network television and featured in national newspapers. So, what was the point in training athletes for such obscure disciplines?

Hamish, being Hamish, stuck to his guns. Of course, he had no idea that slope and air would become Olympic events in the future, but for him it was a no-brainer, nonetheless. He recognised that it was in those disciplines that our best chance of success lay. The facilities in the UK, namely dry slopes and ski domes, simply didn't allow youngsters to develop the technique needed to compete in halfpipe with kids who grew up on mountains.

We would focus on slope and air, he argued, and aim for the X Games. It was the only approach that made sense with the facilities at our disposal. Despite resistance he managed to convince the establishment to give his gambit a chance. Hamish had an idea and, more importantly, a point to prove.

He was joined in this endeavour by Lesley McKenna, a halfpipe snowboarder (and Olympian) who worked as an adviser to Snowsport GB. Together, they created some sort of sorcery. At least it looks that way now.

Lesley had emerged as an international halfpipe rider from the era when British snowboarders got absolutely zero funding from anywhere. They trained themselves and paid their own expenses. Nevertheless, she still managed to qualify for three separate Olympic Games, finishing in a best position of 17th in 2002. Considering how uneven the playing field was, it was quite an achievement.

Like Hamish, Lesley was an intensely thoughtful individual, but she tended to delve more deeply into the psychology and inner motivations of our sport. What was driving us? What did we, as snowboarders, as freesport athletes, have in common? Having grown up from the winter scene in Aviemore, Scotland, she had been immersed in the mountains, in all the white and everything that meant, since childhood.

Small in stature, but with very bright, steady eyes, Lesley had a way of talking about snowboarding that made you think you were doing God's own work. The first time I met her she asked me, 'What do you think "a good life" is?'

I kind of shrugged, felt a bit awkward and avoided the question. I was a 21-year-old kid who liked getting smashed and bombing around on a snowboard. I hadn't expected a Q&A on existentialism, but she really made me think.

'A lot of people make their value decisions like this,' she went on. 'Will it give me more money? Will it give me more status? Will it give me more power?' I thought about lads from school, bullying each other, studying for exams, getting jobs. That sounded about right. 'With us it's not like that, is it? It's more "Am I going to do something new I've never done before. And can I live with the risk?"'

Woah, I thought. *What did she just say?*

'That's how you find contentment, isn't it, Billy? A form of it, anyway. Through risk?'

I nodded. It was like talking to some sort of soothsayer.

Even though the Morzine crew had been so against it, as I learned about the process and history, the opportunity to work with people like Hamish and Lesley excited me. Up to then, my snowboarding life had been totally unstructured and unbound, a way to experience a mad rush that made you want to chase the next mad rush. Hamish and Lesley got that, because they came from that perspective too, but they also had vision.

'People ask what's the point of competition, of being elite?' Lesley said. 'But it's what drives evolution. This sport is developing so quickly. All freesports are. And competition is a big part of that.'

'Some of the kids we start working with,' Hamish agreed, 'would be novices by American or Canadian standards. So, our challenge is to develop all that potential rapidly. I'm taking 14 or 15-year-olds who came from dry slopes, like you or me, then trying to bring them to the same level as a kid whose ridden on snow since infancy, in a fraction of the time. Through analysis, we can measure that progression.'

Part of me was deeply curious about this. I wanted to know how they did it. Up to that point, most snowsport superpowers ran their national teams in a way people would recognise from other sports. Athletes were selected for the national squad, then placed into rigorous training programmes, measuring their performance, controlling their diet and monitoring their free time. They were essentially treated like machines that had to be maintained and sharpened. It was this culture the Morzine crowd so despised because it was antipathetic to the whole snowboarding ethos. It might work in athletics or swimming or cycling, but most freesports athletes didn't see themselves as having much in common with competitors from those disciplines. Our motivations and drivers were completely different.

By the time I was considering joining the team, there had already been at least a decade of clashes between the freesports culture and the sporting establishment. Most famously, Ross Rebagliati of Canada, who won the first-ever snowboarding Olympic gold, in the giant slalom of 1998, confirmed every waster stereotype by immediately testing positive for marijuana.

People from our world looked at that without batting an eyelid. Marijuana isn't a performance enhancer. If anything, it's the opposite. Who cares what the guy does in his spare time? But for Olympic organisers and the general sporting community it was a big deal. Initially, Rebagliati was disqualified and had his medal taken away, a decision that was later rescinded after much hand-wringing and gnashing of teeth. People tutted and shook their heads. 'Look what happens,' the men in blazers said. 'We let the snowboarders in and they do this!'

At the same Olympics, in Nagano, Japan, halfpipe icon Terje Haakonsen, at the time the biggest name in the sport, simply boycotted the event. He found the whole system of qualification and point-gathering, followed by tournament-style competition rounds (as prescribed by the International Ski Federation) abhorrent and refused to have anything to do with it.

For me, the point was that Hamish and Lesley understood this culture clash intimately. They didn't feel the two worlds were mutually exclusive. The traditional sports world had the thesis and the freesports crew proposed the antithesis. We just had to arrive at the synthesis. Their model was for a training regime that utilised the snowboarding ethos – fun and collaboration as a tool for personal progression – rather than replacing it.

I went home, put my Brits gold medal on the mantelpiece and hung out with the Southampton bunch, as usual. Things took an interesting turn on a personal level when I went to a house party with a good friend of mine called Matt Wheeler. It was a typical noisy affair near the water in Gosport, with a bunch of his skate- and surf-influenced crew. They were mostly new faces, so I drank to ease nerves. I've always called alcohol the 'awkward reliever'. As a result, shortly after arrival, the evening's events became very blurry. Somehow, through the haze, I met a girl called Sammi-Jo. Blonde, very cute, and we magically hit it off. Towards the end of the night I got my hands on a little rowing boat and asked her to join me for a midnight cruise. As we disembarked, I tried to kiss her, but she was super shy and ran away. While at home, she and I began spending a lot of time together.

Of course, being back in Southampton meant talking things over with Dad, who was so proud of my Brits win.

'What a result!' He grinned, before following up with the inevitable, 'So what are you thinking to do now?'

I told him about the conversations I'd had with the British team. He seemed impressed, but still, I needed to see some cash from somewhere.

This problem was solved thanks to the ongoing, behind-the-scenes work of my agent, Andy. During that close season, I got an email from Quicksilver, at the time one of the biggest names in freesports sponsorship. They were interested in taking me on as an athlete, particularly in light of my win at The Brits and upcoming association with the British team. James 'Silverback' Stentiford was Quicksilver's athlete manager and had personally recommended me. Their deal offered me £5,000 in my bank account and a card, which I could use twice a year to buy £1,500 worth of stuff from their stores. A British kid who could pull off a backside 1080 was unheard of in 2010, so they were pretty excited.

That was a game changer and a massive boost. I still wasn't making enough money from snowboarding to call it a living, but this meant it was starting to pay for itself. The only drawback was that Quicksilver, being the massive company they were, wanted exclusivity. As they were largely a clothing brand, that would mean dropping Westbeach, who had been with me for the last couple of years. I had conversations with both parties and it was agreed that I would fulfil one more obligation for Westbeach, then switch to Quicksilver.

Westbeach had planned a video promo trip to Lake Tahoe on the California/Nevada border at the start of the following season. I was due to go out there with Nuddsy and McWhirter. Following that, I could make the 1,000-mile journey inland to join up with Hamish and crew in Colorado.

My Morzine days were over. I had moved on, again, and 2011 was going to be an interesting winter.

I sent Hamish a message to let him know I would be accepting his invitation.

'Hey dude.'

'Hey.'

'I'm in.'

At home with Mum, Dad and Ashley. Apparently red shoes and braces were fashionable in 1993.

Mum looking after me following a bicycle accident. I always had bangs and scrapes, but this was a bad one.

Burning around on our Suzuki FZ50 at a wasteground in Southampton town centre which is now the site of an Ikea store.

Performing in my men's four at the national Acro championships. I'm the little one on the top with the bowl cut.

My first time skiing recreationally on the dry slope in 2004. Photo taken by Mum.

Building the quarterpipe at Southampton dry slope after I started working there in 2008.

Backflip nosegrab at Westbeach dryslope contest in Halifax 2010. Shot by Ed Blomfield

'Backflip Billy' doing his thing in a miscellaneous Morzine bar.

The annual 'Battle of Waterloo' was a great Avoriaz event featuring local British shredders. Luke Paull is standing on my right and I am crossing swords with Ben Knox. Also there are Mike Austin, Mark Raper and Joe Chastney.

Sarah and I goofing around in Morzine. Shot taken by James North.

Me, Andy Nudds and Matt McWhirter, outside their apartment in Morzine drinking Sangria and 'Trampagne', our name for cheap champagne.

My first night shoot after a contest at the Stash park in Avoriaz. Mute tailbone.

Me filming my end of season video at the Arare park in Avoriaz with Willy Nangel.

An end of the season shot from Morzine 2012. Alongside me are JJ Jones, Phil, Duncan Ross, Stu Monk, Hannah Kinnear, Liz, Sarah, Sue Garlic, Davina, Tommy Bowers, Crott, Amy Ross and Rohan Anderson.

Me chucking the first backside double cork 1080 done by a British rider in a contest, at the British championships in Laax. Shot by Sam Mellish

On the podium after my Brits win, with Jamie Nicholls and Scott Penman.

Brits pirate night with the crew.

Me, Matt and Andy being idiots in our back garden on the Lake Tahoe, West Beach trip.

Me naked on a rail in Tahoe. Shot by Dan Medhurst.

Big ol' road gap, taken on the *Summit Pass in Tahoe*, also Dan Medhurst.

Sequenced shot of my backside double rodeo at The Freeze in 2012. Shot by Graham Joy.

After my win at the Freeze, messing about in Battersea Power Station.

My Dad on my friend Matt Wheeler's shoulders during The Freeze celebrations. Of course, Dad is wearing his motorbike jacket.

A sequenced shot of my first backside triple cork, taken in Breckenridge after I joined the British team. Shot by Ed Blomfield

Training on the super-trampoline facility in Woodward, Colorado. Shot by Ed Blomfield

Celebrating with Aimee Fuller, the night I got my Red Bull cap and became a fully-fledged Red Bull athlete, a major honour.

Christmas in Breckenridge with the team. Andy, Possum, Paddy, Josh, Me, James, Murray, Dom and Andy

X games bronze medals taste strangely like copper.

At home with my British team gear, after kitting out.

In Sochi with my team-mates. Murray, Me, Ben, Woodsy, Jamie, Emma Lonsdale, Shelly Rudman, Dom Parsons, Rowan Cheshire, Lissy Arnold, Katie Summerhays, Lamin Dean.

Back rodeo off the cannon rail, with Hamish filming, during training. Shot by Nick Atkins

Me with Ben Kilner and Dom Harrington, cheering on Jenny Jones as she went on to take bronze in Sochi, a massive achievement and a great inspiration to me.

Appearing on BBC news after the Olympics with Tony Husband.

A post-Olympics party in my garden at home with the full crew.

Sammi-Jo and I attending the post-Olympic party at Buckingham Palace.

Back on the grind at Air+Style Innsbruck with legends Eric Willett and Sebastian Toutant.

Me at the Red Bull HQ in London, with some freesports legends. Gee Atherton, Chriss Kyle, Sebastian Keep, Joe Clarke, Paddy Graham, Danny Macaskill, Martyn Ashton, Joe Battleday and Ryan Doyle.

On a shoot with the Legs of Steel crew in Austria. Shot by Pally Learmond

Doing a bit of skateboarding in my downtime, during a team summer camp up in Scotland. Shot by Sam Mellish

Part Three

RAISING THE STAKES

'Big air is the most beautiful, insane, stupid, dangerous, death-wishing and beautiful sport ever perpetrated on innocent spectators ... death is always near.'

– *New York Times*

16.

Snowboardin' USA

THE 2010–11 season began with my first time guesting at the annual Ski and Snowboard Show in London, a great, vibey event and a real focal point for the British scene. The show was organised by Spencer Claridge and Stuart Brass, a couple of British snowboard legends, who also organised the British championships in Laax. It took place over several days in October, at a venue called 'Evolution' in Battersea Park.

As well as stalls selling ski and snowboard equipment, the event boasted a real snow 50ft kicker where athletes would perform for watching crowds. It was fantastic fun with plenty of boozy evenings and a real spirit of togetherness. Because the snowsports scene isn't that big in the UK, you tend to meet the same people over and over, which helps form it into a community. The show became a huge part of that, and after that first one it established itself as an annual thing for me, the one event on the calendar I never wanted to miss.

Pretty much immediately after the show wrapped up, it was time to hook up with the Westbeach crew. This sort of carousel of activity, one booking quickly following another, would soon become a regular feature of my life, but at this stage was still new to me. My companions for the Westbeach trip were Nuddsy and

McWhirter, along with a photographer called Bruce. We were all young guys, in our late teens or early twenties, with a travel budget allocated from the company. It just seemed unreal. It was particularly exciting for me as it was going to be my first trip outside of Europe.

I also knew, or at least had been told by others, that the riding in the States would be of a higher level. The snowparks there were some of the best in the world and we would be out on the hill with other boarders whose average technical ability was way above the European norm. Naturally, that added a dose of nerves into the mix. Would my skills stack up against them? Would I look like an English novice and make a fool of myself? The self-doubt I wrestled with throughout my career really reared up and bubbled away in the back of my mind. I may have been about to embark on a cool, pro-snowboarding adventure, but internally I was still backflip Billy, a kid from Southampton.

The four of us got out of the taxi at Heathrow and Bruce said he wanted to get a shot outside the terminal before we flew over. We stood there, posing, the evening sun in our eyes.

'Go on, do something good then!' he said.

I did the old rock 'n' roll 'devil horns' thing with my hand. Nuddsy looked sideways at me.

'You tart,' he whispered. I cracked up laughing.

Bruce filmed us going through the airport and putting our bags on the conveyor. I got a cool vibe from it, a bit like we were a band going on tour or something. Most of all, I sensed we were going to make a top film, a genuine, professional edit like you see in the big snowboard promo videos. That gave me such a buzz.

On the plane over, we started to chat about practicalities. We needed a car to use for the trip, mulled over the possibilities and for some reason settled on a plan of buying one from Craigslist. As soon as we landed, we used the Wi-Fi at the airport to scroll through local ads and found a dude in Reno with a Golf for sale. That was cool, a nice standard car that people drive in the UK. Something we would be familiar and comfortable with.

We headed straight out to the guy's address, which turned out to be a trailer park. The car was a total shitheap, clapped out, with a shonky exhaust. I looked at Nuddsy and Matt, and they looked at me. We all sort of shrugged. It was one of those 'what are you gonna do?' moments. We were there, we needed a ride, so we bought it anyway. It was only $1,000 and we figured as long as it lasted for a couple of months that was fine.

We took the car up to our accommodation, an apartment, quite high up in the hills sorted out for us by Westbeach. The location gave us easy access to the mountains, while nearby was a house full of other riders, some of whom we knew from back home. We settled in the first evening, then drove the Golf up to Lake Tahoe in the morning for our first day of shredding. Unfortunately, we quickly found out that our hasty car choice hadn't worked out the way we hoped. A police officer saw we had no seatbelts, pulled us over, pushed a leaflet through the car window and gave us a very long lecture about the environment.

'C02 levels … preservation of the natural balance … fragile ecosystem.' None of us raised a word of argument but the guy must have talked for ten minutes. The bottom line was that they ran very strict emission laws in the ski zone and our clanking Golf was barred from entry. *Bummer.* We took the loss on the chin and drove it down to a nearby breakers yard. The Westbeach budget didn't stretch to providing transport too, but having already missed out on one day of action we didn't want to run any risks. We used the list of eligible vehicles on the leaflet we had been given to inform our choice and rented a Dodge Ram pick-up truck instead.

As a snowboarding venue, Tahoe was unbelievable, a huge place, with an enormous, shimmering lake as the name suggests.

Around the water were three separate wintersports areas, each of them about the size of Avoriaz. This felt like a whole new level, the *real* snowboarding lifestyle. Snowboarding as people imagine it.

For the whole three months we were there, we rode every day, either on the famous Northstar slopes, with free passes organised by Westbeach, or out in the local area, riding 'street', which we all loved. James North came out to take some snaps and *Whitelines* magazine sent a guy called Ed Blomfield out. Ed spent ten days with us shooting photos for a feature article. For some reason, on one of our street days, I decided to do a handrail naked. Ed snapped it and it became probably my most iconic shot. Being the pro that he is, Ed angled it in a way to conceal my junk and the shot ended up cropping up all over the place. One snowboard resort even turned it into one of those holiday attractions, blowing it up into full size, with a hole where my head was, so people could put their face through for holiday snaps.

The local area was fascinating too. Fifteen minutes down the road was a frontier era town called Truckee with a great diner and a couple of cool bars. A moustachioed barman in one of them told us how Truckee was famous because a posse of settlers travelling into California from Illinois got stranded in the snow there in 1864. Facing starvation, the group resorted to cannibalism to make it through the winter, emerging in the spring with several missing people and miscellaneous body parts. You didn't get stories like that in the Cavern in Morzine.

Of course, after shredding all day, most nights would end up in boozy, smoky carnage back at our flat or the other guys' Elvis ranch down the road. We met other riders who we invited over and had an all-round amazing time.

Beyond the whole experience of going somewhere that cool, one of the best parts of the trip was experiencing night riding for the first time. Riding after dark wasn't really a thing in Europe, but Tahoe's Boreal mountain was floodlit and open 24 hours. Some days we rode all day, then came down, had dinner and went back out to shred again under the moonlight. There was something special about it, something so atmospheric. It was crispier and crunchier. The air felt colder and Bruce got some amazing footage of us against the blackened sky.

That whole Lake Tahoe expedition was an awesome, dreamlike experience and my first realisation of what an unbelievable head-trip snowboarding could be. I got used to riding really big, well-built jumps that outsized anything in Morzine and going super-fast from one feature to another, often for minutes at a time, without stopping. The size of the facilities in Tahoe allowed you to do that.

I knew I wasn't becoming rich in terms of money and wasn't much bothered about that anyway, but in terms of experience … it was almost unbelievable. I saw straight away that I was insanely lucky. How many 21-year-olds get to do that sort of thing at someone else's expense? Snowboarding was a lever to open up the world for me.

Westbeach's generosity meant by the time I met up with Hamish and the British team in Breckenridge I already felt like a pro, which probably helped me to settle in. I didn't realise then, but the Breckenridge area would become like a second home for me. Breckenridge, Copper Mountain and Keystone, with a little town called Frisco in the middle. Perhaps best of all was the nearby Woodward facility, a trampoline, skate and foam pit-based training centre, which was really fun and incredibly valuable. The excellent and varied facilities there meant that Hamish established Breck, as we called it, as a base for the British team for years to come.

Obviously, my win at The Brits meant that I deserved my place, but there were some big names floating around the team at the time and it would have been easy to have felt intimidated. Jenny Jones was already a face on the global scene. She had just won a gold at the Winter X Games and was the number one British snowboarder at the time. James 'Woodsy' Woods had a well-established reputation in the UK, having won the free-ski slopestyle event at The Brits for the previous three years. He really looked the part too, with dreadlock-type hair and facial piercings. He was even a couple of years younger than me as well. There were others too: Jamie Nicholls (of course), Aimee Fuller, Dom Harrington, Ben Kilner and the skier Paddy Graham. Along with Paddy, skiers Murray Buchan, James Webb and Josh Birch were all the same age as me and we got on really well. The main thing was that everyone in the camp was cool.

I especially clicked with Paddy, a slopestyle skier and a really funny, laid-back guy. It was interesting seeing someone approaching one of my disciplines from a different perspective, with two planks on his feet instead of one. Going out on the course with him was fun because he was never super competitive, so it felt relaxed. Even though I was still so early in my snowboarding journey, at 23 I was one of the older guys on the team. I liked everyone, but guys who were just 17 or 18 didn't feel like they were quite on the same wavelength.

The training, once it started, fascinated me because it didn't seem like training. The first day we went up on the mountain I kept waiting for Hamish to tell us all to get in a circle and warm up, like I used to do at acro. I assumed there would be some sort of repetition of basic exercises as there is in most forms of sports training, with a coach barking instructions at everyone for a couple of hours. But none of that happened. We just got out and rode together. At least that's how it felt.

Hamish's philosophy was driven by progression but in an inclusive way, governed by how progression happens naturally and organically, the principle being that you acquire skill together, as a group, although obviously the risk is yours alone.

We operated together on a daily basis, and from an outsider's perspective it would have looked very informal, as if we were just a bunch of friends having fun. But that was deliberate and it was calculated. Hamish wanted the training to feel like that because that vibe brings the best out of snowboarders. Meanwhile, behind the scenes, he beavered away to get a system in place where he could appraise what everyone was doing and what they should be working on to achieve their goals. Profiling, targeting, goal-setting, but he kept it hidden from us. It was used to inform how he arranged activities for us, how he advised us what to practise, without it being the overarching emphasis of everything.

I found all of this truly intriguing. One evening I asked Hamish, over a beer, of course, how he saw his role as a coach. He narrowed his eyes before answering, as he often did when thinking about something. 'If this team is a band,' he said, 'I'm not the singer. I'm not even playing lead guitar. I'm more like a roadie.'

Sometimes he would pull me to one side in the morning and say something like, 'Double rodeo's looking better. Try to hit 20 repetitions today. Maybe pressurise the toe edge a bit more? See what that achieves?'

As always, bit by bit, I felt myself improving. By the end of my first week in Breckenridge I felt I belonged there, in that team, with people who regularly went up against the very best riders in the world. I was one of them.

17.

Fame and Hate

AFTER A couple of weeks working on the triple jump line at Keystone, doing loads of reps and loads of doubles, Hamish started having conversations with me in the evening about where we could take this. We would sit around after dinner, have a few beers, sometimes play cards. Hamish liked to talk a lot about what he called 'the blank pages at the back of the book'. 'What could we put on those pages?' he would ask.

'Dunno,' I replied. 'Anything we like, I guess.' I was still in the mindset of thinking about the immediate future. 'What could I do tomorrow?' That was more my style.

One evening, we sat in the communal hot tub at the back of the house, under the stars, a box of beers open on the decking beside us.

'You know you were on our radar for ages,' he said.

'I was?'

He nodded, a little smile on his face. 'We knew about you since your first year in Morzine. When you spoke to me at The Brits I had already been tracking you for two years.'

'Fuck off!'

'They warned me about you, though. "He's a bit wild," they said. "He's a loose cannon, uncontrollable." They said you've got

138

potential, but you might never fulfil it because you're just too fucking loose.'

I shook my head. What else could I do.

'But I didn't agree,' Hamish continued. 'I watched the way you jump. Underneath that wildness there's a calculating nature, isn't there?'

I swigged my beer. 'I never try anything I don't believe I can do. I'm not suicidal.'

'So, is there anything you've got in mind?' he asked.

'Now?'

'Yeah, while you're here.'

By that point I had been chucking double rodeos for fun for the previous two weeks, landing them nearly every time.

'Actually, yeah,' I said. 'Backside rodeos. Is it possible to go again?'

The backside triple rodeo was a trick that had been talked about in world snowboarding for a few years. Up to that point, no one had done it. Hamish cocked an eyebrow. 'For you, it's possible. Do you want to try it?'

We both knew that if I could pull off a triple rodeo, it would be a world's first, would make a name for me and create a major stir.

'Most people find rodeos harder than corks,' he went on, 'but because you can get so tight it suits you more. Your backflipping ability outstrips riders who may have more technical ability, so I think you can make it work.'

The idea hung for a few more days until it just grabbed hold of me one morning and wouldn't let go. I was on the lift with Ben Kilner, who said, 'Dude, you have so much time on your doubles, you could go triple easy.' He shrugged, totally casual, as if talking about eating a ham sandwich.

'You reckon?' I replied.

When we got off the lift, Hamish was there.

'I wanna do it today,' I said. 'Is this realistic?'

'Why not?' he said. 'Just go for it. It's not one of those tricks you can just huck and see what happens though. You have to intend to land it first.'

We made a plan of how many double rodeo reps I would do before attempting it. I chucked a bunch of really nice doubles, flipping quickly and opening up at the end. On the last one, I went so big and had so much time at the end I had to starfish out, landed awkwardly and went down.

Ben was waiting for me at the bottom and came over to help me up. 'Mate!' He laughed. 'You'd have been safer going over again.'

'Yeah?'

'You easily had enough time for a triple there.'

'Okay,' I replied. 'Okay.' It was time.

I was reaching that point, preparing myself mentally, when the shapers came with rakes to reshape the jumps, a regular ritual every afternoon. It suddenly became an intense moment. Do I go right now, right this very second, and attempt this thing that no one's done before, or do I wait until the reshape and start the whole process again later?

Word of mouth spread down the course like a gust of wind. I could feel a sort of buoyancy in the air. The shapers agreed to wait and let me have one last go. Whispers travelled back up until they reached Hamish. He cupped his hands to his mouth. 'Drop in!' he shouted up.

Instantly the internal dialogue kickstarted. Maybe for the first time ever. *How do you know you can do this? You've got no frame of reference. Who do you think you are, trying for world's firsts?*

Come on, I said to myself. *You're riding these jumps every day. You know them like the back of your hand. Just add another backflip. It's not complicated.*

Yeah, but will I get the airtime? If I try to go over again and I'm not high enough, I could really mess myself up.

You just had loads of time. Remember what Ben said?

Yeah, but that was then. This is now. Every jump's different.

And so on …

Very briefly an image flashed through my mind of the American, Kevin Pearce, landing on his head out of the halfpipe two years earlier in 2009. Pearce is the number one cautionary tale for everyone in the sport, the sort of person your mum would mention while wagging her finger. A super-talented kid, maybe even the best out there for a while, he got himself brain-damaged by pushing things just a bit too hard. He was at the forefront of snowboarding's evolution, jostling with Shaun White for supremacy, stretching boundaries, redefining limits, but it cost him.

That's where I would like to be too, I thought. And suddenly that notion changed my whole thought process. *I would like to be there too.*

I had never admitted that to myself before. This was all just a giggle, wasn't it? A way of venting my internal energy, something I enjoyed. I'm just Billy Morgan, that mad kid from Southampton. But actually, there was a part of me that wanted to make a mark. I wanted to see whether I could do it. Why not? Why shouldn't I? I wanted to be the best I could be.

There's only one way to find out, I told myself. *Have I got the minerals? Fuck yeah!*

I decided I was just going to get up there, send it over again and see. Ben hovered behind me, holding a GoPro camera, as if he sensed that I had been through the mental torture and come through the other side. Maybe he saw it in my body language or something. 'Are you going to do it?' he asked.

'Yeah.' I bent down to tighten my bindings.

'Cool,' Ben said. 'I'll follow on cam.'

I reached out and fist-bumped him. And then there was nothing else for it. It was on.

I dropped in, did two straight airs over the first couple of jumps, reached the third and just 'hooned' it like I had never 'hooned' anything before. Sam Turnbull had a camera too and he stood filming on the knuckle with Aimee Fuller. I could hear her screaming.

'Yes! Go on! Yessss!'

And then I'm up there, up in the place where everything makes total sense and nothing is confused. Everything's rolling around: blue, then white, blue, white, blue, white. My head throbs with each rotation but it's not a bad throb, it's reassuring and natural and then I'm coming down – down to the white. My God, it's happening! I feel I'm going to hold it but there's someone there! There's someone in the landing area! Laid out on the snow like they've been shot. Jesus Christ, I think. I land, instinctively put my hands in the air, then make some last-second adjustments to ensure I swerve around the prone body on the snow.

It was done. 'Oh my God!' I screamed, arms aloft. Ben grabbed me from behind and we hugged. Aimee continued screaming from the knuckle as if she had just witnessed a miracle. It was one of those moments. Something special. Something eternal.

About six years after first getting on a snowboard at the dry slope, I had achieved a world first. We let the shapers do their thing, drove home fizzing with excitement and uploaded the video to the internet. After that, of course, it was time to celebrate.

As I looked back on it through a drunken haze that evening, it felt like it was the randomness and spontaneity that made it so cool. It just seemed to happen – *puff* – like that. Hamish may have felt otherwise, but for me there hadn't been a great deal of planning. It appeared from nowhere, a magic moment on the space-time continuum.

People told me the body in my way on the landing had been Cheryl Maas, a top Dutch boarder. She had gone a minute before me and threw a backside 900, a pretty rad trick for a female, especially in those days, but she fell. Normal mountain etiquette would be to stop and check whether a fellow rider in that position was okay, so I felt a bit bad. I was going too fast, was so stoked, that I just landed, swerved around her and started celebrating. Cheryl was fine about it though, and even commented on the YouTube video afterwards. She said she was pumped to be involved in a world's first, even if only as an obstacle. That was cool of her. I loved that comment.

Once the video had been up a little while and the snowsports world began to react, I started to understand the magnitude of what I had done. Perhaps naively, I thought a world first would bring only appreciation and love. That wasn't exactly the case.

I quickly discovered that although I had never been into the fashion side of snowboarding, lots of people were. I guess, because for so much of its existence it had been a video-based sport, along with the whole self-image, artform thing, some people took the style side incredibly seriously. I landed the world's first backside triple rodeo in a super-colourful Quicksilver jacket. More than anything else it fitted really nicely and I thought it was important to be comfortable when attempting such a dangerous trick.

Of course, colours were 2009. By 2011, the multicoloured look was hopelessly out of date, *darling*. The cool kids were all wearing black on the slopes. And do you know what else? They wore their beanie and goggles *under* their helmet. That was the height of snowpark fashion, but I had my goggles over my helmet because that's how I liked it. To some people that made me uncool. When team members or friends I met on the hill joked about my outfit, I didn't care. It just wasn't important to me. But when you stick a video online that gets hundreds of thousands of views in a few days, you can be forced to re-examine your priorities.

Some Americans, in particular, rained down hate on my video, and as the views piled up, so did the negative comments. I got lots of positive feedback too, of course, but somehow the bad ones were more memorable. A guy called 'Accuser/Opposer' even accused us of faking the trick. Internet anonymity can lead people to make pretty outlandish comments.

'The landing was pasted in from another jump. You can even see how he crashes in one frame, not cleanly edited.'

The best one was written by someone calling themselves 'Haaamey': 'How shit is this video. These feps are such a bunch of faggots. Here's the best fep wearing his best fep clown suit while fepping all over the mountain doing three flip 180s. Please feps, nobody likes you, go back to your homeland and breed with your cousins.'

What a nob! I was never a thin-skinned guy but there's banter and then there's hate. I had never been bothered by people taking the piss, but this felt like some people were angry, genuinely angry, about what I was doing. Was it jealousy? I didn't know. We had a bit of discussion among us about what 'feps' might mean. The best answer we came up with was 'fucking English punters'. That made me laugh at least and we started to incorporate the term into our own banter.

With the hits piling up, ESPN (who own and promote the X Games), ran an article. 'Who is Billy Morgan?' they asked, before answering their own question. 'We wish we knew. He's 22, an Aries and from the UK ... somewhere ...'

Maybe that was part of the problem? As far as the snowboarding community was concerned, I popped up from nowhere. People had never heard of me and the idea of outsiders achieving world firsts, especially British outsiders, was difficult to process.

After a couple of days of grappling with it, I brushed it all off and cracked on. The haters could do their thing and I could do mine. Live and let live. Primarily, I was challenging myself. I wanted to see whether I could do this crazy trick that had never been done before, because I had never done anything like that before. If it's a challenge for you and you overcome that challenge, whatever it is, you've achieved something. That was the way I always saw it, right from the very beginning. It was about personal progression, no more, no less.

In the coming days, I got more and more attention. Emails and messages came flooding in, people called out to me in the streets of Breck as I walked through the town.

'Hey man, are you the triple kid?'

When the camp in Colorado finished, I flew out to Davos in Switzerland for the O'Neill Evolution big air contest. Unfortunately, weather worked against them. They had 90cm of fresh snow, which was way too much to run the comp, so it was cancelled. I was invited to take some powder laps with the crew instead, where I had the honour of riding alongside Jeremy Jones, an absolute legend of our sport, renowned for his big mountain freeriding.

Meanwhile, in the absence of big air, the event itself morphed into a three-day party. At some point during the shenanigans, a Russian guy in a big furry hat spotted me from across the road, did the devil horns sign at me and shouted at the top of his voice, 'Billy Morgan! Do a triple, bitch!' with a huge smile.

Getting recognised by random guys in the street? It was weird, but cool at the same time. This was more than just fun now. I had arrived.

18.

YOLO?

AFTER COLORADO I spent quite a bit of time talking to Hamish and other people about what it all meant. In some ways, I sent shockwaves through the snowboarding world. The video developed an enormous online reach – a million views – which was unheard of for a non-professional production.

Sadly, it seemed that some of the snowboarding community saw it as a sort of infiltration. A vocal minority took the view that the old school of snowboarders who lived for videos and art and lifestyle were somehow threatened by me. Not them as individuals so much. I don't think Travis Rice or Jeremy Jones, who I had just met, were personally offended by my backside triple, but these guys were idols to so many and it seemed their superfans felt a need to attack me in defence of their favourites.

I brushed it off. Even though I was very green in terms of fame and notoriety, and what those things could mean, I understood that no matter what you do, someone will take issue with it. What it showed me more than anything else was how invested and passionate so many people were about my sport.

Hamish told me that when the icon JP Walker did the first double cork back in 2003, the reaction was much the same. Alongside the celebrations there was vitriol and abuse. There were even people driving around with bumper stickers that read 'I'm already against the next cork'. Then, over time, more and more people started doing it, until a double cork became just a standard trick.

We all reckoned the same would happen here and the outrage I had generated would soon be forgotten. It was just something I had to get used to. If I was going to perform on the world stage, to a global audience, this stuff came with the territory. We spoke about plans for the future along with ideas for the coming year. There were a few things Hamish thought were worth trying, but then some news arrived that changed everything in a stroke.

We received notification that slopestyle, one of my events, was to be announced as an Olympic sport alongside slalom and halfpipe for the Games in Sochi, Russia 2014. This was an absolutely huge development for us as park riders. It meant our team would have access to government funding from the National Lottery for the first time. It was also an incredible vindication of the approach Hamish had taken from the beginning.

After discussion, the new official set-up became known as GB Park and Pipe, with Lesley, Hamish and former skier Pat Sharples as team directors. It wasn't a little passion project any more, a bunch of enthusiasts pursuing a dream. Free-skiing and snowboarding now had a real, state-funded, national team.

What that also meant was that suddenly we had a major event on the horizon to focus on. The contrast that had been growing within snowboarding over the previous few years, the division between the video-oriented sponsored space and the competition space, became even more highlighted. It was clear where our intentions lay.

Up to that point our only hope of achieving tangible success lay in setting markers for the sport, as I had just done, or competing in the X Games. Although the X Games were a big deal in the extreme sports world (and still are) access to them wasn't guaranteed. They operated on an invitation-only system and to a large degree were based around popularity. ESPN, who organised the games, wanted riders with big online followings and a filmography of sponsored documentaries behind them. What they didn't particularly want were guys like me they had never heard of.

The Olympics, of course, would be a different matter. Qualifying would occur through FIS World Cup events. That meant that I and other British hopefuls such as Jamie and Aimee could get there through merit alone. The exception to this, the Brit who had massive international kudos, was Jenny Jones. Jenny was already well established, with several X Games medals to her name. She was a real pioneer for us, a trailblazer on the world scene and someone who opened the gates for riders like me.

Immediately, Hamish and the other team directors started being called to meetings with UK Sport to explain their strategy. *How possible is it for the UK to win Olympic medals in this?* That was the bottom line, what those people wanted to know. They wanted results.

Hamish explained that for us, as snowboarders and free-skiers, it was all about the thrill of doing something new, how we felt that getting together with our mates on the mountain and enjoying ourselves was key but, through that, progression would occur. He showed how he was meticulously tracking performance in the background, while allowing us to retain the culture that had brought us all to the sport in the first place. Predictably, he was met with raised eyebrows and scratched chins. This wasn't the usual Olympic approach. The Games were in two years. The authorities expected something regimented and targeted.

'We anticipate that medals will follow,' Lesley told them. 'But medals aren't the sole focus of what we're trying to do with these athletes.'

UK Sport met this philosophy with confusion. Suddenly, these hard-partying, grungy snowboarders had come into their world and they were supposed to just let them continue their reckless ways? What about professionalism? What about sacrifice and self-denial and all those other aspects of standard training practice that were considered so important? They accepted our approach because they felt they had to. But they didn't understand it.

Regardless, the fact that we were now an Olympic set-up added a new buzz to the team and conversations often turned to Sochi and how cool it would be to compete there. Slopestyle wasn't my strongest discipline, of course, but I was happy to take it. At the time I expected to go as number two to Jamie, provided I gathered enough points. His natural technique meant he generally had the upper hand on me in slope and our situation in the UK was pretty clear cut. We more or less knew who the riders for each event would be, barring injuries. In bigger countries such as the USA, the qualifying competition for team spots was almost as hot as the Olympic competition itself.

My new-found near-professionalism, combined with the need to gather points from as many World Cup events as possible, meant I quickly entered a period where I was pretty much always heading off somewhere, with someone. Either an official training engagement with the team, or a promotional assignment with a sponsor. This would become my 'normal' for most of the next decade. It was bewildering at times, but I was always aware of what an absolute privilege it was too.

My permanent base remained at home, in Dad's place in Southampton, but I was rarely there. That first full-on season involved Saas-Fee in Switzerland, a Quicksilver shoot in New Zealand, then another team camp on the Hintertux Glacier in Austria. Hintertux was an awesome location, with a whole string of mountains covered in all that crystalline white, 360 degrees all around to the horizon from the top. It might sound corny but it's a place that has the power to make you reflect on how fortunate you are to be alive. That merry-go-round of locations and experiences eventually led me back home to the UK, when I headed back to London for an FIS World Cup event called the LG Freeze in October 2012.

Sponsored by the white goods manufacturer LG and organised by Spencer and Stuart from the Ski and Snowboard Show, the Freeze was special because it was the only FIS World Cup event to be held in the UK. At the time this was viewed as a recognition of the growing reputation of British riders. There was a scene in the UK for this stuff, a strong scene, and not only that but a UK audience who would turn out to watch it.

On that point, they were proved absolutely right. Spencer and Stuart had built an incredible scaffold next to Battersea Power Station, with a whole festival set-up around it. Because of its urban location and easy transport links, 35,000 people bought tickets, the sort of crowd you might expect for a high-level football match. It's not easy to get that many to come to watch snowboarding on the side of a mountain.

The event was for big air only, which suited me, while the London location meant it attracted a whole host of top riders. That was exciting. For the first time for me, it wasn't just one or two big names in the competition, but lots of them. Scott Penman, who had medalled silver at The Brits behind me, was there, by that time a good friend and team-mate of mine on Drake snowboards. Scott was such a livewire and beyond his multiple talents (rapping, singing, stand-up comedy and being a general legend) he was renowned for always chucking double frontflips. It was like his signature move, the equivalent of my double backflip from the Morzine days.

The Freeze was structured with a Brits-only competition on the first day, followed by the World Cup event the day after. The idea was the top three British riders would then go against the rest of the world in the main event.

Scott and I both qualified for the finals of the British comp, and as we waited at the back of the scaffold, he turned to me suddenly and asked, 'I dunno what to huck for the final, bro, what do you reckon?'

I didn't feel that well placed to offer advice. 'Dunno man.'

'It's the final,' he went on. 'Need to go big. Do you reckon I should try something new?'

I was unsure what to say to him. I had ridden with Scott a little but was uncertain what he was capable of. I thought of my own conversations with Hamish when we decided to add another rodeo to my well-established double.

'How about a triple front?' I suggested. It was the first thing that popped into my head. If he could do doubles comfortably, why not?

Scott's eyes narrowed, as if a gauntlet had just been thrown down. This was his moment. 'Shit,' he said. 'That's what I was thinking.' He fist-bumped me.

I had no idea whether Scott had ever tried a triple frontflip before or how realistic it was for him, but the idea clearly appealed on some internal level. At that time in 2012, the trick was what was known as an 'NBD' – never been done. If Scott pulled it off, especially there, in front of that huge crowd, it would be absolutely mega.

I watched him closely as he headed up to the drop. His face was set with determination. He pulled on his goggles and nodded to himself. You can tell when someone is fully in the moment by the silent contemplation of the jump, as if staring into the eyes of their maker, and he had it, for sure. The official, Colin

Holden, was there, a bit of a character on the British scene. He ran a charity taking underprivileged kids snowboarding and was known as the 'clipboard of power'. He was chief official at the Freeze and, for reasons best known to himself, Colin was dressed as the Tin Man from *The Wizard of Oz*. Scott glanced sideways at him, Colin gave him a signal and Scott exploded into the drop, full of energy, fully committed.

I found myself holding my breath with anticipation, sensing I was about to see something special, but the moment he flew off the kicker, it became obvious Scott had just pressed the 'send' button with not a lot of thought. Although he gathered good speed on the run-in, when he hit the lip, he missed a little bit of pop. I could tell he didn't have enough. He pulled in tight and almost managed to squeeze it around but gave himself no time to open up.

To the untrained eye, Scott may well have looked like the proverbial 'cat out of a cannon', a snowboarding term for a loose and wild effort, as his jump fell apart and he speared himself into the landing, accompanied by a giant gasp from the crowd.

'Please,' I said to myself. 'Please.'

Soon enough, he stood up and waved with his customary broad, cheesy grin. Phew.

For my part, I hucked a standard double rodeo, which went smoothly and qualified me for the final. That was great, but I knew the next day I would be up against some of the best riders in the world and I found it difficult to sleep that night.

This would become a regular feature of my riding career and the first time I truly experienced it. As the stakes got higher and the competition fiercer, I knew I would have to extend myself to the maximum to be in with a chance. In our sport, extending yourself to the maximum always carried with it the possibility of hospital time, or worse. I lay in my London hotel room, eyes on the ceiling until the early hours, mind churning with possibilities.

The next day, I found myself back at the top of the scaffold with Seppe Smits (Belgium), Tor Lundstrom (Sweden), Roope Tonteri (Finland), and a bunch of other top, top riders. In true, snowboarding style, Roope was still steamed from the previous night's revelries and had fallen asleep on some beanbags in the corner.

It was a windy day and the high scaffolding wobbled a little as an official made the call. 'Roope, two to drop!' he shouted. Tonteri remained completely motionless on the beanbag. A minute or so later, the official reappeared, 'Roope, one to drop!' And then, more anxiously, looking left and right, 'Where the fuck's Roope?'

'Er … he's over there,' Seppe said, pointing at the stricken form in the corner. The official shook his head in exasperation, strode over and kicked Tonteri in the leg. Roope's eyelids half opened and he staggered straight up, dropped in, then threw and landed a perfect double cork. The crowd went crazy. Moments later he arrived back up in the lift and flopped straight down on to the beanbag again.

Wow, I thought. *Welcome to the elite.* I was jittering and edgy, probably the most nervous I had ever been. It was the biggest event of my life to that point, and this guy was asleep.

My plan for the competition, what I had focused on in training with Hamish, was a back double cork 1080. At the time it was a popular trick and well established at the elite level. It scored well with the judges and most top riders could pull it off with practice. But like Scott the previous day, I felt the urge to add something extra into the mix for the final. The back double 10 had got me there, which was cool, but a final is no time to play safe.

At the top of the jump, I had a silent dialogue with myself and found myself deciding to add an extra 180 degrees of rotation on to my backside 10, meaning I would go upside down twice with a total of three and a half rotations and land 'switch' (with my back foot forwards). I could perform this with a mute grab (right hand between my feet) thrown in for good measure. That made it a backside double cork 1260 mute.

I had done a couple of sketchy backside 12s in Breck, so had something to build on, although it wasn't close to being a solid trick for me, but that's often the case in these situations. It was time to live up to my reputation and go YOLO.

I dropped in and hucked it, came up a little short on rotation but landed right at the bottom of the landing area. As I turned to face the crowd, I was aware of them going completely mental all around me.

'What do you reckon?' I asked Hamish on my way back up to the top. 'Second?'

He shrugged, half-smiling, as usual. 'Maybe,' he said.

For the only time in my life, I may have had a bit of home advantage. The crowd wanted me to win, and as the last few riders chucked their jumps, word began to spread around that I was in pole position. It didn't seem truly feasible. I was still a novice on the pro circuit, a relative unknown. Could I have beaten Tonteri, Smits and the rest? With the comp over, Roope and a few of the riders were already tucking into some booze.

'Great jump, man,' Roope said. 'Great jump.' He was knocking back a glass of some crazy green stuff. I felt honoured.

'And your results of the LG Freeze Big Air 2012,' the tannoy blared. 'In third place, Tor Lundstrom. In second, Marco Grigis … and your winner … Britain's Billy Morgan!'

It was unreal. I looked out through the crowd and saw my brother. Next to him, Sammi-Jo was perched on my dad's shoulders. My family had never attended an event before. What a show to bring them to.

19.

Big Win? Big Celebration ...

WHAT A rush! My first World Cup win. A bunch of friends and well-wishers charged over and picked me up. I found myself thrown around for a bit before the organisers called me up to the office and gave me £5,000 cash in £20 notes. I made it rain money, throwing a bunch in the air, because I thought I should do something like that, then quickly gathered it all back up. Ryan Matthews, one of the organising team, offered to keep the money in the safe for me. I agreed that was a more sensible course of action than taking the lot to the bar, grabbed a handful of twenties and went out to party.

As soon as I hit the public area outside, a bunch of drunk Brits rushed over to congratulate me. Within minutes I was pretty shit-faced and sending it in the drum and bass arena with Scott and the boys. Lots of punters came up to me and introduced themselves, usually with the opening line, 'No way, it's Billy Morgan!' I must have posed for a hundred selfies.

Once the music finished, the official after-event was an invitation-only boat party, but after a brief chat with my mate Matt, Sammi-Jo, my brother and my dad, we confirmed by group consensus that we would enjoy ourselves more at the venue. The DJs might have packed up but that didn't mean there was no more fun to be had.

Attracted by the hulking structure nearby, we all wandered into the disused leviathan that is Battersea Power Station. Something about the vast, disused space was much more enticing to us than a knees-up on a riverboat.

Dad and Sammi-Jo started a little fire with some bits and bobs and hung out in the middle of the station. Dad had had a few brews as well and was getting into proper Mad Eddie mode. Ash, Matt and I went off to explore, ran through a doorway and could barely believe what we were confronted with.

We stumbled into a big function room with a sort of events tent. They were obviously setting something up in there and we picked our way through into the backstage area, where we found a whole room full of fire extinguishers. We grabbed a couple each, chasing each other around and spraying CO_2 powder, laughing our heads off. It was like a *Call of Duty* deathmatch. I managed to fill one of my eyes up with powder and Ash rushed me off to a disabled toilet and washed it out. Luckily, I was fine. We swung around on the lighting rigs and leapt off to the floor below. Things began to get pretty 'loose'.

The main part of the building was properly 'rad', two football pitches in size but so dark you could barely see your hand in front of your face. There were huge holes in the floor, which had filled with water, and it had this weird, semi-industrial smell. It was like a film set for some mad horror movie. Curiosity kicked in and we decided to explore. In fact, it was more than that. We *needed* to explore, despite being pretty steamed.

A bit of further wandering brought us to the entrance to the lift shaft, which rose up to the bottom of the chimney stacks. Of course, there were no lifts any more, so we started to climb the scaffolding on the outside of the shaft, using the poles like a ladder. It went on and on and on. The building is about 60 metres high, while the chimneys on the roof stretch up for another 100 metres.

After ten minutes of solid climbing, the floor had disappeared below us and the scaffolding ended. Matt clearly began having second thoughts and suggested heading back down, but Ashley and I weren't finished. At the top of the scaffolding, two parallel poles connected it to the building, attached by brackets. On the other side of the poles was a scaffolding platform, placed at the base of the chimneys that looked out over the river. We both sat and looked at it. There was a moment of silence.

Ashley turned to me. 'YOLO?' he asked. I nodded.

In true Morgan family tradition my brother shimmied across first, hooking his legs over the poles then using his hands to pull himself along. Until he reached the other side, all that lay below him was 60 metres of air, then the ground. One wrong move and he would be a headline in the next day's *Evening Standard*. Being Ashley Morgan, of course, he didn't make a wrong move, reached the platform on the other side, sat down and gave me a thumbs-up.

I grinned, got on all fours and edged my way along. For a moment, our old mate James Kingston popped into my mind. He would have loved this. Matt stayed behind, clinging to the relative safety of the main scaffolding, shaking his head. 'You boys are nuts,' he said. It was pretty gnarly, to be fair.

Ash and I sat together on that platform, hung our legs over the edge like we were dangling our feet in the Thames and looked out over the London night. What a view! We could see right past the twinkling city and out over the South Downs beyond. Matt snapped a few pictures of us on his phone from below.

'Well?' Ashley asked after a while. I nodded and one by one we shimmied back across, then started to pick our way back down the scaffolding. We were maybe a third of the way from the top when a torch beam criss-crossed around us.

'Oi!' a male voice called out. 'I know you're up there.'

We froze. For some reason, we thought maybe if we stayed still, he wouldn't be able to see us, but shortly after he shouted again. 'I can still see you, you know!'

We continued down, and as we neared the bottom, we could pick out a man in uniform, a security guard. All three of us understood that timing was everything in this situation.

'This is a criminal offence!' he shouted. 'You're trespassing on private property!'

By waiting, then moving, waiting, then moving, we managed to avoid being apprehended, reached the floor and ran off. Dad was where we had left him, warming his hands on the fire he had built.

'Fucking hell, I'm glad you're back,' he said.

We pointed up. 'We went all the way up there!'

He smiled. 'Yeah, well stay down here now, will you?'

All of us went back to Matt's van, chilled for a bit and had a few tinnies. We had made it a memorable evening. My first World Cup win, followed by a once-in-a-lifetime adventure. What more could you ask for?

Three weeks later, back in Southampton, Matt was leaving his house to go to work and found himself immediately surrounded by police cars, then arrested on a charge of trespassing and criminal damage. At the time, he was due to emigrate to Australia and couldn't risk a criminal record. The only way to avoid it was to pay £3,500 in damages, so we did the decent thing and split it between us.

For quite a while, we all wondered how the police had caught up with Matt. Other than Dad and Sammi-Jo, the only one who knew we were in there was the security guard, but he hadn't seen our faces or anything from which to identify us. In the end, like so much else in the early 21st century, our answer came from social media. Matt put some pictures of us at the top of the chimneys on Twitter. After the fire extinguisher wreckage was discovered and the security guard made his report, police knew where to go.

This may be the internet age and people of our generation may well be used to putting everything from pics of their meals to relationship details out in public, but some things, we told Matt, were better not shared online.

20.

The Complexities of Success

FOLLOWING MY win at the Freeze, Hamish put some feelers out to see whether he could help advance my career as a snowboarder. Now that I was entering and even winning international-class big air comps, there had to be hope of bringing in a major sponsor.

Sure enough, following Hamish's enquiries I received an exciting email from a guy called Rich King, athlete manager at Red Bull, who I had met a few times before. This was shortly followed by a phone call, and King sounded super upbeat when we spoke.

'Hamish tells me you've got a strong work ethic and really positive attitude,' he said.

'That's kind of him,' I replied. 'I'm very committed to my snowboarding.'

'Well, we'd like to give you some support to help you achieve your goals.'

That conversation led to a meeting at the Red Bull offices in Covent Garden and ultimately to a deal. It seemed they had been looking for a UK snowboarder for a little while, so the timing was perfect. Initially, they would start me as an 'unbranded athlete', meaning they would offer some support in the form of medical expenses, strength and conditioning or help with travel and filming projects.

'Let us know if you're doing anything cool,' they said, 'and we'll do whatever we can to help.' They sent me a couple of crates of Red Bull down to Southampton as a welcome gift but, notably, I hadn't yet earned the prestige that comes with the Red Bull hat.

This is one of those things that might sound silly to outsiders, but anyone involved in extreme sports fully understood the significance. The energy drink manufacturer had been a long-time supporter of freesports, with an impressive roster of athletes, from surfers, to skaters, to climbers and motocross riders. Their name was intrinsically linked to the highest level of the scene and for many years they had forged a reputation for cutting-edge videos and web content. We all used to watch their output back in the Morzine days when doing our own vids, and usually, if you saw a viral video on the internet that blew your mind, Red Bull had something to do with it. Their level was what we all aspired to, so an association with them was a massive badge of honour.

The fully fledged Red Bull athletes wear the branding on some sort of headwear (usually either a beanie or a cap). They would be expected to have it on for any public engagement and doubly so if there was going to be photography or videography involved. When you reached that stage, you were a fully fledged representative of the brand.

There was no denying it from that point on. A world first, an Olympics to aim for and a Red Bull partnership? I felt I was on the right track. At 23 years old, at the tail end of 2012 and still relatively early in my snowboarding career, it was a great position to be in.

The Sochi Olympics were scheduled for February of 2014, meaning that we had just over a year to prepare. Not only that but we had to make sure we met the qualification criteria, meaning we had to be ranked in the top 40 in the world, which for a lot of Brits was challenging. Ranking points were gained via the FIS World Cup events, so for obvious reasons we decided I would spend 2013 focusing on slopestyle, with only a couple of big air meets to keep me ticking over, for potential prize money and glory.

To get things underway, I finished 2012 with a trip out to Sölden, Austria with my buddy Paddy Graham, who was also a fully fledged Red Bull free-skier. Paddy and I had bonded a lot during British team training camps in Breckenridge. We were regular drinking buddies and got on really well.

Paddy had a side project, a crew called 'Legs of Steel', who were chucking out some epic video content. They were in Austria to shoot segments and take some stills and it was my first time seeing how a fully 'legit' crew operated.

They had a private jump, meaning no interruptions or having to worry about punters milling about on the knuckles. They had an octocopter drone recording some of the video content, which resulted in unbelievably classy-looking aerial shots. Most impressive of all was the use of a team of snowmobiles instead of ski lifts. There was a queue of snowmobiles with ropes hanging off the back at the bottom of the jump, like a taxi rank. To go back up to the top, all you had to do was hold on to a rope and you would be immediately pulled back up. This was at least ten times quicker than the standard way of doing things and meant you could get so much more riding done.

It was a great opportunity to get amazing footage of my hardest tricks, so I really pushed myself. The back triple got plenty of repetitions. At one point, Paddy and I swapped equipment and I surprised myself by actually managing to pull off a backflip on skis. I don't think it was the most graceful of manoeuvres, but I landed it.

Legs of Steel cut some fantastic edits and it felt like a genuine privilege to see my riding displayed on footage with such high production values. The other riders were awesome too, guys such as Thomas Hlawitschka and Benny Maier. I must have watched the clips a hundred times the next day in the editing studio at the Legs of Steel house in Innsbruck.

It was a great way to end the year and led me into the Christmas break with a massive feeling of momentum. Of course, it was cool to have some downtime and hang out with Sammi-Jo and the rest of the Southampton crew. Our crowd of friends hadn't changed and there was a bunch of parties and pub nights, but my heart was still in the mountains. Whichever continent they were in and however far from my birthplace they may have been, snow-capped peaks under clear blue skies now felt like home.

The following year, 2013, began with another Breckenridge training camp. I already felt like an integral part of the team and it was so good to see all the guys. Aimee Fuller, Katie Ormerod, Murray Buchan, Jamie Nicholls, Jamie Trinder, Sam Turnbull, Ben Kilner, Dom Harrington and, of course, Jenny Jones. There was also Jack Shackleton, a former team member, who had become Hamish's assistant coach. We had crossed paths before but not spent a lot of time together. As he was only a year older than me, we connected instantly and became 'homies'.

About a week in, I managed to rack up a Keystone code violation for speeding and spraying a safety sign with snow as I turned a corner. The slope officials suspended my pass until I attended a deathly boring safety course, which reminded me of being at school, except I didn't have my old mates there to mess around with. I found myself sitting in a meeting room with six or seven other riders, while a po-faced woman with red cheeks droned on about the importance of staying in control at all times, showing consideration to other slope users and observing signs and warnings. I managed to stay sane by chatting with a helicopter rescue officer at the back of the room.

'What are you doing here?' I asked him.

He looked a little sheepish. 'I got done for a ski speed violation on my day off,' he replied.

I found it hilarious that one of the highest-ranking safety operatives had fallen foul of their own rules and we bantered away to pass the time.

In one sense that course was effective, though. The sheer tedium of it served as a powerful deterrent. There was no way I could sit through another one of those and I promised myself never to speed or spray a sign again (at least until tomorrow).

While back in Colorado I took the opportunity to take a break from the relentless slopestyle events that I was entering to pick up points, to focus again on big air. Over time I had become strongly attracted to the idea of attempting a backside triple cork 1440. As usual, I chatted to Hamish and we began building up to it, heading down to nearby Woodward to use the foam pit there. Hamish was sure the trick was in reach if we broke it down and worked towards it systematically.

They had a superb training facility at Woodward, the super-ramp and foam pit meant you could practise new tricks without fear of injury. This was huge help in developing the necessary muscle memory to pull off the more gnarly stuff. We worked hard on making sure I had the right rip to get over and around three times, then land. It took several days of repetitions before I felt like I was ready, but we got there.

Ed Blomfield from *Whitelines* magazine had come out to write a piece on the team and shoot some footage. He had previously taken the iconic pic of me naked on a handrail in Tahoe and would be there to witness my attempt at the triple.

A back 14, at the time, certainly fit the gnarly category, although it wasn't quite another world first as the Canadian Mark McMorris landed one in 2011. I remembered watching the McMorris video when it was released and being mind-blown by it, feeling that it was miles and levels above me. In fact, I think it was this that made me want to land one so much. If I could, it would be like a message to my former self. *You see 2011 Billy? You see what you can do?*

Despite the word 'triple' in the full title, the trick actually consists of four complete rotations: three vertical flips (each of which constitutes a full 360 degrees) and one full lateral spin. The spin constitutes another 360 degrees of rotation, hence the total of 1440. In technical terminology this makes it a gyroscopic trick, meaning you're rotating around two different axes. This makes it extremely difficult, even for someone like me with an acrobatic background. It's one thing to flip and then spin, but to do both simultaneously is a real brain scrambler. If you think of a waltzer ride at a funfair, where the carriages move in a circular fashion on a track, but also spin individually around their own fulcrums as they do so, it might make it easier to understand.

The back 14 was a real mark of my evolution. There were similarities with the triple rodeo in the sense that both tricks involve being upside down three times while airborne, but the cork element added a level of high-end technicality. I knew within myself that it would have been beyond me a year or two before. That was exciting. The sheer progression it demonstrated gave me a high like no other.

I psyched myself up for it by trying it early in the morning. With any trick you've never done before, there's always an issue with how you conceive the jump in your mind. With most jumps I can fully visualise the trick all the way through, but for this, it was unknown territory. After the first cork, it was impossible to conceptualise where the knuckle would be in relation to my eyeline. I call this the 'black spot', meaning I had no real idea how the middle part of the trick would feel once I had started the process. This meant, to some degree, hucking it.

I did three double corks to warm up, got a fist-bump from Ben and went for it. In the air it felt unlike anything I had ever done, although I seemed to remain aware of where I was. My feet hit the ground first, as they should, but I washed out and ended on my arse, for safety. By complete coincidence, the legend, Shaun White, was riding nearby at the time and, as I hauled myself up from the snow, he appeared out of nowhere, spraying Ben and I with snow as he ground to a halt.

'Holy fuck, dude! Are you alright?' he asked.

'Yeah, I'm fine,' I replied with a grin.

'That was so *sick*!'

With a fresh fist-bump from Big Shaun, I got some final words of advice from Hamish.

'Stay over your board more and really take the pop, so you've got more time to chill at the end and spot your landing.'

I nodded excitedly. Both of us knew that first one was close enough. As I sat on the world's slowest two-man chairlift back up to the top, I tried hard to stay in the right mental state and keep my buzz, visualising the trick, rehearsing the process. It wasn't easy.

On the second attempt I got more of the pop, immediately feeling higher than the previous attempt. I watched the knuckle go past my vision once, twice, then after that I got the visual marker that I needed, opened up and stomped the landing, handling all the compression through my knees. Ben stuck the camera in my face. I simply couldn't stop grinning, a feeling that lasted for at least the next few days. God, how I had come to love Colorado. I had performed the two best individual pieces of my snowboarding life there. To me, Colorado meant stoke.

Outsiders may not get it, but although the triple rodeo was a world first, the triple cork was personally more important. By the time I landed mine in 2012 and the video went up on the internet, along with assorted media coverage, including a feature article in *Whitelines*, only McMorris, the Norwegians Torstein Horgmo and Ståle Sandbech, Canada's Sebastien Toutant, Japan's Yuki Kadono and the man himself, Shaun White, had landed one. Other people began to put my name up there in that sort of company. For my part, I still felt like an imposter, to some degree. I practised the tricks I thought I could make work but knew other parts of my riding technique were very basic. Those other guys could do a bit of everything.

To celebrate, we ended up in a multicoloured cocktail bar called Cecilia's and somehow managed to lose Murray Buchan. At the end of the evening we caught a ride home, wondering what had happened to him. Early the next morning, the phone rang.

'Hello, do you know an individual by the name of Murray Buchan?' a very bored-sounding American voice said on the other end of the line.

'Yes.'

'This is the drunk tank at Breckenridge police headquarters. We found him on the road last night.'

We all cracked up laughing.

'It's too cold out there to be wandering around drunk, so we had to bring him in.'

We all got in the van and went to pick him up. Murray emerged from the station looking very sorry for himself with a $150 fine in his hand. 'Not bad for a night's private accommodation in Breck though, eh?' he said. Legend.

That stay in Colorado finished up with the US Grand Prix event at nearby Copper Mountain. It was another beautiful spot (they seem blessed with them in the USA) about 75 miles west of Denver, with 2,500 acres of rideable slopes. It's been a favourite for Hollywood over the years, with two Jim Carrey movies filmed there, *Dumb and Dumber* and another simply called *Copper Mountain*.

The Grand Prix utilised a standard slopestyle set-up and I was so used to the Colorado riding conditions by then that I felt completely at home there. I finished a creditable second in my heat with a score of 91.3 and the following day came fourth in the final, with the only downside being that I fell on the last jump of my first run, smashing my arms on the ground and breaking my wrist. I had a cast fitted immediately, and although it was inconvenient, the injury wasn't enough to stop me riding. I headed back to the UK with a finalist's certificate from the Grand Prix and a positive feeling about where things were heading.

While back at home, I attended a Red Bull gathering with Paddy and some of the other guys at a cliff-diving World Series event in Pembrokeshire, South Wales. It was another unbelievable location called the 'Blue Lagoon', sitting beneath an ancient cathedral on a cliff. Red Bull liked to pull their athletes together like this so that people with similar mindsets and lifestyles could bounce ideas around and learn from each other.

After the event finished, most of the athletes got into it at a small after-party at a local bar. When like-minded freesports athletes are thrown into a room together with a bar tab, it typically ramps up pretty quickly. Out of the melee, Paddy tapped me on the shoulder, with Rich, the athlete manager standing next to him. He had a massive, cheesy grin on his face.

'They told me to give you this,' Paddy said, holding up a cap. 'It's yours, dude.'

'Well done, Bill!' Rich said. 'You've earned it, bro.'

'You're still a douche though,' Paddy whispered.

I thanked both of them, wishing I had had a beer or two less at this point, put the hat on and said a few words of acceptance. I had just become an official Red Bull athlete.

That meant from then on I was required to wear the hat whenever and wherever I was riding. That would instantly indicate to anyone else that I was an 'elite' rider. Although my face was becoming better and better known among the snowboarding community and I had a fair amount of press, until then it had still usually been possible for me to keep a low profile and shred around without being recognised. The hat would change all that.

I soon learned that going out with Red Bull kit carries huge status and respect but also exerts pressure. I might, for example, want to go out to practise something quite simple. We all need to sometimes, but if people saw me with my Red Bull helmet on, it felt like they expected me to be doing triple corks every run. That added some different pressures to my days on the hill.

21.

Living with Injury

BY MID-SEASON, the points situation looked promising, but I still wanted to hit as many events as I could, to keep racking them up. There were still a few months to go and every top 20 placing was worth something. The plaster cast was beginning to annoy me and I wondered whether it might be having a tiny effect on my performance. Even if it shaved off two per cent, that was something I didn't need at that stage. While still at home, I told Dad.

'How does the wrist feel?' Dad asked.

'It's fine now.'

'Sure?'

'One hundred per cent.'

'Right, let's get that off now,' Dad said.

He came up with a typical Mad Eddie solution. We went out to the garage, he put my arm in the vice and cut the cast off with an angle grinder.

Being released from the cast did give me a boost. It felt great to have full movement in my wrist again and the knowledge that I could use my hand to break my fall if I wiped out. While the cast was on, that was something else I had to consider. When falling I would have to purposely roll on my shoulder or use my elbow, so as not to put weight on the injury. That stuff is unnatural and occupies space in your consciousness. It can also lead to further damage, which is always the biggest danger of competing while injured. The need to compensate for impairment in one part of the body can often cause harm to others.

It proved well timed because February took me to Russia for the Olympic test event. I was already quite widely travelled but had never been to Russia, and at first it was difficult to know what to make of it.

'I think I packed the wrong clothes,' I said to Hamish, as the coach drove us from Sochi airport through the town.

'What? No speedos?' came the quickfire response.

Sochi is actually a coastal resort on the Black Sea, complete with beaches, palm trees and ornate 19th-century buildings. Driving along the beachfront felt a bit like being on the Côte d'Azur in France. Soon, we left the coastal area and were whisked up into the imposing Caucasus Mountains, rising away, 90 minutes from the town. Tall, snow-capped and surrounded by belts of wispy cloud, this was much more the view I had expected. I couldn't think of anywhere else with two such disparate sides to it. Sochi was a summer seaside town with a snowsports resort built above it.

The mountain athletes' village was yet to be fully finished but looked impressive, with the large Olympic rings logo everywhere. Vladimir Putin himself had a large part to play in preparing the Games, we were told, as Sochi was one of his favourite spots. The Russian president had a house in the area.

I enjoyed my visit to Russia, did some riding and a fair bit of touristy mooching around with Hamish and Jack. For me it helped build anticipation for the Games the following year, but already there were rumblings from some quarters about the conditions. It was set to be the warmest Winter Olympics ever held and some of the snowsports fraternity questioned the suitability of the location. For my part, if I qualified it would be my first Olympics and I couldn't have cared if they staged it in Egypt. I was just excited at the prospect of being involved.

I then hopped on another plane, for a trip to the Czech Republic for a World Cup event being held at a remote town called Špindlerův Mlýn. Situated in the middle of the Krkonoše mountains, I found it a weird and unsettling place, very small and very quiet. Fog would close in at night to the point where visibility was reduced to a metre or two and it was pretty eerie. I didn't sleep well while there and found the riding conditions difficult. It was super cold and the slopes were in the shade all day, making for bulletproof snow, which you really didn't want to fall on to from any sort of height.

While there, I began to feel pressure building inside my head. My instincts were to ride with caution, to preserve myself for the World Cup at the end of the season, but suddenly I was a Red Bull rider, potentially an Olympian. Everyone in snowboarding and even some outside knew who I was. Riding cautiously wasn't the expectation. It's the never-ending battle between how you see yourself and how you're perceived by others. That's not always an easy thing to square in your mind.

A swirling wind made for all sorts of problems getting on and off rails or jumping. I struggled a bit, fell a couple of times and missed out on the final. That was disappointing in terms of points, but in truth it was a relief to get out of there.

My final competitive outing of the season was set for the end of March in Spain, meaning I had the annual 'Snowbombing' festival at Mayrhofen in Austria first. Snowbombing is an event that essentially captures the collision between the free-ski, freestyle snowboarding scene and music, a very natural relationship. Every year about 6,000 Brits descend on this quiet Austrian village, getting smashed at night and going riding during the day. Needless to say, Snowbombing always had its casualties.

As British team members we received free invitations to the event and fresh snowfall made for some great fun on the slopes in 2013. My favourite day was the 'ride with a pro' day when they teamed up each professional snowboarder with one of the public, to try to pull off a trick on a small jump together. I had great fun with a beered-up guy called Carl from Bristol, who wanted to learn to backflip. It took a few attempts, but we got there in the end. Of course, the nightlife, as usual, was off the hook. Normally, Snowbombing marked the end of the season and an opportunity to go completely wild, but I reined myself in, knowing I had my final World Cup event in Sierra Nevada.

Sierra Nevada took place at the same time as The Brits, which were being held in Tignes that year. After a disappointing heat in which I just scraped through in sixth place, the conditions changed, becoming soft and slow for the finals, which meant all the riders were fighting for speed. That actually worked in my favour, as one of my slopestyle issues was that sometimes I struggled remembering how fast to go for each individual jump. Different jumps and different conditions require different speeds, dependent on which trick you want to land. Without that to worry about, I just pointed the board, went for it and managed to nail my run, which included three doubles, alongside all the rail features. I ended up on the podium, in third place behind Max Parrot and Yuki Kadono, outscoring some really top slopestylers in the process. My first World Cup medal meant I ended the season on a huge high.

Combined with my results from the latter half of 2012, the Sierra Nevada result meant I accumulated enough points to finish the 2013 season officially ranked number two in the world in slopestyle. Once again, this was absolutely massive for me. Slopestyle wasn't even my preferred event and it meant there was no longer any real doubt. I would be Britain's slope representative in Sochi, along with Jamie Nicholls, who was very close to securing his spot too.

Yet, before there was even much time for all of that to sink in, Gary Greenshields, the new athletes' manager at Quicksilver, whisked me away for a film shoot in the Italian Alps, with a bunch of European pros, including legend Eero Ettala and Ben Knox's brother Sparrow Knox, a super-fun guy with some rad style. The whole thing was a sick media trip on a private park. I remember feeling during this period that I was living in a kind of bubble. A fantastic, fun-filled bubble, but a bubble, nonetheless.

The normal world that I had come from, the world where people went to school then grew up and had jobs, where life could sometimes be boring or repetitive or mired in routine, had evaporated around me and been replaced by this other world, where everyone was young and cool and lived for white and stoke.

Lesley spoke about it with a wise smile and said this was what life was supposed to be, the 'good life' of stretching boundaries, and that through progression we found meaning. Whereas, when I first met her, I had struggled a little with her philosophies, now I felt I was really beginning to see that. It all made total sense. But then, the universe shook things up. I twanged my knee on the last day in Italy, but that was just the start of it. My little bubble was about to pop.

In April I was booked in for a close season, Red Bull UK summer camp at the snowdome in Castleford, Yorkshire. We did gym sessions, strength and conditioning during the day, then rode at night. Aimee and Paddy were there, along with Katie Summerhayes, a slopestyle skier. On the second day, while having had a really good session on the rails, I headed down to the

174

bottom of the lift and, on the way, frontflipped off a box. It was just a regular, single frontflip, but I messed up the take-off.

I knew immediately I had messed it up but felt happy and relaxed in the air. A frontflip is such an undemanding manoeuvre, and if you mangle it, you just land on your back and it's fine. It's a bit like the snowboarding equivalent of a forward roll. My tail hit the ground first and my right knee folded inwards. I felt a weird pop. Immediately I knew it wasn't good.

It was one of those accidents you have all the time as a park rider and think absolutely nothing of it. I guess, by the law of averages, if you fall off a bit of equipment a thousand times, sooner or later you'll do some damage.

I tried to stand but it was hard to put any weight on my leg. I felt a wave of fear, as if my body had scanned itself and knew this wasn't a straightforward knock. I ended up laying on a bench in the changing room, being examined by a physio.

'Hmm,' he said, screwing his face up.

'What?' I asked him.

'You're gonna need to get this checked. I think it's blown.'

I felt sick. Knee ligament injuries are very common in snowboarding due to all the impacts and it seemed we were fearing the worst. Hamish and the rest stood around making faces of concern.

Red Bull got me to a Game Ready cold compress machine and, as this was potentially quite serious, they put me up in the hotel door next door to the training centre. I was booked in for an MRI the next day, where it turned out things were even worse than we suspected. I had snapped the anterior cruciate ligament (ACL) and ruptured the medial collateral ligament (MCL). An operation was clearly required.

This was something of a disaster. Recovery from knee ligament surgery is so unpredictable. Some people heal quickly, others much less so. As with any operation, there could be complications or delays. A lengthy spell of rehabilitation was a definite and no one could accurately predict a timescale, but doctors advised we would be looking at a minimum of six to nine months of recovery. At that point, the Sochi Olympics were eight months off. If we went through with the operation, I would almost certainly miss them. A sense of impending dread bubbled up inside me.

'There has to be an alternative,' Hamish declared. He conferred with Red Bull and with Alison Robb, the team physio. Alison was a really integral part of our set-up and had a way of approaching physiotherapy that almost made it enjoyable. Ultimately, a plan was devised that would temporarily swerve an operation by wearing a bespoke knee brace and doing intensive gym sessions, focusing on quadriceps, glute and hamstring exercises. The idea was that, by building the muscles around the knee, those muscles would compensate for the work that should have been done by ligaments. It was risky, but worth a try.

22.

A Miracle Down Under

ALISON AND Red Bull collaborated on a programme for me. I was sent to Darren Roberts at Harrison Ross in Manchester, one of the country's leading physiotherapy clinics, for three-day sessions every other week. Darren was ex-Parachute Regiment and had great banter. He knew how to make strength and conditioning appeal to freesports athletes, for whom it may not have come naturally.

Meanwhile, Alison looked for a physio in Southampton and booked me in to The Quays diving centre for sessions with a guy called Dean Cook, who worked with the Olympic diving team. Dean also ran the Dynamics Physio clinic, which I ended up spending more time in than my house when I was back at home. Cook linked up with top orthopaedic surgeon Andy Williams about my case and combined with a strength and conditioning coach called Matt Dickinson. They started me training with the divers, weight training, soft tissue massage, doing single-leg hops on to boxes and things like that. I wore a pressure cuff when performing leg press repetitions, which temporarily cut off circulation and increased the intensity of the exercise. This was a way to increase leg strength rapidly. Yet even with the weight of all that knowledge and experience behind me, I knew it would still be at least a couple of months before I could think about riding again.

Under other circumstances, I may have got a little down about it, although I'm a person who tries to find the positives in every situation. But while all this was going on, a letter came through the mail to my dad's house in a fancy, embossed envelope. I opened it up to see the five rings logo and an opening sentence of 'Dear Mr Morgan, welcome to the British Olympic team.' Immediately I took it around to show Mum.

'You've done so well, Billy! I can't believe you've made something so huge out of doing what you love!' she said. Her eyes were wet with tears and we hugged. As we held each other, I could literally feel the pride and emotional energy pulsing out of her. At that moment, I truly began to realise what a massive, massive deal this was. Snowboarding had always been my thing, which meant a lot to me, but Mum's reaction showed how it was now becoming something more – something that could mean a great deal to others, too. That was down to one thing: the stature and cachet of the Olympic Games.

The letter invited me to get kitted out in London, which suddenly made everything seem very real. I travelled down and met up with all the GB Park and Pipe crew. We went through a huge fitting room, going from one person to the next, being measured, trying on different items and ended up leaving with three massive bags full of red, white and blue Adidas, Team GB kit. I had never seen so much stash in all my life.

Still unable to ride, in May I flew out to Kaunertal in Austria for the annual 'Board Test' event, a sort of industry get-together, where sponsored riders and public try out new equipment, although lots of people go just for the craic, too. This was perfect for me as I could see everybody, hang out with the brands in the tents on the mountain and still feel involved, without actually snowboarding. The scene is very much like that. As well as the top riders there are thousands of casual participants and many others who may not even ride much at all. They're attracted to the sport for the travel aspect or the culture and musical tie-ins.

Kaunertal is famous for its bar called the Pfiff Alm, and as I wasn't able to get out and shred, I spent much more time in there than is advisable. Scotty Penman had moved to Rome Snowboards and I was hanging out with him and the other Rome riders. They were a particularly reckless crew, Jesse Smith, a guy called Monkey and Angus Leith, a real character, known for being the lynchpin of the Wee Breck Bastards crew, or WBB for short; a bunch of Brits who hung out in Breckenridge making cool video edits. They were very much at the forefront of the core snowboard set who shunned the competition scene and still did things the old, stylish way. Rome had set them up with a house in Kaunertal and, needless to say, things got pretty loose.

A favourite game involved six dice and a shot, which had a super-hot Naga chilli in it. If you got it, you had to chew it five times on either side of your mouth. The dice were out at some point every evening. I've never understood why people play drinking games for nice drinks. What's the point in a drinking game where you lose and you're like, 'Oh no! I have to do this shot of Baileys!' In that Rome house they knew how to play drinking games. No one participated hoping to lose.

One night after playing we headed down to the Pfiff Alm and sunk a few more. It was metal night, with a full-on mosh pit going and things were getting very sweaty and out of hand. Angus had just finished his pint and I shouted, 'Smash it on my head!'

'You what?'

'Go on, smash the glass on my head! On the top!'

It may be a national stereotype, but being a Scottish dude, I assumed Angus would know how to glass someone without hurting them. Hit, then retract, allowing the glass to explode without dragging it down their forehead. Angus was hammered though, and, of course, messed it up.

'Shit man, I'm sorry!' he cried as I staggered back, laughing, with blood streaming down my face. He had managed to cut my cheek and nose, avoiding my eye. When reflecting the next morning through my hangover, I realised that was possibly one of the closest calls for no reward I've ever had. Sometimes I found, just like my old man, I couldn't help myself.

Fortunately, there was then time for much-needed recuperation, with a long summer holiday in Indonesia. I spent a month over there with Paddy, Murray, Scott, Rob, Liam Russell and Matt from home, soaking up sun and generally resting my body.

This led up to a New Zealand trip where I had a good four weeks to tentatively start riding again. To begin with, I was pretty nervous, as perhaps is natural. If I found the knee wasn't strong enough, I was done and the Olympic dream would be over. I had to wear a knee brace manufactured by a company called CTI, and this piece of equipment would become an ever-present companion throughout my riding over the next few years. In the absence of ligaments, I simply couldn't ride for long without it.

I discovered quite quickly that although the knee functioned with the added muscle instead of ligaments, it got sore, tender and swollen very quickly. I needed to ride as much as possible to get my legs back, but once I suffered a few big impacts I would need to rest. This resulted in Hamish coining the phrase 'knee tokens'.

'You've probably done enough today, Bill. You need to save your knee tokens,' he might say. Or maybe, 'That was a heavy hit, you spent most of your knee tokens there,' or even, 'This event's worth spending a few knee tokens on.' It was a way of making light of a situation we all knew was delicate. If I overdid it, I risked another lengthy spell on the sidelines.

My first major expenditure of knee tokens came in the Kiwi Winter Games in August, where I shook off the cobwebs by qualifying for the final. After that, it was over to Australia for the Mile High comp. That was my first trip to Australia and great fun. Fellow slopestyle and big air athlete Rowan Coultas had just joined the team, and although he was much younger than me, we got on very well. Sharing a car from the airport, we were super excited to see kangaroos running wild in the fields beside the road. We asked Hamish to stop, got out and spent half an hour chasing kangaroos before resuming our journey.

The months of rest and gym work seemed to have really done the trick. I felt so stable on my board and won the big air by landing the first triple cork on Australian soil. To pull off a trick of that magnitude relatively early on in my recovery from injury was a great marker for me. Essentially, I was back to my best. I also came second in the Mile High Slopestyle, pocketing $6,000 in prize money. This was a fantastic validation for all the work our medical team had put in. I basically had no ligaments in one knee, but still found myself on two podiums. The combined planning of Red Bull and GB Park and Pipe was achieving something I would previously have thought medically impossible.

We spent a few more days in NZ after the comp and I did some filming with a crew called 'Diaries Down Under'. They decided it would be cool to shoot me on one of the world's gnarliest bungee jumps, the infamous Shotover Canyon Swing in Queenstown. At a height of 109m, the jump effectively involved a 60m freefall off a cliff, before swinging around 200m above the Shotover River. The sheer height of it all excited me and it proved to be another fabulous experience. The Australian continent as a whole has such a different vibe to Europe.

As I was about to leave Australasia and embark on the long journey home, I received another unexpected boost. After checking in at the airport, I opened my email inbox to find a message from ESPN: 'X Games invitation'.

Woah. This was a major deal. Despite breaking on to the scene with the world's first triple rodeo in 2011, I hadn't received X Games recognition before. They wanted me to compete in the Winter X Games in Aspen, Colorado in January 2014. Of course, my first response was to call Hamish. It was an incredibly exciting offer, but would it be a barrier for Sochi, bearing in mind my injury?

'No, come on, let's go and do it, but we'll just think of it as a warm-up for the Olympics,' he said.

I went back home, continued my physical therapy and reflected. Despite 2013's problems and the toll snowboarding was taking on my body, 2014, and certainly the start of it, was going to be absolutely huge. X Games in January followed by the Olympics in February was about as big as it was possible to get. How had all this happened? It only seemed like yesterday I was working at the dry slope and counting my pennies to go to Morzine.

I was lucky that at home I had Sammi-Jo and Dad and all my old mates to hang with. As I headed towards what I knew would be the most significant year of my career so far, I looked back on my whirlwind rise with satisfaction. I may have become a real name on the global snowboard scene, but in Southampton I would always just be 'Billy'.

Part Four

THE REALLY, REALLY BIG STUFF

'A man is a success if he gets up in the morning and goes to bed at night and in between does what he wants to do.'

– Bob Dylan

23.

The High Life

SHOWN LIVE on ESPN, the X Games had long stood as the biggest thing in extreme sports. My first experience of it in Aspen was nuts. A huge event, full of freesports people (who tend to be loud and loose), with concerts and parties all over the place. Hamish flew over with me and Aimee Fuller, who was also competing. Of course, Hamish was a veteran, having been to both Aspen and the X Games many times before, with considerable success, having taken Jenny Jones there multiple times. By then Jenny already had five X Games medals, three of them gold.

We met Gary Greenshields, who was now the Quicksilver international team manager, at the airport. Just to add another point or two to the eccentricity tally, Quicksilver had set their riders up to stay at a house that was rented from the singer, Cher. This proved to be a proper head-trip.

The superstar owned a sort of giant chalet in Aspen, which she rented out most of the year when not using it. The place was full of weird contents, especially mannequins. She must have had a thing for them. It had huge windows, offering spectacular mountain views, in every room and tapestry-style wall coverings made out of some kind of gravel. I had never seen anything like it. In one room hung a huge mirror surrounded by antlers, which felt unearthly, even a bit biblical, while on a shelf below the mirror sat several urns full of ashes.

'Who do you reckon's in there?' I asked, pointing at the largest one. Aimee shrugged and took a picture of it on her phone.

'Maybe it's Sonny?' Hamish suggested. Cher's famous song-writing husband, with whom she first made her name in the 70s, had died in 1998. I recoiled at the thought and found myself backing away.

In the hallway stood a stone washstand, draped in a rosary, crosses and crucifixes. I don't know whether it was intentional. Only Cher could explain the vibe she was going for, but the general aura seemed pretty spooky. The *pièce de résistance* was a nativity scene made from dead, stuffed squirrels in a glass case. They even had little clothes on, like a nightmarish tableau from a Beatrix Potter story. It was against the wall in the dining room, where you might expect to find a TV set, or even a fish tank, and we spent a good while staring at it.

In my bedroom I slept in a giant four-poster bed with red velvet drapes. The first morning I woke up in a panic, momentarily forgetting where I was and thinking I was in some sort of gothic horror scene. All this weirdness added to the feeling, again, of things having gone up a level. You didn't get to stay in crazy pop-star houses at The Brits.

Along with myself, Hamish and Amy, other guests at the house included plenty of other big-name riders, notably Iouri Podladtchikov from Switzerland.

Aspen itself was high-end, like Knightsbridge (the London area where Harrods can be found), but with snow. Boutiques, exclusive eateries, an opera house – I spent a couple of days cruising around the town on pushbikes with Hamish, just to get to know it.

I lapped it all up, as I always tried to do, believing you need to be open to every experience, but in terms of the impending competition, I was fully charged to be there. At least partly this was because Shaun White was set to ride the slopestyle too. I had become used to mixing with big names by then and there were some I even considered friends, but White was a guy whose fame transcended the sport. To many on the snowboard scene he was an iconic figure, the Muhammad Ali or Cristiano Ronaldo of our world but rumoured to be atypical for a snowboarder: quiet, intense and super professional. Of course, by then I had already run into Shaun briefly in Breckenridge and found him cool, so to me he was a sound dude, while his travails with public image were something I could sympathise with. It can't be easy to come across laid-back all the time if people are constantly asking for your picture when you're trying to train. Regardless of any of that, the opportunity to compete alongside Shaun was something I considered an honour. I would be able to share a stage with the biggest name in our world.

As the scheduled Games opening of 24 January approached, we got to check out the athletes' village. Everything was free for us there, which was great. I left with my board bag full of handy things such as cereal bars, high-end SPF lip balm and orthopaedic insoles for boots. They were usually £250 on their own. There were three full-time physios who you could book in with. Prior to my injuries I hadn't made my peace with that side of things yet and always found close contact uncomfortable. I hadn't believed in the benefits of soft tissue massage and saw it as a bit of hocus-pocus, but the knee injury and all my sessions with Alison, Dean and Darren helped to change my mind. It was all part of becoming more professional. If there's one descriptor you could definitely use for the X Games, it's professional.

We were also able to get out on the course, which was the best I had ever ridden, an amazing set-up at a place called Buttermilk

Mountain. By that point, Aspen had held the Winter X Games for something like ten years straight, so they really knew how to run an event to get the best out of the athletes.

On my practice runs I found I was struggling with frontside spins, which had always been my weaker side and was opposite to my natural spinning direction. Switch backside (riding with my left foot forward with my back to the jump) was another I always found difficult, and by this point in my career, when I was competing regularly with elite riders, I regretted not practising them more when younger. Muscle memory is such an important feature of our sport. If you practise things early, they become engrained in your body to the extent they become instinctive, which is exactly what you need when you're in the air. When I started out, though, I just did whatever I could and kept doing it. It was another example of the limitations of my background.

Maybe the pressure was getting to me, but piecing my run together was proving quite difficult. The middle rail feature was messy and the only option on it, for me, was a gap to the down rail. I wanted to miss the first section and land on the down, which was awkward, but I needed to land that rail to have enough speed for the first jump. That meant I had two things to practise and had to make a decision about which to focus on. That stressed me a little and meant I didn't get enough practice on the rail.

Altogether, the course had three rails and four jumps, so I planned a run based around a cab 270 on, 270 off on the first feature, then a back 270 to down, followed by a gap to back lip. That took me straight into a front double 1080 with an indie grab, my trusty double back rodeo 900 melon grab, a cab triple 1260 mute grab and finally a back triple 1440 mute. The cabs, double backside rodeo 900 and back triple were all secure. (A cab is a sort of backflip with a half spin while grabbing the toe edge of the board. The name comes from legendary skateboarder

Steve Caballero, who is credited with pioneering the direction of rotation.) I knew that I was most likely to fall on the front dub 10, but more or less managed to pull the whole run off in practice.

There were 16 of us competing in the men's slope, and alongside Shaun White, the Canadian trio of Mark McMorris, Sebastien Toutant and Max Parrot were all hotly tipped. The idea was that the 16 would be cut to eight after the first two runs, for the final.

Sadly, for me it turned into one of those days where nothing quite worked. On my first run, I stuffed up the rail by going too big and barely touching it. On my second run, I nailed the rail, which felt amazing, but was scrappy on the front 10, which was too small. That gave me an okay score but only got me into ninth place.

Ninth was what was known as an alternate spot, meaning if someone was unable to make the final for any reason, I would be in. So, there was no party for me that night and I was back up early the next day, eager to have another crack.

Hamish encouraged me to use it as the best training day ever, by treating it as if I was still in the competition. I warmed up by spontaneously chucking out one of those unplanned but super-satisfying combinations, managing back-to-back triple corks on the final two jumps of the run. This caused a major buzz. Almost instantly, videos started circulating online. It was the first time back-to-back triples had been landed on an X Games slopestyle course.

From there, I pushed hard and got through my complete run another time, but as the final drew near, it became clear there would be no pull-outs. I sat on the sidelines, had a few beers and enjoyed the show. Of course, there were tinges of disappointment not to have made the final, but as ever I took all the positives I could from the experience. Just as I had in practice, Max Parrot threw back-to-back triples in the final and ESPN went crazy, pushing hysterical coverage about it. Hamish and I laughed at that. Hamish had even sent them a recording of my back-to-back triples from earlier in the day, but they still ran with the story of Max doing it first. Ultimately, he did it in the competition, whereas I did it in practice. Cometh the hour, cometh the man, I guess.

I got a little drunk and watched Shaun White win the halfpipe, which was rad. It was actually refreshing to sit and watch some really high-end technical tricks without being preoccupied about my own riding. White, as ever, was mind-bendingly good.

As I left the arena later, I actually found myself on a little high, despite going out in the heat. My knee had withstood the competition, the Olympics were around the corner and I was the first guy in history to throw back-to-back triples on that course. My time in Aspen put me in a really positive frame of mind for Sochi.

To mark the end of the Games, I went out to a Red Bull dinner at a fancy restaurant. Chase, the US Red Bull athlete manager, encouraged me to order an $85 steak from the menu, something I would never usually have dreamed of doing. The whole Aspen experience had been a taste of the high life.

The only downside to competing in the X Games was that it left so little time to prepare for the Olympics, although we knew and understood all of that before committing. Hamish felt I needed to get the front 10 dialled in to be really competitive in Sochi, because judges like to see a variety of frontside and backside tricks, and up to that point all my best tricks had been backside. I practised it tenaciously in my last couple of weeks before leaving for the Games and finally nailed it about two days before flying out.

Unusually for me, as I boarded the plane to Russia, I did feel an increased weight of expectation. Although I had experienced pressures before, this was at another level. Rather than going out on the slopes and other riders expecting big things from me, it now seemed that nearly everyone did. As this was the Olympics, coverage reached beyond the snowsports world and out into the mainstream.

Suddenly, I was all over the media. BBC and Channel 4 News both interviewed me, along with most of the national newspapers. Needless to say, I also received a lot of attention from local outlets around Southampton. The general perception among journalists was that I was a serious contender. A line I kept reading everywhere described me as a 'top British medal hopeful'. I had finished the year second in the world rankings, after all, and had the world's first triple rodeo to my name, so I suppose it made sense, but internally I didn't think in those terms. I knew the field and how good those guys were. I found it hard not to doubt myself.

I also knew from experience that, in a competition situation, so much depends on what happens on the day. Most of the guys were capable of beating each other in the right circumstances. As a result, I wasn't thinking of going all out for a medal. I just wanted to put my best run down, land a triple, and see what happened. I knew I *could* win a medal, but I didn't necessarily think that I *should*.

Having people outside of our niche, people who didn't understand either the technicalities or culture of snowboarding, put forward their expectations was strange. I accepted it as a symptom of the level I had reached. It was a positive thing! But at the same time, I tried to put it to the back of my mind.

24.

Huck It!

NOW FULLY operational, the Sochi Olympic Village resembled a small town, as would be expected for a facility built to house 6,000 athletes from 85 nations. Divided into three sections, it had its own restaurants and fast-food joints, round-the-clock dining rooms serving food from around the world, a fully fitted games room and a 24-hour gym.

The cafeteria on its own was virtually an eighth wonder of the world. About three football pitches in size, it had almost any type of food you could imagine. It was really difficult not to pig out on everything. You could get a curry for starter, Chinese for your main course and a steak for dessert, if you wanted to, then head over to the snack stand and load up on cakes and biscuits. One of the things us park riders are really lucky about is how lax we can be with our diets compared to athletes in other disciplines. The endurance sports, especially downhill skiers and speed skaters, have to be so careful over what they eat. We more or less get free rein.

Before heading out, the British team had divvied up into pairs and I roomed with Murray Buchan, a halfpipe free-skier from Edinburgh. We're roughly the same age and good mates, despite me regularly winding him up. Not only is he a great guy and easy to get on with, but he's also tidy. People find it surprising, considering my reckless, daredevil reputation, but I like an orderly room. It's probably Dad's military tendencies rubbing off on me. There's nothing worse than getting up in the morning and not being able to find your stuff amongst all the pants and socks.

Life in the athletes' village was interesting, although regulated. We soon realised that we were viewed not just as sportspeople but ambassadors. British team officials would take note of what you were wearing and take issue if anything was amiss.

'Excuse me, but you don't seem to have your gilet on. Please go back to your room and get it before going for breakfast.'

It was hard at times not to react and tell them to get stuffed. At 23 years old, it had been a while since anyone checked my uniform and such a schoolteacherish approach didn't sit well with the snowboard ethos. It was just one of those things we all had to accept. If you wanted to participate in the biggest sporting event in the world, this was the baggage that came with it.

Sochi began with a mini-crisis when I unpacked and realised I had left my knee brace in England. There was no way I could ride without it, so an emergency courier was dispatched to bring it out. Of all the possible reasons to have to withdraw from an Olympic Games, leaving something at home would have been probably the most embarrassing.

The day after arrival, I, Murray and the other slopestyle competitors were shuttled out to inspect the course. It looked decent to me, although they were still in the final stages of building it. All the rails were in place but the jumps were only roughly shaped. The features had been built to accommodate both the ski and snowboard slopestyle competitions. Skiers prefer whippier jumps and longer rails, so the organisers tried to compromise by pitching the course somewhere in the middle. This created jumps and rails that were big by snowboard standards. I rubbed along with that just fine, as I've always been okay going big, but not everyone was as happy.

Conditions were great, still and bright, but the perfect weather didn't stop a flood of negative comments from riders prior to the competition. The Sochi snowpark was called the Rosa Khutor Extreme Park, and for some of my fellow competitors, 'extreme' did seem to be the operative word. In the practice days before the Games began, loads of boarders finished their runs shaking their heads and screwing up their faces, the general consensus being the jumps were too steep and the course too dangerous. Just to underline the point, the Norwegian Torstein Horgmo, a three-time X Games gold medallist and originally a street rider who grew up on gnarly street rails, shattered his collarbone falling from a rail at the top of the slopestyle run. I felt he just rolled the dice wrong, but afterwards my old buddy Roope Tonteri, from Finland, gave a TV interview in which he expressed the views of many:

'It [the course] looks pretty sketchy, the rails are sticky. I think they wanted to make big kickers and it's not really good for riders and it's not really safe. I just don't want to get injured. It's not really a fun course to ride.'

The media soon picked up this ball and ran with it. All of us, as slopestyle competitors, were bombarded with questions trying to get us to say the course was crap. I always avoided answering them. From my perspective the course was decent and I didn't want to be insincere. It may have needed adjustments or tweaks, but this is completely normal. I didn't get what all the negativity was about.

Behind the scenes, everyone was whispering and getting agitated. In fact, such was the level of concern that when the course builder, a Swede called Anders Forsell who worked for the FIS, went back out with a work crew to trim the tops of the jumps, add snow to the knuckles of each landing and smooth the transitions, the media again carried it as a big story. I felt sorry for him. This process is standard at most slopestyle competitions and it's common for the course to be modified up until the last minute. I saw it as another symptom of slopestyle's novelty status. As a brand-new Olympic event, even some of the snowsports crowd didn't properly understand it. Forsell became a controversial figure in the media, even giving interviews where he defended his design by saying that the Sochi weather was warmer than normal for a snowpark, so he created big jumps as a precaution against melting.

We spoke about it within our team and felt it was a storm in a teacup. The rails were on the big side and the jumps were also big, but it's an Olympic slopestyle event, so what did people want?

All of this created an atmosphere of even greater tension than there would have been usually. This was already the first-ever Olympic slopestyle competition and the internal dialogue was babbling away in my inner ear, purely because I knew the world was watching. But the course issues added another element. I already felt some creeping doubts as my front dub 10 wasn't a solid trick for me yet. Now I would also have to pull it off on a bigger-than-average jump. Despite that, I headed into the competition in positive mood. Slopestyle was literally the first event held at the Olympics, so once we had a couple of days of practice in the bag, there was no more time for analysis. We were on.

The Olympics ran a three-round competition: qualifiers, semis and a final. Slopestyle rules dictated that we got two runs, and whichever scored the highest was kept as your score. When the time came for my qualifier, in truth I was absolutely shitting it. My heat was full of huge names: Mark McMorris (Canada), Yuki Kadono (Japan), Chas Guldemond (USA) and Scottie James (Australia). My old imposter syndrome kicked in, big time.

The draw was made, and as luck (or bad luck) would have it, I came out first, meaning I was the first rider in the first competition of the Olympic Games. Perhaps it played into my hands by not giving me the opportunity to overthink, but I dropped in and smashed it. I performed the standard run I worked out with Hamish for the X Games but swapped the front 10 out for a front 7, to make things easier on myself. A day later the same thing happened in the semi-final, where a near-perfect run of 90.75 saw me placed first.

In the weird psychology of these situations, my strong first run made me even more gung-ho for the second. If planning things logically, I would have taken the view that with qualification assured, there was no point taking risks, but if anything, the effect was the opposite. Knowing that barring a freak second round in which everyone rode out of their skins I was assured of a place in the final freed me.

Behind the scenes Hamish had urged caution, but as I stood with the official at the top of the slope, waiting to take my run, as I got that tunnel vision and the strange, empty feeling came over my body, as the crowd and the mountains and the flags melted away, leaving me alone amidst all the white, the urge to express myself, to let it all out, to be the most Billy Morganish Billy Morgan I could be, overwhelmed me. I was supposed to be there, doing that at that time and nothing else mattered.

When the signal came, I flew down into the drop, breezed the first rails, locking on to them perfectly, then threw a smooth backside rodeo off the cannon. That wasn't straightforward at all. It was a hard trick on that feature, but I landed it perfectly. The next couple of elements whizzed passed in that magical way everything does when you're flowing and, with only the last two jumps to hit, I knew this was my best slopestyle run ever. I chucked a cab triple underflip off the first and landed it, then flew into the second exhilarated, barely conscious, doing and feeling but not thinking. I launched into a frontside 10 but ended up short of rotation on the landing. The compression jolted through my ligament-less knee and I touched down with one hand.

Suddenly, all the flow and stoke and euphoria building inside me abated, as if every gland in my brain that had been pumping out hormones stopped at the same time. I came down off the cocktail of internal drugs in my system and looked around at the crowd, aware of them again. Colin Holden (the clipboard of power) was there waving his distinctive three-and-a-half-fingered hand in the air. (He lost some fingers in a mysterious accident when he was younger.) For a moment, I caught his eye. It felt like that moment at the end of the night in a club, when they switch the lights on and you know you're going home. The sky was grey. The magic had gone. If only I had kept my hands off the ground it would have been an unbelievable run. If only, but no. I shrugged and trudged away.

We had a couple of days to relax between the semi and the final. Jamie qualified too, which meant I had a homie to ride with and made it a great outcome for UK Park and Pipe. I was stoked to be in the final, which was the result I had been aiming for, but now I found myself there, I could relax and enjoy it. A weight had been lifted from my shoulders.

On the day of the final, conditions were perfect again. The weather was bang on and the course ran smooth and fast. There had been some fresh snow, making the ground soft rather than icy. The complaints from the beginning of the Games were forgotten and we seemed set for a great competition.

We chatted with Hamish in the athletes' waiting area. As always, in a two-run contest, the idea was to start solid, get a mark on the board in the first run, then you can really let go in the second. I felt I was riding well, but at the same time had no jitters or nerves or anything. You need a bit of that beforehand to get you into the right mental state. You need fear to get into flow. But I just stood chatting with Hamish and Jamie in a condition of strange calmness.

On my first run, I opened up with a mistake, coming off early from the first rail, then got myself together again, only to fall on the backside rodeo off the cannon. It being a throwaway run and the whole world watching, I picked myself up and tried a backside 1620 on the last jump, probably because I had nothing to lose. It was my biggest backside trick and I had only done it once before, but pulled it off, slapping the floor when I landed. If I needed it on another run it was worth having a practice shot. The crowd went bonkers when I landed it, but the fall and other mistakes made it a poor run and the judges gave me just 38 points. To cap it off, I wrenched my elbow a bit on the back 16.

On my second run I managed the rails nicely enough but got overexcited and went super big on the front 10. I bounced off the ground and heard the crowd moan. That was it. I was done.

In the end, I finished tenth, and in truth can't even say I was disappointed. I was so happy to have made it in the final, which had been my original goal. Jamie nailed his run containing both a frontside and backside 14 and came sixth, so it was considered a strong showing from the Brits. To cap it off, Jenny Jones won bronze in the women's event, becoming the first British athlete to win a medal on snow and an incredible inspiration for us all. Jenny's outstanding result really brought it home to me. She had been a top performer for years and achieved great results at the X Games, but to see a Brit actually win an Olympic medal proved to all of us that it was possible. She had worked so hard for so long and actually pulled it off. We could throw our hats in the ring with the Canadians and Scandinavians and even compete with them. Jenny proved that.

Hamish, Lesley and the whole team were ecstatic with the medal. It really showed we were going places. The mechanisms were working and that would mean there would be less resistance and more support from the authorities in future.

Afterwards, Jamie and I were interviewed live by the BBC, and at the time I remember just feeling relieved it was over. The Olympics had loomed so large over my life since they were announced, and it would be nice to go back to talking and thinking about something else again. With Jamie smiling magnanimously beside me, I tried to explain what had happened to an interviewer who clearly expected me to be gutted. That pre-Games tag of 'British medal hopeful' still weighed heavily on my shoulders. Quite simply, having fallen on my first run, it was a 'go big or go home' type situation, but I couldn't make it work. I tried to articulate that for the camera.

'I knew that maybe if I landed my run, it'd put me up there on the podium,' I said into the microphone, smiling. 'So, I just thought, I'll just huck it!'

The interviewer nodded awkwardly and there was a pause as Jamie and I stood there grinning away like idiots. We were completely unaware, as we waited on the side of the mountain, but the producers were going mental in the interviewer's earpiece and duly cut the transmission. BBC pictures reverted back to Hazel Irvine in the studio, who shook her head and issued a solemn apology to viewers for my 'offensive language'.

As we left the slope and headed back to the athletes' village, I found myself embroiled in a frenzy of controversy. There had always been this suspicion that snowboarders were wild and unpredictable and, according to some people, I was supposed to be one of the wilder ones, but using the F-word on a live BBC broadcast in the middle of the day? When children could be watching? What sort of example was this? This was a serious disciplinary matter. It wasn't the conduct expected of an Olympian! The establishment were outraged.

Of course, anyone who knew anything about snowboard terminology knew that I had said 'huck' not 'fuck', and that although they were very close rhymes, the two words had quite different meanings. 'Hucking yourself', in our lingo, simply meant to relinquish your fear and throw your body wholeheartedly into your run without fear for potential consequences. Replace that first 'h' with an 'f' and … well, I don't think I need to explain that.

'Go on dude, just huck it!' It was a phrase we used literally every day.

Fortunately, the online snowboard community came to my rescue and the BBC website, along with their social media channels, were deluged with messages explaining what I actually said and what it meant.

There was something very interesting about the whole thing and not just because it showed a level of prejudice towards snowboarders. 'Huck it', after all, really denotes a strengthening of resolve, a determination to go all out. It's a casual, slang way of saying you're all in. Do or die. On the other hand, in the same context, 'fuck it' would mean you're giving up if anything. They were pretty much opposites. That meant not only did the BBC think I had used profanity on air, but they also misrepresented my message. I hadn't given up at all, I had put my body on the line for one last shot at glory.

Happily, the misunderstanding was cleared up and I was absolved of wrongdoing. My friend, Jim Stewart at Butta Waxboard (a wax company), had some 'Just Huck It!' T-shirts made up. We all wore them around for a while.

As slopestyle was one of the first events at the Olympics, we then had the whole of the rest of the Games to really make the most of it without the looming dread of competition. We checked out loads of other sports and I particularly enjoyed the figure skating, which has a lot in common with acro. The British pair of Nick Buckland and Penny Coomes especially captured my imagination. They skated well and were unfortunate to only finish tenth, as I had.

The Games finished with a massive after-party in a three-floor club. The bottom floor was open to the public, the middle floor only for those with Olympic credentials and the top floor was for VIPs. At some point during the usual booze binge, I went to the toilet and found the seat was broken, so I decided to pick it up and wear it around my neck. I re-emerged back on to the dance floor area with it to rave it up with all the spectators, wearing the toilet seat like a necklace. Obviously, everyone found it hilarious and snapped pictures of me on their phones. Being the 21st century, before we even got back to the village for bed that night, the pics were all over social media and then picked up by the press.

'He may not have won a medal, but Billy Morgan finished the Olympics with something around his neck' was the standard line. Work hard, play hard; party animal Morgan, clown prince of snowsport, the joker in the pack. I guess it's cool to have a reputation for something.

25.

A Gymnast on a Board

WE FLEW home from Sochi on a high, landed at Heathrow and made our way back through the airport in our British team tracksuits. Members of the public called out to us as we passed through arrivals:

'Well done, guys!'

'We're proud of you!'

It was a wonderful feeling and underlined the perception I had got from Mum. The Olympics, through its sheer scale and reach, was a way for my snowboarding to impact on the lives of others. That was massive for me.

In the main hall of the airport, I was met by a guy called Adam Phillips from the Wasserman sports agency. I had split with my long-term agent Andy Sherman-Mills before the Olympics. Andy had brought me as far as he could and recognised I needed someone with greater global reach now that I was a recognised elite rider. Wasserman had been keen to come on board to assist with my career development and had set me up with some cool sponsors such as Samsung, who gave me a new Note 3 mobile phone. Of course, in true Billy Morgan style, I had forgotten about the meeting with Adam and he came running across the arrivals area with a sheaf of papers for me to sign as I was getting into Sammi-Jo's car. We chatted for a while and he seemed a really amiable guy.

You might think that after an event as big as the Olympic Games you get some downtime, but in the middle of the season you don't get much chance for that. I had a bit of time back in Southampton with Dad, Sammi-Jo and all my mates. We had some house parties and resumed some Southampton nightlife, but it was just a brief respite. Very soon, the cycle of flying off to this and that place kicked in again.

I got to witness my team-mate Katie Ormerod land the world's first female double cork 1080, in Stubai, Austria. This was an absolutely sensational achievement, especially as she was only 16 years old at the time. Once again, it was evidence that the approach taken by Hamish and Lesley was the right one and that our team was becoming a genuine force on the world stage.

From there, over the next year and a half I competed in almost every slope and big air event going, and in the process steadily became one of the main names on the world snowboard tour. I was never an out-and-out superstar but had a sort of cult status among the sport's followers. That suited me just fine.

I won the annual 'Spring Battle' in Flachauwinkl, Austria a couple of times, taking over from Seppe Smits, who had won it for three consecutive years prior to that. Battle was a super-cool event and almost like a fusion of the two sides to snowboarding: the video-based and the competition-based riders, with a €16,000 first prize for the winner. All the invited riders lived communally in two big chalets and it was a very social, media-centred competition. Rather than having runs, each rider had five days to film and submit their best run. The format really suited me and was so enjoyable.

After my first win there, we came down the hill at about 3pm and went straight to an après bar, where we had one too many celebratory beers. For some reason, an extremely talkative parrot was perched on the next table, which we all found hilarious. We went back to the rider accommodation, trying to hide our level of intoxication before heading to the after-party/prize-giving at the bar. Riders talk of the ten per cent rule in which you're supposed to put ten per cent of your comp winnings behind the bar, which nobody ever does. But as I was a few drinks deep at this point I ordered 100 shots of Jägermeister for the crew. Combined with the unlimited Vodka Red Bulls, it got all of us heinously smashed. At one point I gagged Hamish with a napkin and bashed his face repeatedly against a hairdryer on the wall in a playfight. I've no idea why. It seemed funny at the time. Anyway, he was fine.

From there it's really a blur of comps, video shoots and drinking sessions, beautiful mountains, resort towns and big ramps. I hit Andorra, Spain, Finland, did some more filming with the Legs of Steel guys in a few places, went back to New Zealand and Australia, where we linked up with the Kiwi crew who we were pretty tight with. We had become friends with one of the groms, Noah Regan, whose mum Gizelle worked for the Wanaka tourist board. She hooked us up with some of the local attractions and I had some amazing experiences. I went up in a 1946 biplane, wearing Biggles goggles, and looped the loop. I did my first skydive, went bungee jumping again, did the canyon swing, went on the Shotover Jet boat. Josh Birch came out to shoot and it was wonderful to step off the merry-go-round for a month and be a tourist.

In March 2015, I rode the Air + Style event in Los Angeles too, which was cool, although quite a strange event. On arrival, as we drove through the city, Hamish turned to me and said, 'We should definitely rent Harleys.'

That sounded like a plan, so prior to the competition starting, Hamish, Jack and I spent two days cruising around the city and up into the Hollywood hills on the biggest, most outlandish motorcycles imaginable. It was unbelievable fun.

On the first day of practice, as all the other athletes were driven in on the event buses, we arrived on our Harleys, causing quite a commotion. The competition itself was an unusual one. The temperature in LA rarely dips below 20 degrees, even in winter, so it's not the most natural location for snowsports. The sensation of preparing to jump while under hot sun was a strange one, while the snow they prepared for us was constantly melting.

I took a big slam in practice and cracked a couple of ribs, so ended up pulling out of the comp, which was a shame, although the LA experience helped to cushion the blow. We watched Shaun White's band play at the after-party, then burned off on our Harleys again. Rock and roll lifestyle, all the way.

It was like being on a fairground ride or something. I never had time to stop and reflect. Events wise, I won a few, lost a few, made some money, made some friends. It was a whirlwind time of pure fun, constant improvement and, I guess, to a degree, what every kid with a board, a backwards cap and a pair of baggy jeans dreams about.

Like a kid playing guitar in his parents' garage then ending up on MTV, I had come from the most basic of origins, a tatty old dry slope that was like riding on a load of turned-up toothbrushes, to the top of the sport. I stayed in hotels, got driven here and there. I was living 'the life'. International travel, shredding around, doing my thing, not a care in the world.

People say that it's human nature to never be satisfied, to always find something to complain about, but I was fully aware of the position I was in. I knew it could have turned out so differently. A kid like me, with few qualifications and no real money behind him, what would I have done? I could have hung on for a few years, earning minimum wage at the dry slope, or I would have ended up on the nine-to-five treadmill. My friends back home did various things – military jobs, gardening, office work, building. One worked in a bank. Snowboarding was my escape from all that. Of course, there were things I missed, especially hanging out with my mates at home, but what an incredible gift I had been given.

Despite that, during this time, anxiety began to creep in around the edges of all the fun. Quite often the fear got to me – the fear of serious injury, or even death. It didn't come to me on the mountain because I didn't allow it to. Up there you might even use your fear to access the 'flow state', but once you're in it, as soon as you're flying, fear is forgotten. The times when the fear ate me up were my times alone. I would lie in bed, sleepless for hours, especially in the run-up to a big competition. I think partly that explains why I liked to party and get wasted so much, too. Maybe it's why most snowboarders do. As much as anything else, it was a distraction.

When you're riding or getting drunk, that inner voice is silenced. It's when you're staring at the ceiling, thinking about what you'll try to pull off tomorrow that it comes. If you're always pushing it, stretching your boundaries, especially if it's something major, something you've never done before, there's uncertainty. You don't really know. You don't know if you can do it. You don't know if you'll be okay. No one does. That's the worst bit. Sometimes I suffered insomnia for weeks, somehow nodding off, then waking up with debates raging in my head, devils on one shoulder, angels on the other.

That's right. Happy-go-lucky, renegade Billy, the one with balls of steel, the one fazed by absolutely nothing. The one who liked to get wrecked and stick fireworks down his pants. You know what the truth is? Half the time he was scared absolutely shitless. They just never put that in the papers.

Red Bull decided it would be cool to set up a video series·of weekly episodes called 'Hill-Billy', following my snowboarding life, a sort of vlog. My mate Josh Birch was filming and the idea was he would follow me around the world with a camera, 24/7 style, to create a fly-on-the-wall documentary vibe. Obviously, it was quite intrusive, and as my mental state became more and more delicate, it became difficult to handle. When you're not great in your own mind, having a camera on you while you eat breakfast can be hard to cope with. While we were doing some filming in Beijing, China, around the Air + Style big air contest, the anxiety reared up and really got on top of me. I started having mini panic attacks, feeling breathless and faint. I went through a phase where I didn't even want to get out of bed. It got so bad, I pulled out of the contest in Beijing. Obviously, it impacted on the vlog project, too.

'Look,' Josh would say, 'go and stand over there next to that security guard so we get a funny shot.'

'I can't do it.'

'What's wrong with you?'

'I just can't do it, okay.'

It was a side of my character only those close to me saw. Mortality is a bitch.

As a result, the Hill-Billy project was sidelined. For a time I considered therapy or maybe hypnosis as a means to settle myself but decided against it. I reckon that sort of thing is a rabbit hole that just goes on and on once you begin it. I didn't want to become dependent on treatment, so forced myself to live with it. I felt it was the only option.

Along with my reputation for unpredictable behaviour and hedonism, which only told half the story, something else had stayed with me from my early days. Within the hardcore snowboard community, the perception remained that I was a 'hucker 'n' chucker'. Maybe a far better hucker 'n' chucker than most, but a hucker 'n' chucker, nonetheless. A kid with guts who could throw and land big tricks but without natural style or feel for what he was doing.

As I became better known, people looked into my past, which I was open about anyway. They all wanted to know how a kid from Southampton got to mix it with the elite. I spoke about it often in interviews, how my acrobatic training helped me. The thing was, I said, that I had aerial awareness programmed from a young age, so I didn't have the natural fear of going upside down or twisting in mid-air that a lot of beginners had. That gave me a head start and helped me develop quickly. If you can throw yourself off a springboard in a gym and spin around three times, it stands you in good stead for doing it off the side of a mountain. It also enabled me to calculate my risks. I had a pretty good idea of what I could get away with.

As this information became widely known, that I was a latecomer who began as an acrobat, it led to a phrase that was repeated more and more often. Billy Morgan? He's not a *proper* snowboarder. He's just a gymnast on a board.

A gymnast on a board.

It was repeated so much that it almost became a slogan. Yes, I trained in gymnastics from six to 14, but then I snowboarded from 14 to 23. In big air they always talked about the DEAL scoring system – difficulty, execution, amplitude and landing – those were the component part of how tricks were scored. I always did okay on those criteria but that didn't satisfy everyone.

I don't truly know, maybe it's physiology, but one guy can do a trick and it looks super easy and chilled. Another can do the same trick, pull it off, but it looks messy and hucked. His arms don't look tidy or he lands in an ugly way. A lot of connoisseurs are looking for grace. They want 'gangster-steeze', like a laconic

West Coast rapper, but in the sky. The contradiction is that they also want big tricks – massive, gnarly jumps, but performed with effortless ease – that's the snowboarding holy grail. My acrobatic background meant I could use my body to land tricks my peers couldn't. The problem was that because I knew I could do that, I used my body too much.

'Wow man!' someone would say out on the mountain. 'That back dub was stomped!'

'Thanks, dude.'

'Bit wild though.'

From a very young age I had learned to control my momentum in the air and had been conditioned to flip fast. That's an important feature of most somersaults and spins, but to please the old order I had to generate it without looking like I was doing so. It just didn't work like that for me.

I spoke about it with Hamish, who always said that more flowing form would come with time. We were very candid with each other about the limitations of my technique. I knew I wasn't a natural stylist like Horgmo or Rice or any of those guys, and in truth he often made fun of me because of the way I turned or performed other manoeuvres. To me that didn't matter because it wasn't what I was about. But it did matter to some people.

Perhaps it was partly for this reason that Hamish and I began to talk about doing something really big, really noteworthy, something that would drop a boulder into snowboarding's lake. The triple rodeo had been cool and had launched me on to the world stage three years before, but other triples had been done, before and since. How could we push that on?

Since the first doubles had been landed around the turn of the millennium, moving through to triples in my era, the possibility of quadruples had been an ongoing snowboarding fantasy. It was like science fiction; in the future we'll all live in oxygen bubbles and have flying cars, and snowboarders will be 'hooning' quads.

The perceived wisdom was that as progression took its natural, inexorable course, someone would attempt one. The thing was that nobody knew whether it was humanly possible to land a trick that ambitious. What would that amount of rotation and airtime do to your brain? How would you cope with the G-force? Would your balance hold up well enough to land it? Would it be too much rotation to kill? How big would a jump need to be? How much speed would you need?

For your typical casual rider, someone who might get out on the slopes and chuck a nice backflip on a good day, who dreamed of one day landing a double, the notion of a quad was something completely out of this world. Even among elite boarders, many thought triples were the extent of human capability on a board. To them the quad was nothing more than a chimera, a fool's errand. If we, as the snowboarding community, were all Captain Ahabs, on our own personal quests of discovery, the quadruple was Moby Dick. A conversation topic, a tantalising 'what if?' But maybe something that should stay in the realms of the theoretical. When spoken of, it evoked a strange mix of awe, horror and titillation.

Of course, for guys like me and Hamish that made it unbelievably attractive, and throughout 2014 and 2015, as we travelled here and there, with the Olympics behind us, we often spoke about it. We had to factor in the knowledge that my injured knee wouldn't hold together forever. At some point I would need a major operation and a lot of recovery time. Was it something we could attempt first?

'Do you think it's possible?' I asked him one night back in Breckenridge over a glass of red.

'Theoretically, anything's possible.'

'Theoretically?'

'Yes.'

'But really?'

We were sitting around a flickering log fire with our feet up. A few other team members were flopped on a sofa nearby, playing games on a laptop.

'With the right ramp, it could be. The question is more that if we decide to work towards this, whether you actually ever do it or not, would that journey be valuable to you?'

'How do you mean?'

'Like the process of trying to see if maybe you could. Do you think it would help you in other ways?'

I thought about it for a moment, watching the flames dance. 'Yeah, of course. Long-term it can only stretch me, make me a better rider. It would make triples feel chill, for a start.'

And then, after a few moments' more thought, I added, 'As long as I don't kark myself!'

Hamish laughed. That was obviously the answer he wanted. 'So, let's try,' he said.

26.

Redefining 'Possible'

WHENEVER POSSIBLE we spoke to Red Bull about our vague plans. They were always supportive of my goals, but a huge, seismic snowboarding event (if it came off) captured on film and performed by one of their sponsored riders was right up their street. If it happened, it would be a legendary moment. What kind of sponsor wouldn't want to be part of something like that? Their only concern was feasibility. Obviously, they weren't keen on investing money in equipment and filming if it was all just a silly pipe dream.

So, Hamish set to work, sketching out plans on his computer, with the dimensions of the jump that would be needed, the angles, the size of the landing zone, like some sort of mad scientist. Often, I would find him absorbed in his laptop in a corner somewhere and ask what he was up to. He would look up, nod, and I knew. Hamish was incredibly protective of that machine and under no circumstances was anyone ever allowed to touch his laptop.

He wasn't a guy ever given to overt displays of emotion, but secretly you could tell he was excited by it. No one invests that amount of time in something otherwise, and he began scoping actual possibilities, considering locations and dates to bring this thing out of make-believe and into the real world.

By early 2015, we knew that if we were going to have a crack at it, it would have to be soon. My supply of knee tokens was nearly exhausted and the injury was beginning to cause me a lot of trouble. Although the ruptured MCL had healed, the missing ACL meant the cartilage was starting to grind. Even with the copious amounts of physio from Alison releasing the muscle pressure around the knee, it still made the joint stiff and meant, for the first time in my life, I had to regulate my riding. A couple of hours here, an hour and a half there. If I overdid it, the pain was too much and I would be forced to rest.

In late March 2015, Paddy Graham got in touch to say he was doing a shoot with his Legs of Steel crew in the Arlberg region in Austria. By then, Legs of Steel had developed from a rad bunch of shred mates into a fully fledged production company. Their projects were highly ambitious and reached a massive audience.

This particular shoot involved some wild mountains, an enormous up-and-over jump and a helicopter. I spoke with Hamish and we decided to head over there with Rowan Coultas, who had been on the team for a few years by then and had become something like a younger brother to me. We all had more than a little curiosity about the exact dimensions of the jump and whether or not it might be quad-friendly.

The shoot was set up in a breathtaking location near a village called Zürs. They had constructed a jump in a valley, surrounded by snow-laden peaks, on one of the hard-to-reach areas of the mountain. Their plan was to shoot with the helicopter coming up the valley to reveal the massive jump, while a train of skiers did their tricks back to back. As always, it was such a pleasure to be invited to come and hang out with them, but this time with the added subtext of whether we could also use their jump for the big one.

As soon as we arrived, Hamish headed over to the jump, had a good look, did some mental calculations and came back looking a bit glum.

'The landing is huge, so we could go deep,' he said. 'But I think as it's such a step up, it will mess your visuals up.' In Hamish's estimation it wasn't really viable, and because of the way the landing spot was raised, there wouldn't be enough airtime to do what he hoped, as I would only be able to see the landing spot halfway through the jump. Nonetheless, as we had travelled there specifically for that purpose, it felt wasteful not to give it a go.

My ribs and back were still tender from the slam in LA, and as I tried a couple of doubles and got used to the set-up, the pain got worse. We had to face facts, on that ramp I was nowhere near getting a quad. So, we cut our losses. I relaxed and just shredded around, had fun and got some really dope shots from British photographer Pally Learmond.

After a couple of days in Arlberg, we prepared to leave, feeling a little disheartened. It was close to the end of the season and I was due to go in for surgery on my knee very soon. It would be a while before we could think about attempting a quad again.

'Maybe,' Hamish said, 'if the demands are so specific in terms of equipment, this thing isn't so possible. Perhaps the only way to do it is to have a jump custom built.'

It seemed that the ship had sailed, so I mentally prepared myself to let it go, head home and face the knife. No sooner had I made that mental shift than we received a phone call from Red Bull. They had heard about the Arlberg disappointment but said a last-minute opportunity had come up to try for a final time in Italy. Over the phone, Hamish asked for as much information about the jump as possible. There was no point driving to Italy for another disappointment, but the information he received was unclear.

'Nine-nine? The Nine Knights?' I heard him say down the phone. He made a strange face. 'Okay then ...' He put the phone down and turned to me with optimism in his eyes.

'What do you think of this?' he asked me. 'There's a load of snow lying around at the Mottolino snowpark in Livigno, Italy, left over from the Nine Knights event. Red Bull are up for pushing the snow for our jump. It sounds promising.'

'Yeah?'

'I think so. If there's going to be a time to try this and land this, this is probably it.'

'Well, I'm going into hospital next week anyway.' I grinned.

So instead of heading home, we drove to Italy. As we made our way there, workers began to dismantle a massive jump that had been concealed inside an enormous 'snow castle', with a huge polystyrene sword sticking out of the top of it. Even as we arrived, Red Bull's crew were still reshaping the jump according to Hamish's very precise instructions. I wasn't told at the time, as Red Bull didn't want to pressure me, but they spent about £15k on that team, hiring a German company called Schneestern to work 40 hours straight, using winches, cables and all kinds of machinery. Once they had finished, they sent Hamish some pictures. He had a good look at them and turned to me wide-eyed.

'It's good,' he whispered. 'It's really good.' The words seemed to hang in the air.

Time continued ticking, however, and all the preparation meant we had just one day, 15 April, to get this thing done and film it. I was due back in England two days later for surgery. Very fortunately, on the morning, the gods smiled and we had good weather. If it had been windy, we would have been screwed.

We left our apartment in Livigno. As we headed up in the Mottolino lift and the jump rolled into view, I got chills. It looked absolutely perfect. In the morning there was a sheen of thin snow in the sky, sparkling under the Alpine sun. There was no one else on the mountain and all was quiet apart from the sound of distant snow cannons doing their work somewhere. It really felt like a moment, like something divine. A sense of inspiration began to spread through my body – half nerves, half excitement – exactly the internal cocktail you need. Stoke.

The unusual thing for me was turning up and knowing that we just had the one day to do it. All the other times that big progression had been made in my career, with the triple rodeo or cork, for example, I had been riding the jump for a while. Every day I rode the same jump until I knew it intimately. I knew the speed at different points and felt really comfortable with it, until I got to the stage where I could try something really progressive.

We headed out to the jump, and as I sorted my bindings and readied myself, there was a definite sense of tension. We had talked about this thing for so long and it was potentially a defining moment. Now it was here, and it was ride or die, maybe literally.

By this point, the Legs of Steel shoot had finished in Arlberg and Paddy had driven over from Austria too. He, Hamish and Rowan were with me. A tight little squad. It felt so right. All the elements were there and we exchanged nods and words of encouragement.

We got up to the top, rolled down and had a little walk around on the jump, just to try to become familiar with it. Some of the shapers were still out, even then, applying some finishing touches. We had a quick discussion about how we wanted the day to work, just to make sure everyone was on the same page. The plan was to warm up, do a bunch of triples, then get the guys to do a reshape, do two more triples and go for it. The crew then went to stand on the side with the photographers and filmmakers.

I headed back up to the top and began the process of speed testing. On any new jump, no one ever knows how fast to go, so there's an inevitable process of trial and error. For that reason, speed testing can be pretty dicey. Every rider who has ever reached any sort of level has a story of inflicting some major physical damage on themselves through speed testing. It was lucky Paddy was there, and with his years of experience behind him, he offered to help out.

Generally, the way a speed test works is by dropping in, as if you're going to hit it, then stopping as late as possible. You ride up the jump, reach the lip and make a judgement about what feels right. For some reason, Paddy decided to reverse expectation, flew down the run-in, sent a huge 360, overshot it massively, did a 540 instead, fell and hurt himself. Fortunately, it wasn't bad, but that was enough for Paddy. He stood up and waved his arms in a gesture of 'that's me done for today'.

I took a turn after that, went a bit slower and just scraped over the knuckle. Rowan had a go after me, struck the happy medium and nailed perfect speed. Hamish and I were buzzing at the bottom.

'Sick!' Hamish said.

'Yeah,' I agreed. 'There's some airtime there. That's rad.'

From there, I knew what I had to do.

I went back up on the lift and Rowan and I took turns working the jump, developing towards triples. Things progressed very nicely and quickly and I found myself chucking triples sooner in the day than normal. After landing the first couple, Hamish met me at the bottom and said, 'Now you need to do a triple, get it done quick, then open out at the end, so you've got a bit of time as if you're going to go over again.'

I tried that a few times and couldn't really do it. I don't know why. It just wasn't happening. I remember landing after one of these runs and hearing the shapers, who were waiting around to do the start work, having a conversation.

'It's impossible,' one said.

'Never gonna happen,' replied the other.

For some reason, hearing their negativity spurred me on. *Fuck that*, I thought as I headed away. *I can do it.*

At that point, Hamish decided to call the reshape in. I took a break for an hour, ate something and tried to clear my mind of analysis. We were nearing the point where overthinking could become a burden.

Once the reshape was over, I did another straight air as a kind of speed retest, because speed requirements can change when the jump is modified, even if only slightly.

I chucked another couple of triples and Hamish bounced up to me on the chairlift and said, 'You've got to wind it up soon, Billy.'

Now or never.

I kind of thought about doing another triple, just one last one, but the thought seemed to strangely extend itself. I stood there, alone at the top of the jump, thinking but not thinking, and found myself in that moment, just staring, not saying, not listening, just being.

Rowan rode down and appeared behind me.

'Mate,' I said, 'I'm just gonna go a bit faster and rip it.'

Rowan didn't reply.

'I'm good, right?' I asked.

'Fuck yeah, boyyy! You got this,' he said.

So, I dropped in, just a little faster and higher than I had before, making sure I stayed on top of my board. I took everything the jump had to give me.

Hurtling down 39 degrees of slope, 80 metres of it, wind on my cheeks, that alpine smell, the white, the intoxicating white, then faster, faster, faster … I hit the ramp, twist my obliques and crunch my abdominals to initiate spin. I'm generating 68 newton-metres of torque as I start to fly. Then I crouch and grab my board. The tighter I tuck, the faster I rotate, but my direction isn't perfect, so during the first cork, as the ground disappears and the sky fills my vision, I stick my left arm out to adjust my rotation. Then I need more. More of everything. More rip, more speed, more rotational force, so as I begin the second cork, I pull my arm into my chest. This enables me to turn as quickly as possible, so I can complete all five rotations (four flips and one spin) before landing. That's a lot of rotating. I'm averaging 1.7 revolutions per second, over and over, around and around, then the ground's there and I throw out my arms and straighten my spine to slow down. I bend my knees as I land and the impact sends about 200 kilos of savage force through each leg, causing one hand to drag the ground, easing the compression. I was in the air for 2.9 seconds and travelled 41 metres over the snow. But that's all done and this is the moment now. This one. Just this one. I've done it.

Of course, in real time, most of that last paragraph didn't happen. Not that I was aware of. Not in any deliberate or conscious sense. Flow kicked in and I entered that state of simultaneous absence and presence. I felt myself going big, then held on and watched the spot I had thought about. It went around four times, then I found myself back on terra firma, slammed the brakes on and did a big left-hand turn to stop. Momentarily alone on top of a mound of snow, I punched the air. I had survived.

Paddy skied down from the knuckle where he had been filming and hugged me.

'Yesss!' was all I could manage to say. I was shaking with adrenaline.

Hamish slid down the landing over to us. 'So quadruples *are* possible then?' he said. 'Who knew?'

27.

How I Killed Style and Ruined Snowboarding

ROWAN APPEARED out of nowhere and joined the bro hug. It was an incredible feeling and, of course, I knew that it would cause shockwaves around our world.

Rumours circulated that Max Parrot was in Whistler, Colorado, also trying to land a quad. That meant there was something of a race on and it seemed we had won. Once we had all finished whooping and cheering, Hamish took me to one side.

'Stay with Row,' he said. 'Let's get him doing this front trip.'

'Yeah.'

'Start going through the movements for a cab quad. And if it's feeling nice, let one go. Then you could do two quads in one day. How sick would that be?'

For Hamish there was more to be gotten out of this day, but I felt I had climbed my mountain. It's difficult to remotivate yourself after such a climax of adrenaline. In truth, I didn't feel much like pushing it, but I definitely didn't want to leave Rowan hanging. He was only 17 at the time, and if he pulled off a FS triple 14, which only four other guys had ever done, it would have been a major, major achievement.

With my quad in the bag, from that point on our roles reversed. The focus was on Rowan and I was like his alternate rider, chucking out jumps between his attempts, to keep the momentum going.

Rowan had a couple of very unlucky swings at his trick, landed on his bum a couple of times and just needed to dial it in and get it right. He felt he was short on rotation, so on his third big attempt he opened up, but lost his awareness and hit the landing on his side, skidding sideways on the snow. It was a terrible, terrible fall.

When somebody slams that badly, an eerie silence descends while everyone waits for some sort of indication of what's going on. From the top I didn't hear anything. A couple of awful, soundless seconds passed, then people began sprinting towards him. I immediately rode down, and, as I neared, could hear the most gut-wrenching howls and screams. It was obvious that Rowan was in huge amounts of pain.

'Is it a good idea to move him?'

'Shall we take his board off?'

These sorts of questions were being asked in panicked voices. Unbelievably, nobody out on the hill had any painkillers and another agonising couple of minutes passed as we waited for the medical team to arrive by helicopter. Immediately they administered some heavy-duty medication that effectively knocked Rowan out.

Ro-bag, as we called him, was airlifted away and the celebratory mood of my achievement disappeared with him. Normally after something like that we would have found a bar and got smashed, but that no longer seemed appropriate.

During the wait for word on Rowan's condition, we found a café with Wi-Fi in Livigno and began looking at some of the quad footage. It was important to upload something, even if it wasn't very good quality, and put it online, just to place our marker. For all we knew Max Parrot had just landed a cab quad in the States and was about to go public. For my world first to be recognised, there had to be proof, and a video posted on the internet was the simplest way.

We took a section of quite rough footage from Hamish's camera and sent it to Red Bull to post, while all the proper filmography went off for professional editing. That night, we were actually due to stay back in Mayrhofen and I offered to drive Rowan's car back there as otherwise it would simply be left behind. Hamish, meanwhile, got in the helicopter to be with Rowan in hospital. Still in sombre mood, I began the eight-hour drive alone back across the Alps, with my phone in a cup holder next to the driver's seat.

As I wound around the mountain roads, lost in my concern for Ro-bag, I became aware of a constant buzzing and vibrating next to me. My curiosity piqued and I found a layby to stop, picked up my phone and checked it. Predictably, the little video that went out had absolutely blown up in no time.

I had prior experience of this sort of thing, from when I exploded on to the scene with the triple rodeo in 2011, but if anything, this time the reaction was greater. Red Bull wanted a day or so to edit their footage and our vid didn't clearly show the whole jump, but word quickly began to spread of an unverified quadruple landed by Billy Morgan in Italy. Before the official video had even gone live, message boards and social media were awash with conspiracy theories, rumours and expressions of disbelief.

We found out that Rowan had dislocated his right hip, a nasty injury but one he would recover from in time. He was still young, and although the damage was pretty bad, it would all be part of his journey, something to add to his snowboarding experiences.

Yes, he karked himself and had to be scooped up, but that's how it is in this sport. Everyone gets scooped up, sooner or later.

Once the Red Bull edit hit the internet too, which clearly showed all parts of the jump from take-off to landing, I went through maybe a month of being the most talked about rider in the snowboarding world. The global media latched on immediately. All the major British and American outlets ran stories. *The Guardian* called my jump 'snowboarding history', the BBC 'snowboarding's biggest ever trick' and *The Telegraph* said that I had entered 'the history books'. The *Washington Post* said I had landed 'an impossible jump'. *Time* magazine called it 'an amazing feat', while Hamish's aunt phoned him from Melbourne in Australia to say we had just been on the TV evening news down there.

All this mainstream coverage was very nice, superficial and adulatory. For outsiders who knew nothing of snowboarding's foibles and sensitivities, the fact that I had managed something once considered impossible was simply a great and notable achievement. They wrote and spoke about it in the same way they would if a sprinter broke the 100m world record.

The backdrop, of course, is that while this was going on, I flew home, had my knee operation and was in recovery. In some ways that gave me a welcome rest from the circuit after a hectic few years but in others it was less positive, as it gave me time to reflect on some of the comments being made on the web. I didn't spend much time reading them myself, but other people told me what was being said.

Predictably, within the snowboarding community, the reaction to my quad was somewhat uncertain. There were many praising my achievement and welcoming it as a symbol of progression, but there were just as many more either picking holes in the jump itself or condemning what I had done as an act of heresy.

Lots of critics pointed out that I touched down briefly with one hand as I landed, which would lose me points in a competition event. I laughed that off by saying I was just testing the snow temperature, but others went further still.

Agnarchy, an online magazine, described my jump as the 'death of style'. It decried the 'spin to win mentality' (meaning whoever does the most flips gets the most points) as being anathema to the snowboarding spirit. Snowboarding should be about more than that, they said, and riders like me with my 'huck at all costs mentality', would make snowboarding 'much more sterile, predictable and unwatchable'.

The way I saw it was that in the previous few years spectators had been complaining that too many big air competitions turned into triple cork contests. So, sterility and predictability had clearly existed before my quad, too, but hey …

Yobeat, another snowboarding webzine, compared the state of snowboarding after my jump to a clinically obese person who needed to stop overeating. 'How did we let ourselves get to this point?' they asked. They discussed how pointless and attention-seeking they thought my jump was, before writing, in conclusion, 'Hopefully this doesn't become the standard, cause no one wants to watch that shit, it looks gross. Hell, no one even wants to try that shit, do they?' When I was shown that article, I actually found it pretty funny, to be fair.

Meanwhile, comments on the Red Bull edit on YouTube, which garnered hundreds of thousands of views very quickly, ranged from the positive: 'Keep up the progression! Love it!' To the mixed: 'Have to like it for the insanity of it, but I dread what comes next from it. I'll stick with sick methods and powder runs.' To the outright insulting: 'The Winter X Games has just become more lame than it already is. 2016 is gonna look like a speed run game play of Sonic the Hedgehog,' and, 'God damn

On scooters on a hilltop on the island of Lombok near Bali, with Matt Wheeler, Luke Walker, Rob Taylor, Liam Russel, Scott Penman, Paddy Graham and Murray Buchan.

Frontside handplant in the halfpipe in Perisher, New South Wales, Australia. Shot by Matt Georges.

With Jack Shackleton and team physio, Alison Robb after they gave me a haircut in Perisher.

Jack filming my run at Spring Battle at the Absolut Park, Flachauwinkl.

On the podium after my Spring Battle win, with Roope Tonteri, Sebbe De Buck, Clemens Schattchneider, Seppe Smitts and Antoine Trushon.

On the hunt for the elusive Quad, in Zurs, Austria with the Legs of Steel crew. Shot By Pally Learmond.

The Quad.

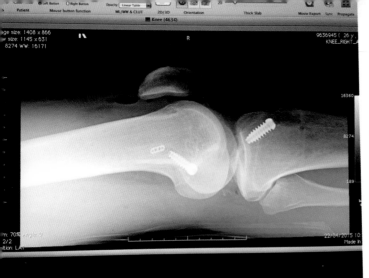

An X-ray of my knee, post ACL op.

Rebuilding strength in my knee, with strength and conditioning coach, Matt Dickens.

A way of making rehab fun, doing Acro with Hanh Delpierre, who I met at the gym.

The crazy stuffed squirrel display case at Cher's house in Aspen, Colorado.

Ripping up the streets of LA on Harley Davidsons with Hamish and Jack.

Doing a naked handplant in a photo shoot for the now defunct Sport *magazine.*

At a Big Air event in Fenway Park, Boston, USA. The sheer scale of the jump can really be seen in the background.

Season closing got weird, Wanaka, New Zealand 2017. Jack and I decided to let our hair down. Shot by Mark Clinton

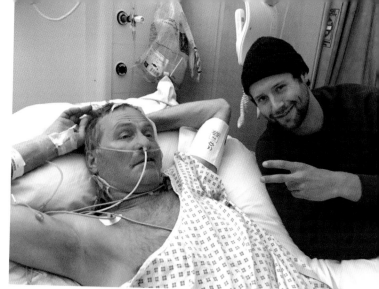

Visiting Dad in hospital, following his aneurysm.

Mum visiting Dad at the rehab clinic in Southampton.

Ashley pushing Dad on his first walk
out of hospital. 'Don't go too far,' the
nurses said.

At the top of the Pyeonchang Slopestyle course with Lesley, Hamish, Jack, Jamie, and Brown. Superstar Max Parrot lurks menacingly in the background.

During practice for Big Air in the 2018 Winter Olympics. Shot by Sam Mellish.

At the top of the run. The calm before the storm. It's mountain time. Shot by Sam Mellish.

Hamish, Jack and I analysing my jump for speed by watching footage. Shot by Sam Mellish.

Backside triple cork with a nosegrab, in the heats in Pyeonchang. Shot by Sam Mellish.

After confirmation of my bronze medal, celebrating with the people who had supported me for so long. I'm hugging Jamie, Amy, Alison, Jack, Rowan and Sam Mellish, the official Park and Pipe photographer.

Me celebrating with a Union Jack borrowed from a crowd member after my bronze medal success. Shot by Sam Mellish.

At the medal ceremony with Kyle Mack and Sebastian Toutant. It was really beautiful to share that moment with guys who were not just two competitors but also friends. Shot by Sam Mellish.

With Paddy Graham, shredding in Essex during the long British winter of 2018. It was cool riding the UK streets, without competitive pressure. We were shooting a video with Red Bull.

On a shoot for Jacamo clothing, one the many things I have done since I left the snowboard tour.

Although my competition days are done, I hope I can keep shredding for the rest of my life. Shot by Theo Acworth.

Doing these things with people I love isn't something I want to become a thing of the past. Shot by Theo Acworth.

I hate where snowboarding is going. This is gymnastics, there's no style.'

Perhaps the crowning moment of the anti-quad campaign was a guy who made a sort of online wanted poster with my face on it, with the slogan that I had 'ruined snowboarding'.

By then I had learned to cope with all of this and was still able to revel in what I had achieved. I got loads of supportive text messages and calls from fellow pros. I did lots of interviews with really positive people. My sponsors were stoked, especially Red Bull. My family and friends were stoked, which was lovely, and my jump made it on to a compilation video on YouTube called 'People Are Awesome'.

As mentioned back at the beginning of this book, snowboarding is a freesport that grew out of people going out and doing whatever they wanted on their boards. That's the whole basis of it – *do your thing*. All the different forms of snowboarding, the big mountain stuff, the street stuff, all the various park stuff, it all still existed. It wasn't as if just because I had done a quad off a big ramp that snowboarding in its entirety was reduced to being about quads and big ramps. I wasn't restricting anyone else from boarding however and wherever they wanted, and I would never dream of doing so.

If people wanted to ride powder, go ahead. If people wanted to ride street, fair play. If people wanted to hit the halfpipe, game on. So, if I wanted to go off big jumps and try lots of spins and flips, why should that be a problem? It felt like some of the internet snark brigade were the ones forgetting the true spirit of snowboarding, not me. Who were any of us to place limitations on anyone else?

I had some conversations with various snowboarding journalists, where I put my point of view across, but was always careful not to be too strident about it. To me there was no real debate to be had, so I didn't want to appear to be engaging in one.

Of course, the whole 'style versus spin' dispute was nothing new, but my quadruple had reintensified hostilities. Because of what I had done, the dispute was closely attached to my name. I had become the embodiment of 'spin to win'.

As the argument ebbed and flowed, all the stuff about my gymnastics history kept being dragged back up. I told one journalist that I was never as good at gymnastics as I now was at snowboarding. Yes, I could do flips and throw myself around, which was impressive at a party or something, but I wasn't a competitive-level acrobat and hadn't been since childhood.

What really pushed me on in the snowboarding world wasn't the fact I came into it able to do a standing backflip, but my work ethic, my desire to learn and my willingness to open up and see where it led, to pursue it into the unknown. It was an attitude that I had my dad to thank for. The ability to ignore the devil on one side telling you to be afraid and listen to the angel saying 'give it a go, it'll be fun!' All I ever wanted was to take something really difficult and get good at it. I played to my strengths and that was that.

Eventually, after more than a million views, the quad furore began to gradually die down. At the same time, I completed my initial period of healing from the operation, entering the rehab phase. I took it seriously and laid off the booze, knowing that alcohol harms recovery. I did badly miss getting out and moving, but I had to be realistic. I knew it was unlikely I could get back on my board until at least the end of the year.

28.

Post-Quad Life

ALL THE time back at home convalescing really cemented things with Sammi-Jo. We had kept the candle burning whenever I was back, and for reasons of emotional support, it helped so much having someone with me right then. The recovery period from a serious injury can be a difficult time, mentally, for any athlete. Ultimately you're deprived of doing the one thing that gives your life meaning above all else, so during periods like that you really need solid friends and family.

All around me, it was reassuring to see things continuing on their standard trajectory. Dad had got into paragliding as his latest obsession and was still drinking and partying despite his advancing years. Mum, as ever, was always there with a kind word or a supportive hug.

As soon as I was able, I began doing some exercise with the leg, under the supervision of Dean Cook at the clinic. To start with it was gentle stuff, straightening the knee and short walks. This soon progressed to cycling as a beneficial, non-impact activity. I bought a road bike and started going on longer and longer rides, eventually making my way up to 20 miles. I surprised myself by finding I actually enjoyed this. I had always thought of straightforward pursuits such as running or cycling as boring, but

I enjoyed the contemplative state it created. There was something soothing about it. I even bought some proper cycling gear, sailing dangerously close to becoming the stereotypical MAMIL (middle-aged man in Lycra).

The aim of all of this was to reach a point where I could fully extend my leg without pain. Once I got to that point, I could lose the crutches I had been using to get around and walk under my own steam again.

That was important, as towards the end of May I was invited to the post-Olympic garden party at Buckingham Palace, along with the rest of the British team. I didn't want to go there on crutches. Sammi and I got dressed up and went to hang out up there for the day, even though that sort of thing isn't really my bag. I'm not a great lover of formal occasions, but we met up with Ben Kilner at a nice pub and had a few gins beforehand. It was actually a cool day out. We got to explore the public areas and it was great to see athletes from other sports who we had lived with in the Olympic Village. The Queen did come out at one point and everyone queued up to shake her hand, which was nice enough, I guess. I hung back at that stage, not really wanting to get involved. *'Yes ma'am, thank you ma'am.'* It's just not something I'm particularly comfortable with.

Around then I started to feel solid enough to begin going back down to the gymnastics club. I went with an old friend of mine called Mike Butcher, who really went out of his way to support me. With his help I began the first steps towards throwing myself around again. I also continued my strength training at the regular gym, where I met a female Vietnamese fitness enthusiast called Han. We spoke about my background and she said she had read about the increasing popularity of acro yoga online. She asked me to try it with her. We got really into it, while the skills needed also helped with my recovery. Between her and Mike, things felt like they kicked up a notch. I've always been a person who works better with the help of others and all of this started to coalesce into a more layered programme.

UK Park and Pipe sent me a TRX machine that I set up at home. Squats, leg press, hamstring curls, then hopping on and off objects, lots of single-leg work and even an obstacle course with a box, hoop and BOSU, over which I had to hop-stick, then land, hop, hop-stick. The idea was to reintroduce the knee to a variety of movement and impact, to slowly get it as robust as possible again.

A couple of months of all that stuff and I actually felt better than ever. The combination of such a variety of training methods led to what I perceived to be the best physical shape of my life. The knee felt fantastic, although I knew I still couldn't attempt anything too risky with it. The aim was to get back on snow in the winter months, maybe around November but, as often happened, something came up that made my need to get riding again all the more urgent.

On 8 June 2015, I had just finished a gymnastics session with Ashley and a few other friends. We were on our way out of the gym and back out to my car when my phone began buzzing like mad in my pocket. I lifted it out and saw about 30 messages from different people, along with notifications from social media, all telling me the same thing. It was massive. One of those stop-what-you're-doing-and-take-stock moments. An 'oh shit' moment. Not in a bad way but in a significant, this-changes-everything way.

The International Olympic Committee had issued a press release definitively confirming a rumour that had circulated since the previous year. For the next Winter Olympics, slated for Pyeongchang, South Korea in 2018, big air would be included as an event.

I had never made Olympic success my ultimate goal and was already pleased with what I had achieved in the sport, but Sochi had shown me how much the Olympics meant to others. While there were never any guarantees with anything, and I was competitive in both, I knew that in a competition format my chances in big air were far greater than slopestyle. This could be a massive, massive opportunity.

For the next few months, I continued rehab with Dean and kept a low profile. By October I felt strong enough for a jaunt out to Stubai in Austria to give the knee a proper test. I hooked up with Ham, Jack and the rest of the guys, which was amazing. Riding back up on the lift for the first time choked me up a little as I gazed out over the peaks. I was home again.

For a few days I stayed away from jumps or rails and just rode piste with Alison. She kept the reins on me and helped managed my knee, especially the swelling. She had always been good to talk to about family and relationship issues and felt like my travelling mum. By the end of that trip, I progressed to little rails and boxes, which the knee withstood. Of course, by then I was absolutely frothing to get back on it. It was almost as if I had joined the team anew, for a second time, and could see the progression some of the other riders had made while I had been gone. The whole trip was refreshing. I felt good for the winter and was sure I was going to be ready.

But something did bother me while I was there. Something more important than my knee or how I would prepare for the next Olympic Games. There were places where rock was visible, where I knew there had been ice and snow on my last visit. Perhaps because I was more relaxed, just riding, not so focused on my tricks, it gave me more time to see. Sometimes I would look across the valley at the other slopes and notice great stripes of grey beneath the ice. Our world was clearly and quickly changing.

Occasionally I had conversations with other riders who had all noticed the same thing. There seemed little doubt that over the years, the snow and ice had thinned.

Of course, we had all heard about the effects of CO_2 emissions, of the seriousness of global warming, but seeing its results with your own eyes was something else. That part of Austria is one of the most renowned snowsport spots in the world, an area of incredible natural beauty. People had been skiing there for centuries. But it was absolutely undeniable. The Stubai glacier was shrinking.

29.

Back on the Grind

CHRISTMAS OF 2015 was spent in Breckenridge with the team. Sammi-Jo came out for the six-week stint this time and I loved having the opportunity to properly show her this part of my life. I had such a long lay-off the previous year that I didn't want any more downtime for a while. I felt I wanted to get back on it, find my form again and maybe even up my game.

In early January it got pretty stormy in Colorado, meaning mountain riding had to be suspended. Not wanting to sit and twiddle his thumbs, Hamish had the idea to set up a little jump in the back garden of the house we were staying in, which was great fun. Adam, my new agent, had set up a sponsorship with Chipotle, the Mexican burrito company, which gave us a free party, with a massive spread of food and drink for a one-off event. I booked it in and a day of chucking backflips in the garden turned into an evening with a bunch of American, Kiwi and other riders joining us at our place for hot sauce and beer. Things got pretty loose and at some point after the meal we threw Tim-Kevin Ravnjak, a Slovenian kid known as TKR, off the first-floor balcony into the snow. The next morning, I woke up fuzzy-headed, checked my emails on my laptop, and had another of those stop-what-you're-doing-moments: 'X Games Oslo 2016 invitation'.

My hangover disappeared in an instant, replaced by butterflies. My second X Games. In our world it's such an honour to be invited. *Okay*, I thought. *I need to get a bit serious.*

The X Games gave me something major to focus on and build towards and was pretty much the biggest thing happening in freestyle snowsports in 2016. My lead-up began in January with the Laax Open, a slopestyle event with a €75,000 first prize. I went into it riding well, but the course was an unusual one in which the bottom feature was basically a big quarterpipe on to a bank. This was always likely to be a problem.

My transition skills have never been the best and I chose a basic trick called a 'crippler', a backflip with a frontside 180, to cope with that part of the course. I landed a few in practice, just about managed it in the heat and made it through to the finals, where I ran two perfect runs, both with two triples and a decent double cork. Sadly, the crippler got me both times. The silly thing was that, compared to what I was doing on the rest of the course, the crippler was considered an easy manoeuvre. The sad truth was that my halfpipe skills were just not up to snuff.

The event commentator, Henry Jackson, a well-known and respected figure on the circuit, was flummoxed. 'Mate, what were you playing at? You were on for a podium there!' he told me, grinning. 'I don't know what to say to you. You really need to practise your halfpipe!'

All in all, I took huge positives from that event, though. It was my first bit of serious competitive action since the injury and I made the final.

After the competition was over, I stayed in Laax and hung out with Jack for a week. We were 'ride or die' homies by then and it was a cool little time because all the other riders had left, so we had the course to ourselves. We spent an amazing few days shredding and got loads of practice in, often coming down off the mountain by midday, as we already had enough laps in the bag.

While there we stayed at a place called The Capricorn, a budget backpackers hostel run by a long-haired stoner dude called Benny.

'Ven are you going to go and ride ze powder?' he used to say, in his heavy accent. 'Go to ze mountains. Ze snowpark is for pussies, ja!' He was a hilarious character and we enjoyed several boozy nights and barbecues with him.

Benny served a special hemp beer, which was super strong, called Hanfbluete. Every day I would come down off the mountain, turn to Jack and say, 'I'm definitely not having a beer tonight. Need to take it easy.'

Then Benny would pop up with his infectious grin and say 'Hanfbluete? Komm schoen!' and I just couldn't resist. After a solid day on the hill you would be mad not to.

During that week I spontaneously decided to change my grab from a mute grab to a nose grab on my BS triples. The mute grab was too standard at that time so it would be a way to differentiate myself from the crowd. I was having such a good week, so just hucked one with a nose grab and it came off. I knew that would give me extra points in a competition format, which was super useful with the X Games approaching. The interesting thing, as so often happens in freestyle snowsport, was that this important improvement came about from me and Jack having fun, rather than arising from specialised training and regimented schedules. That week with Jack in Laax, for me, encapsulated how snowboarding works. You simply can't replicate that vibe in a performance camp.

After leaving Laax, I headed straight out to South Korea for the test event in Pyeongchang, where the 2018 Olympics would be staged. It was certainly an interesting venue for a massive snowsports competition, located in a rural region of sheep herders, dotted with Buddhist temples, 80 miles east of Seoul and only 40 miles south of the border with North Korea. When we arrived, they told us that recently the North had sent a load of balloons filled with propaganda leaflets sailing over the area, so the South Korean military had blown them to smithereens with machine guns. We kind of smiled and nodded, not sure how else to react. By this point of my life, I was pretty widely travelled, so felt unfazed by any geographical or cultural quirks. In fact, South Korea fascinated me. It was so unlike the shiny resorts of Europe and I liked being somewhere where everything was written in a language I couldn't read. It gave the place a mystique.

The location wasn't really ideal for skiing and snowboarding, however, sitting just 800 metres above sea level. The South Koreans had invested time and money in ensuring every possible facility was top notch, but although they had built great sites for the various events, along with a superb athletes' village, it still gave the impression of being artificial. This was a remote, agrarian place having Olympic status thrust upon it unnaturally.

At that point, still more than a year away from the Games, there were roadworks everywhere. The pre-existing, single-lane mountain roads were inadequate for Olympic traffic and had to be widened or replaced. They were constructing a high-speed rail link from Seoul too, with excavations and orange cones everywhere. I couldn't help but think of some of the famous Olympic white elephants of the past – Rio, Athens and the rest – areas that had invested masses of money in preparing for the Games only for the facilities to fall into disuse and disrepair afterwards. This uneasy feeling was heightened by the knowledge that the South Korean plan was to demolish much of what they had built as soon as the Games were over. The main stadium cost $109m and was only going to be used for the 16 days of scheduled competition before they brought bulldozers in to flatten it. Was that a sensible use of resources? Was Pyeongchang the sort of place that really needed state-of-the-art winter sports amenities, and infrastructure for moving tens of thousands of people around on a daily basis? It didn't look like it to me. But that, I guess, is the lure of the Olympics. The Games have the power to bring to a country recognition and esteem that governments badly want.

The slopestyle course they constructed was awesome, really well constructed and gave a positive feeling for everyone who rode it. Unfortunately, in practice I overshot the last jump, landed on my arse and subluxated a rib, meaning I stayed off the slopes for the rest of the time to allow it to heal. The X Games were following on almost immediately afterwards and I was a little concerned at having another injury so soon after such a major one. I got home and booked in to see a specialist, who tried to pop it back in, but too many days had passed and it had already semi-healed, so it was left floating. It didn't bother me in truth, and I barely felt it.

Oslo 2016 proved to be both my second and final X Games appearance, which is something I sometimes reflect on. Even though I was doing world-leading stuff at the time and was internationally known, I was only invited twice. I guess that's how it goes. As far as ESPN and their commercial partners were concerned, I was from England, I wasn't one of the cool kids and I never bothered to cultivate much of an online following. I can understand that. Some guys put as much effort into their Instagram and Facebook pages as into their riding, but that was never my thing.

I arrived in Oslo a little nervous. Injuries can get you like that and my fear was that a big competition would spur me to push myself too hard, then possibly reopen the injury, or do something even worse. I adopted the mindset that I was simply going to put some solid tricks down and see what happened. No internal expectations, no pressure. Of course, that wasn't how the media or the snowsports public saw it, and now that I was the quad man, people expected major excitement every time I appeared.

In the heats I chucked a nice backside triple cork with a nose grab, as I had practised in Laax. It got me some decent points and finals qualification, without too much stress. There was a lot of buzz around the venue about me trying a quad in the final. I think some people even expected it a little bit, but I didn't fancy it at all. The Oslo jump was excellent, and a decent size, with a good landing area, but I didn't feel I would have the airtime. I threw the same trick in the final as in the heat, with a cab triple underflip on my other run. It's a scary trick and not easy to pull off, especially in a competitive situation, so landing it after such a long period of inactivity the previous year felt great. The rotations felt so comfortable, I landed smoothly and cleanly and found myself in second place.

As one of the first riders to jump, there followed a long wait for all the other guys to take their second runs, but I was absolutely stoked to ultimately pick up a bronze medal, behind Japan's Yuki Kadono and Max Parrot from Canada, two of the sport's real big hitters. What a boost that was, so soon after my rehab, to find myself on a podium at an X Games with those two. I did feel a little fortunate, as in truth I had held back slightly, but a medal is a medal. Up to that point the only other Brits to pick up X Games medals were the legends Jenny Jones and Woodsy Woods, a cool little club to join.

The rest of the season passed much like the previous two. Once you're on that World Cup circuit, everything becomes a bit of a blur. Compete-party-travel-practise-compete-party-travel-practise; Austria-Canada-New Zealand-USA-various spots in the Alps, all mixed up between video shoots, sponsor meet-ups and interviews. With the Olympics themselves happening so early in 2018, the plan for winter 2016 into 2017 was to consolidate, keep my slopestyle and big air ticking over, as I would be competing in both, and stay on the grind. I felt like a veteran by this stage, and purely in terms of age, I suppose I was. At 28 I was at least five years older than most other guys out there.

Having done several years on the circuit, I knew what it was like, going from place to place, week after week, racking up ranking points. I had been to all the big ones already so felt prepared. I came third in a World Cup event in Špindlerův (a great event for the Brits in which Jamie Nicholls took gold with an epic run and Katie Ormerod came second in the women's event), third in another at Mönchengladbach and second in Spring Battle at Kaunertal. Things were looking good.

I also knew the closer we got to the Games, the more hyped up the media would get. Now I had done the quad *and* won an X Games medal, that old 'Brit medal hopeful' tag would be even weightier than last time.

30.

Brains and Knees

I DON'T know whether it was the added pressure or maybe residual anxiety from my injuries, but I went through another psychological wobble towards the end of the 2016–17 season. I rode in a grim event in Quebec, Canada, where conditions were awful, freezing cold and icy. It felt unsafe, even more so than usual, and I restrained myself on purpose, not wanting to get hurt.

Shortly after, I was back in Sierra Nevada, Spain for an FIS World Cup event and found myself sinking, emotionally. It's not that anything bad happened. That particular event actually held very positive associations for me, as it had been my first-ever World Cup podium finish back in 2013, but my tricks weren't flowing and I just wasn't feeling it. I spoke to Hamish after the heats.

'You know what, Ham,' I said, 'I just don't want to do it.'

'How come? Are you jet-lagged?'

I shrugged. 'I'm just not feeling it.'

I was fortunate to have an understanding coach. Some team managers in some sports would tear strips off athletes who showed that kind of attitude. But Hamish always understood the psychology of snowboarding, the need for flow and stoke, without which it just doesn't work.

'Alright,' he said. 'Sack it off then. We'll go down to Malaga for a few days.'

It was so refreshing to leave the circuit behind, spend some time on the beach and re-energise. It also proved to be an excellent decision from Hamish. In my next event, the Cardrona World Cup in New Zealand, I made the final and picked up further points, meaning my place in South Korea was assured.

I went back to Southampton, where Sammi-Jo and all my old mates helped me relax and prepare for what was coming. The 2017–18 season was all about the Games, simple as that. Hamish and Lesley carefully decided the events we needed to compete at. Everything felt very targeted.

Back at home, old Mad Eddie had been up to his usual shenanigans – a few nights out, plenty of things he shouldn't have been doing in his sixties – then took himself off for a bit of hang-gliding. He had been out for a session near Brighton, literally about to launch himself into the air, when he suddenly collapsed to the ground. Dad was rushed to hospital, where it was discovered he had suffered an aneurysm.

At the time I was in Laax with the team for the British championships. I didn't compete in big air at The Brits, as I had outgrown it to some degree, but had fun entering the boardercross competition, just for laughs. It was a nice end-of-season get-together more than anything else.

While there, enjoying the vibe, I received an unexpected phone call from my grandmother. Grandma was in floods of tears and told me what had happened to Dad. Immediately I sought out Hamish.

'Dude, it's a fucking aneurysm, what do I do, do I go home?'

'Yeah, mate, just go,' he replied.

I went straight to the airport and booked the first available flight. On the way I thought about what this could mean. I wasn't entirely sure what an aneurysm was. I only knew it was something to do with the brain and could be very, very bad news.

I got a cab back from London to Southampton, went straight in to see Dad in hospital and was soon joined there by Ashley. Ash had been all the way over near Bahrain with the Navy when he heard of Dad's plight and had conjured a small, logistical miracle to get home, involving a rigid-hulled inflatable boat, a US warship, a Chinook helicopter and finally a commercial airliner.

Dad was a sobering sight. Doctors had already stopped the bleed but put him in an induced coma as he awaited further surgery. He was being kept alive on a ventilator. Tubes snaked everywhere. As Ashley and I sat with him, I couldn't help but think about some of those Mad Eddie moments from my childhood. Someone so alive couldn't just die, could they? After an hour or so, they wheeled him away for the next phase of his surgery, leaving us staring at an empty bed. Ash and I didn't talk much and I found my mind turning and turning while Dad was gone. As much as death, the possibility that he would survive the surgery but end up permanently disabled also haunted me. All of my life Dad had been a larger-than-life character. It would be tough to handle if that changed.

An aneurysm, it turns out, is similar in effect to a stroke and is caused by a burst blood vessel in the cranial area. As with anything of that nature, there were no guarantees, but Dad survived the operation. Doctors said the prognosis was unclear. They had stopped the bleed but couldn't tell how much damage had been done. It was impossible to tell, they said, whether his life would ever return to 'normal'. He had high blood pressure too, which didn't help, possibly related to his lifestyle.

It was fortunate, in a sense, that all this happened right at the end of the snowboarding season. I was able to put competitions and ranking points and all the rest of it out of my mind and make Dad my number one priority.

The operation went well. Ashley and I sat with Dad, talking to him, although he was completely unresponsive. Doctors told us that even while unconscious he could probably hear, and our voices might help to revive him. By the end of the first week, he began to emerge from the coma and open his eyes. He saw me and Ashley sitting there and seemed to react to our presence.

'Shit!' I said. 'Let's call the doctors.'

When the doctors arrived moments later, Dad used his left hand to claw at the tubes in his nose and mouth, as if he was trying to pull them out.

'You better wait outside,' the doctor said.

For the next few minutes, we stood in the corridor, until they opened the door and let us back in. All the breathing and feeding equipment had been removed from Dad's face and he was able to smile slightly. A wonky, weak-looking smile, but a smile nonetheless. We went over to the bed and Ashley and I held his hands for a while.

That moment of hope and normality only lasted a few seconds. Without the artificial assistance of the life support machines, Dad's heart and oxygen readings dropped dramatically. As soon as the doctors noticed this, we were told to leave the room again. This time the wait was longer, and when they eventually let us back in, the scene was much as before. Dad had been returned to his induced coma and the tubes were back in place.

'Sorry,' the doctor said. 'He wasn't ready.'

Fortunately, that initial awakening did prove to be the start and not the end of Dad's recovery. The next day, he opened his eyes again and from that point on spent more and more time each day in a state of consciousness.

The worry during those early days was that the prognosis from there remained so broad. Doctors talked us through a spectrum of possible outcomes, ranging from being wheelchair-bound, non-verbal and requiring round-the-clock nursing, to something approaching a full recovery but with a probable speech impairment.

Ashley and I spoke about it a lot and agreed that being able to use the toilet independently was a key marker. If Dad recovered enough to be able to do that, we figured he could have a decent life and be happy. If not, and he either required assistance to use the toilet or had to wear a kind of adult nappy, as he did in hospital, it would be awful.

'Dad would fucking hate that,' Ashley said. I nodded in agreement. You can't go from the level of free-spiritedness Dad always had to wearing nappies and eating baby food forever and deal with it. The transition would just be too great.

A few days after his first awakening, the doctors removed his feeding tube. He still didn't have enough control over his hands to feed himself, so Ashley and I took turns to give him his meals. He was being brought what amounted to baby food, basically, pureed vegetables with a little meat or fish mashed in, and we would spoon it into his mouth for him. As bad as it was, Ashley and I tried to make light of the situation. We made little jokes, believing an atmosphere of banter and fun might trigger a positive response somewhere in those damaged neurons. We sometimes took him to the toilet and cleaned him up, a situation Ash referred to as a 'Code Brown'.

'Unconfirmed reports of a Code Brown in the vicinity of Edwin Morgan's arse. Immediate action needed. Over.'

'Copy that, sir. I'm going in.'

We shaved his facial hair too, a strangely intimate thing to do to your own father. Grandma reminded us that Dad was very particular about that and always liked to be clean-shaven, so we made sure never to leave him more than two days without a shave.

Before long he began to regain some movement down the left side of his body. As soon as possible we gave him things to hold in his left hand, encouraging him to practise movements and grip. After a couple of weeks, Dad left intensive care and was moved to a ward. Eventually, a month on from the aneurysm, he was allowed to leave Brighton hospital and was transferred to Southampton General.

From there, he was soon moved on again to a specific stroke and aneurysm rehabilitation centre, which was only half a mile or so from his house. With his condition steadily improving too, this took the burden off Ashley and me to some extent. While Dad was in Brighton, we had been riding back and forth on motorbikes, day and night, to spend as much time with him as possible. With Dad now so close to home, other family members such as Grandma and Sammi-Jo could become much more involved.

The proper physical rehab began. The rehab centre were excellent and wheeled Dad into the exercise room to get him on to the parallel bars to see whether he could support his own bodyweight. He was under strict instruction not to try to move of his own volition, though, with an alarm button next to his bed should he need anything. About a week after he checked in, I arrived at the rehab centre to find the nurses at their wits' end.

'We don't know what to do with him,' they said. 'We might need to restrain him or something.'

It turned out that Dad had completely ignored protocol, tried to get out of bed on his own, managed to sidle along by the wall, then used the sink for support by leaning on it with his left hand. Dad's bodyweight ripped the sink out of the wall and nurses had rushed in to find Dad on the floor surrounded by broken porcelain and a small flood. As the nurse relayed the story, I couldn't help but smile. Not because of the damage, but because the incident proved that despite any physical impairment, the spirit of Mad Eddie lived on.

I also spent a lot of time working with Dad on rehab, feeling I had some expertise after my own experiences of the last few years. I was allowed to put Dad in a wheelchair and take him outside when I visited, so I would get him to perform repetitions of little exercises. I focused a lot on the right side of his body, which had been unresponsive to begin with. Getting him to wiggle toes, then turn his ankle, bend the knee and so on. As he got stronger, I incorporated some light resistance bands to help the muscles build, and day by day and bit by bit his condition steadily improved. Fortunately, his continence returned too.

At this point I knew I had a decision to make. Ashley's compassionate leave ended and he was back on duty in the Middle East, which meant most of the visiting and everyday input for Dad was on me. I spoke to Hamish on the phone and conferred with the rest of the family. Sammi-Jo insisted I should rejoin the team and resume riding. Snowboarding was my job, after all, and like any competitive athlete, my time at the top level was limited. If I passed up this Olympics, I might regret it for the rest of my life.

On the other side, Grandma was equally definitive. As far as she was concerned, I needed to forget about riding altogether and focus on Dad. Family comes first and all that stuff. I could understand her point of view but felt the truth of the matter probably rested somewhere between those two extremes. Sadly, Dad's speech hadn't recovered well enough for him to give his view, but I reckoned I could guess what he would say. Everything I knew about Eddie Morgan told me one thing: he would want his son to be fully sending it at the Olympic Games.

So, with a residual feeling of guilt, I took my first trip away since his aneurysm, in August, when I spent some time in New Zealand with the Wanaka tourist board again. As I got out there and got back on a board, I felt straight back in the mix, as if a switch had been flicked in my mind. Alongside everything else it gave me, riding served as distraction from everything that had happened. While there I focused especially on my frontside doubles, knowing I needed a cool frontside trick for the Olympics. It was yet another wonderful month of shredding and I left New Zealand feeling reborn. While I was there, Sammi-Jo picked up the reins with Dad, visiting him with Han from the gym, who helped continue the physio work I had been doing.

From there, spells at home were interspersed with other trips abroad, the focus very much on Olympic preparation. Towards the end of November, Hamish phoned me with that sense of urgency he always possessed when something big had cropped up.

'There's a slot on the Mammoth airbag in like four days' time.'

'Okay.'

'I really think we should do it.'

This proved to be an absolutely crucial period of pre-Olympic training. Probably the most crucial, on reflection. A week's airbag training in Mammoth, California with the Austrian Anna Gasser (another ex-acrobat) and Aimee Fuller was followed by more in Mottolino, Italy, near where I had done the quad cork the year before.

The airbag had been developed by Hamish and was something of a pioneering move in European snowsport in 2017, requiring £150k of funding that he acquired through UK Sport. By that point, Jenny's medal in Sochi, along with my world firsts and the achievements of guys such as Jamie and Woodsy, meant Hamish's philosophy gained a lot of credibility with the authorities.

It wouldn't have been so easy to wrangle such large slices of investment from them before.

The airbag consisted of nine pieces that weighed over a ton each and had to be hand-stitched together, then dragged into the right position. It changed the game for us massively, giving us the freedom to try ambitious new tricks with a much-reduced fear of injury. This provided me the perfect opportunity to hone an elite-level frontside trick, to complement the range of backside moves I had developed over the years. Under normal circumstances, it takes years to develop a new trick to the point it can be competitive in elite competition, but the airbag shortened that considerably.

This sort of training is now standard practice for slopestyle and big air athletes and our development of it is another example of Hamish's intuition. He had actually conceived this idea and designed it on his laptop nine years previously. The guy was way ahead of his time.

I went to work, hucking tons of frontside triples, which felt unnatural and weird to me initially, but I knew if I could nail them, I would be in great shape for the Games. While away, Sammi-Jo sent me daily updates and videos of Dad's progress, so I could see his improvements as I focused on making my own. Despite the differences in our situations and locations, I still felt a great synergy with him. Mad Eddie was getting better. And so was I.

While in Mottolino, I did manage to twang my knee again, landing awkwardly after trying the new trick. I hit the bag and a ripple in the material caused the board to stand up beneath me and spin me around. Instantly I felt a pop, some tension and a weird heat inside the knee, which made me feel slightly sick. Fear coursed through my body.

Oh God, I thought. *Not again.*

Hamish came jogging over. 'You alright?'

I shook my head. 'Help me off the bag.'

Of course, I stopped riding and a couple of days of panic ensued. At that point we were only six weeks out from the Olympics, so anything major would mean game over.

Alison Robb came to the rescue again and I was flown to London for an emergency appointment on 21 December. The clinic performed an MRI, which confirmed a sprain to my lateral collateral ligament. Fortunately, it was relatively minor and manageable, although another reminder of the fragility of the human body. At the time, I was only 28, but it seemed that interruptions caused by injury were becoming an ever-present feature of my career. A week on from the fall and after physiotherapy with Dean, Alison said she was happy enough with my take-off and landing mechanics for me to fly to South Korea. However, there remained substantial doubt over how fully I would have recovered by the time of the slopestyle, which again was scheduled to be the Olympics' first event.

By this point Dad had recovered to the stage where he was able to walk, albeit unsteadily and mostly with support. His speech had also returned to some degree. He wasn't able to hold a complicated conversation but could ask for a cup of tea or respond 'yes' or 'no' to simple questions. His recovery had advanced enough that he was able to return home for Christmas, which was amazing.

I also made an internal commitment, an unusual one for me, to do 'Dryanuary', figuring I should try to give myself every possible advantage. A month without booze couldn't hurt, could it? All this meant that by the time I headed to the team kitting out in Manchester in January, I felt good, both mentally and physically.

Once again kitted out as a Team GB Olympian, I headed over to Laax for a few days, just to make sure the knee was functioning. I had three fairly solid days there, felt great, flew home on 31 January, then out to South Korea on 2 February. This time I adopted the mindset of appreciating the little things, trying to enjoy the whole experience. Instead of feeling self-conscious walking through the airport with my Team GB tracksuit on, I savoured it. I was aware that this would probably be the last time I did this. You can never say never, but the idea of competing in big air and slopestyle at the highest level when 32 years old didn't seem too likely.

As I walked around the stadium during the opening ceremony, with a great platoon of us in red, white and blue, following the flag, I turned to Hamish. 'Mate, this is gonna be fun,' I said.

He smiled. 'I was thinking that,' came the reply.

31.

Heart and Seoul

AS WITH the last Olympics, the South Koreans put slopestyle at the very start of the Games, with a ten-day gap between the slope final and the first big air practice. I was cool with that. It would give me time to get my head (and maybe my knee) together between the two events. As a precaution, Hamish brought the talented Scottish youngster Matt McCormick along as a reserve. He was next highest on the points list and could ride the events on my behalf if my injuries flared up again and prevented me participating. This was a big deal for Matt, who was capable of riding an Olympic Games, but as it stood there was no slot available for him. We all knew that, as a young guy, there would be plenty more opportunities for him in future.

What no one seemed to mention during the build-up was that climactic conditions in South Korea at that time of year weren't particularly conducive to performing technical manoeuvres on snowboards. The slopestyle proved more or less a washout.

It would be more accurate, I guess, to describe it as a blow-out. Strong wind made for incredibly difficult riding conditions. Apparently, this is standard during January and February there. They even call it the 'windy season' in the same way that some places have a monsoon season. As anyone who grew up riding outdoors in the UK can confirm, swirling, eddying gusts are not ideal when negotiating rails and jumps.

The course itself was really cool, with lots of big features and skewed, banked take-offs, which favoured the technical, creative riders. I knew on that basis I wouldn't be among the favourites and just held on to my standard mantra: *Just put your run down. Just put your run down.*

In practice, all of us were battered by the insane winds. It made judgement virtually impossible as you would go into a jump having no idea how much force or whip you needed to give yourself. The wind could come from any direction, at any time and at any velocity. You start a jump in relative stillness, get airborne, then find yourself up against a vicious headwind, a booming tailwind or sideways gusts that had the power to destroy equilibrium in a heartbeat. It made everything a complete lottery. Pretty much close your eyes and hope for the best. Katie Ormerod, who had been on top form and was potentially on for a podium finish, broke her wrist on the first practice day, then followed that by suffering a shattered heel on a rail feature the day after. She was forced to withdraw, and the foot injury was serious enough for there to be questions over her riding future. Like Sochi, where there had been concerns from some riders over course design, there were vociferous calls from various quarters for the competition to be postponed. As is standard, it seems, the organisers wouldn't listen.

When the heats began, everyone struggled, literally everyone, and I wiped out twice. I fell on my first run, going too big off one of the skewed jumps because I misjudged a headwind. On the second run, wind howled at me from the side and wrecked my balance, causing me to fall after a frontside 1080. Those gusts were incredibly tough to deal with. It was deafening and disorientating. Game over.

In a typical contest, three quarters of the field fall or make a mistake, especially when trying ambitious stuff, but in the Pyeongchang slopestyle it was way more. That's the catch-22 of competition, isn't it? You work for something for years, but if the gods frown on the day, it counts for nothing. I failed to qualify for the final, finishing in 22nd place. Jamie Nicholls didn't make it either, coming in 16th. It was disheartening, especially for Jamie being such a strong slopestyle rider. In the women's competition, Aimee Fuller had a similar experience. After the decision was made to put all the ladies in one final, the weather was no better and it was washed out for them too. Through all this, I clung to the one big positive I could – my knee had held up. I would be riding in the first-ever Olympic big air.

With the slopestyle done, Hamish, Rowan and I had a quiet drink with Rowan's family. I remained philosophical about the whole thing. Slopestyle was never my stronger event anyway, so there was no point dwelling on it.

With ten days to go until big air, Hamish had one of his brainwaves. 'You know, if you fancied getting out for a bit,' he said, 'now would be the time.'

'Yeah,' I pondered. 'Good call, bro.'

Just as I had the previous year in Spain, I figured the best thing to do was to have a little break and give the inner dialogue a rest for a bit. It had worked for me then.

We collared deputy coach Jack and an American wax-tech called BJ, who Jack was sharing the wax room with. BJ seemed cool but was something of an unknown quantity. We organised ourselves a hotel down in Seoul and figured we would go to see some of the real South Korea.

On the way back out of the hotel, I approached the receptionist. He only looked 25 or so but seemed to speak about ten languages fluently. I later learned this was another South Korean Olympic initiative, that all workers likely to come into contact with tourists – taxi drivers, waiters and hotel staff – were sent on intensive language courses. Pretty mental.

'Look man,' I said, 'we wanna go out and we're not after anything standard. I don't want to go to the Irish pub and eat at Pizza Hut. Where do we get a real experience? Where do the locals go?'

He creased up his face a bit, thought for a while and replied, 'For four young guys like yourselves the obvious choice would be Yeong Deung Po.' He wore a little smile as he said it.

'Cool.'

We thanked him, got him to write it down and jumped in a taxi. The driver smiled too and gave a knowing nod. As soon as he dropped us off, we understood all the non-verbal signals. Yeong Deung Po was what we Europeans call a red-light district.

We wandered through a couple of streets of plain shops with dodgy-looking characters standing around. They smiled and offered us assistance as we passed. After a while we found a street that wasn't full of pimps or drug dealers, but rather strange rows of little white tents, standing on the kerb.

'What the hell?' Hamish said, so I approached one, lifted the flap and opened it. I don't know what I expected to see, but the interior took me by surprise. Inside was a display of seafood, some of it alive, squirming and wriggling, beside meat cuts and shelves of bottles. In one corner, a tiny old lady stood by a wok. She bowed at me. Two chubby, middle-aged South Korean guys were her only customers at that point. They grinned and waved as we all filed in. It was obvious from their glassy eyes and rosy cheeks that they were completely shit-faced.

Before long we had all ordered food and chucked back a few glasses of soju, a strong distilled spirit that reminded me of vodka. A few glasses of that and we overcame the communication barrier with our fellow customers, using hand gestures, nods and smiles. They indicated we were supposed to down each shot in one. If that's the custom, then hey, we had no problem with that.

From there it turned into one of those hazy, beautiful, timeless evenings where complete strangers with no common language somehow bantered their way through the course of several hours. We ate a bunch of delicious, freshly cooked food and knocked back far more soju than was sensible.

Sadly, the mood was ruined towards the end as our American friend kept shouting 'fuck you!' at the end of every anecdote. He didn't mean it aggressively. It was just an American thing. One of the South Koreans would say something in painstakingly broken English and he would roll up laughing, bang his hand on the counter and shout, 'No way, man! Fuck yooouuu!'

The South Koreans' mastery of English didn't stretch far at all, but they knew what 'fuck you' meant, while the nuance of context got lost in translation. As it was clear that anger was starting to bubble, we kept telling BJ to tone it down, but the guy was way too smashed to care. Eventually one of the South Koreans had to restrain the other to prevent a fight and we decided at that point the time had come to say goodbye.

The next few days went off in a less boozy fashion, exploring, eating weird stuff. We visited a couple of temples and marketplaces and other typically tourist stuff, but most importantly I achieved my number one goal. Respite. Headspace. A release of pressure. I completely forgot about the Olympics, the disastrous slopestyle competition and, despite the alcohol and whatever anyone may think about elite athletes drinking, it did me the world of good.

When we finally returned to the village, I wanted to keep the relaxed vibe going. Dryanuary hadn't done me any favours in the slopestyle, so I didn't see the sense in continuing to restrict myself.

Glass is banned in the athletes' village, as is booze, but I brought in a plastic water bottle full of vodka, which I kept in my room for the closing ceremony. In the previous Games we had really enjoyed playing table tennis as a means of relaxation, but despite our requests, a table hadn't been provided in South Korea. Jamie and I circumnavigated this by pushing a couple of dining tables together and making a net out of boxes and books. It was better than nothing.

These distractions were important because the expectation level for big air was far higher than for slope. Yes, I had plenty of decent slopestyle runs under my belt and had been number two in the world at one time, but all my top moments had come in big air. Not only among the British media, but the snowboarding world at large, I was considered a very live contender. If things went my way, I could be up there, for sure.

Big air practice was scheduled for 16 February and I woke up in the morning to find I had a blocked ear. The team doctor confirmed I had an ear infection, which wasn't great news and could have been problematic, especially as there's a close link between ear health and sense of balance. He treated it with a bit of syringing and antibiotics and fortunately it didn't cause too many problems.

Practice went well and the jump was perfect, although a touch on the small side. My trustworthy backside tricks were flowing and smooth, but my normal cab triple just wouldn't work. Hamish suggested I try a couple of front doubles and a couple of cab doubles, see which felt better and choose one of them to go alongside my backside triple.

As soon as I tried the frontside stuff, it worked beautifully, which isn't a usual experience for me. I landed two frontside double 1080s, then a triple, and the decision was made. That would be my alternate trick for the competition.

The morning of the heat, 21 February, I arrived on the mountain in good form psychologically, feeling fresh and ready. I saw a few of the other guys and buzzed off the vibes, the snowboarding camaraderie.

For the previous few years, the stock trick in the top big air events had been a backside 1440 triple cork. Mark McMorris had been the first to do it, in 2011, but since then all the top guys had nailed it, to the extent that it sometimes became difficult to differentiate. That made the style of grab all important. I had focused on this a lot in practice and perfected my nose grab, which we knew would stand me in good stead.

There were murmurings that several guys were intending to go for more risky tricks and a lot of media kerfuffle about someone trying a quad. We didn't think that was quite possible. At 19 metres to knuckle, the jump wasn't big enough and the landing area certainly wasn't. Anyone attempting a quad would have to get their trajectory and height correct to within a couple of centimetres or they would leave the arena in an ambulance. Bearing all that in mind, Hamish and I conferred. Naturally, he had analysed the variables and produced this incredible document on which he mapped out every other athlete's most likely performances. We would use it to devise our strategy. Hamish was never more Hamish than at times like this.

That level of obsession and attention to detail is unreal, but all his prep work meant he had a good idea of how many points I would need to progress. Together we decided I would go for the backside 1440, like most of the field, but if I went big, as I usually did, and smashed the nose grab, it would get me the most points for a 1440 and see me through. The 'go big or go home' approach could be saved for the final.

If elite sports strategy was a degree programme, Hamish could get first-class honours. His whole analysis proved scarily accurate.

I came sixth in my heat, meaning I qualified. No more and no less. The five who finished above me all landed harder tricks, others fell, while most did the standard backside 1440 triple mute. I beat all of them purely through my nose grab and extending my landing down to the end of the landing area. Unbelievably, I made the Olympic final without really having to push myself.

32.

Cometh the Hour ...

THE NIGHT after the qualifiers was quiet. I spent some time playing table tennis on our makeshift table with Murray and Rowan, then tried to keep myself in performance mode from then on. As usual, I struggled with sleep. I had done since before the big air practice runs but was used to the mental and physical fatigue by then. Once you get going, adrenaline trumps tiredness every time.

Olympic final morning began with a 6am alarm and, unbelievably, a shot of vodka. I woke with a serious thirst, grabbed what I thought was a bottle of water from the bedside table and took a swig. Disaster! In my half-asleep state I sipped from my secret vodka stash by mistake.

'Oh shit! You fucking idiot!' Momentarily enraged, I cursed myself over and over.

Despite what anyone might say or write about me, I was never enough of a waster to drink booze before an event. Going back to the Morzine days, lots of guys smoked weed before hitting the hill to ride. Not me. I learned very early on that my riding was negatively affected if I did anything like that and, to me, the riding was always the most important thing. I liked getting a buzz on, sure, and would engage in all kinds of shenanigans after an event, but never before. There's no way you could carry on like that and compete at the highest level, especially when you're up against elite nations who are ruthlessly professional in all aspects of preparation.

Other international teams are super, super strict. They follow diet plans, have shrinks, fitness coaches, technical coaches and various others. They have media training. Even their downtime is regulated. While my rivals probably started the day with a protein shake, aloe-vera juice, ginseng tea or something like that, I started mine with a mouthful of hard liquor.

Whatever, dude. It's all good. Don't think about it.

After spitting out as much as I could, I felt a touch unsettled; I got dressed and went straight to the food hall. Murray came with me for moral support and, as always, the sight of the buffet instantly improved my mood. The 24/7 catering was one of my favourite aspects of being an Olympian. From the first day we arrived in the village, our coaches stressed how important it is not to overdo it.

'Just take it easy,' they would say, as if it was the simplest thing in the world. 'Eat as you would normally at home. Don't go mad.'

But that's hard advice to follow when you're confronted with a huge choice of dishes from every continent and it's all free. The morning of the final, nerves added to my usual hunger, and after my muesli I made my way through an English breakfast.

'Sure you've had enough?' Murray asked. 'Maybe you ought to take some bread rolls with you in case you get hungry between jumps.'

For a moment, I thought he was serious, but ultimately, I do think people overstate the importance of that side of things. In my opinion, sports nutrition should be adjusted for the needs of each particular sport. In snowboarding we're not running marathons or throwing punches for 12 rounds. What we do takes serious mental toughness but flying down mountains isn't physically as taxing as cycling up them. Our nutritional needs are therefore not the same as people who do those things.

Our discipline is skill-based. A level of fitness is essential, of course, but not so much as to involve long-term self-denial. Key attributes are attitude, technique and balls (I mean that in the metaphorical sense; female boarders need them too). Lungs with the capacity of hot-air balloons are not really necessary, and because it's a mental game, I always felt it's important, to some degree, to eat what makes you feel comfortable. Worrying about this or that nutrient, aminos and omega-3s doesn't serve much purpose. In snowboarding and especially big air, you need to put yourself in the right frame of mind. That's the number one priority.

Feeling much more settled, we boarded the bus for the 15-minute journey to the arena. I got out on to the hill and went through my regular stretching/hopping and warm-up routine. Nothing too intense, just a few lunges and single-leg hops to increase the heart rate and tell my body that the time had come to start doing stuff. Then it was up into the waiting area and that disastrous first jump.

Maybe it was the occasion, maybe it was psychology, but somehow on my most reliable trick, the backside triple that I had landed consistently for years, I went too big and blew it.

'Fuck, fuck, fuck!' I hissed as I climbed back to my feet in the landing area. Fortunately, there were no microphones nearby, but anyone watching on TV could have lip-read my self-recriminations. I was so annoyed with myself. Competition riding, especially big competition riding, is all about producing your best stuff when you need it. It was no good chucking amazing jumps in practice then blowing it when the heat was on. That was exactly what I had done.

From there I had a mountain to climb. And I knew it. It was a terrible, terrible start. By failing to land my go-to trick I put huge pressure on myself. I would have to land the frontside triple first time, instead of giving myself two attempts to pull it off. Based on previous stats from training, there was a 22 per cent chance of me nailing it on the first attempt. No one needed to spell it out for me. The reality was clear. Odds weren't in my favour. The bottom line was that I had two jumps left in the Olympic Games, one of them on a fairly new, unreliable trick, and they both had to be perfect.

Hamish got in my head and told me to think of it like starting again. Forget that first jump. It never happened. It was just practice. 'We go back to the start,' he said.

And that's back where this book began.

I got back to the waiting area, sat down and watched on the screen as Sebastien Toutant flew into a frontside triple 1660 and absolutely smashed it. For a moment there was a shocked silence in the athletes' area, before all the Canadians started whooping and cheering. Now we had an Olympic final. The elite business had started.

Toutant's first-round effort was a really impressive start, an unusual trick that starts frontside but lands switch and garners big points. With me, Carlos Garcia Knight (NZ) and Michael Schärer from Switzerland yet to score and languishing in joint last place, Seb Toots had laid down a marker. Max Parrot, who had picked silver in the slopestyle event, smashed his first jump too, while Norway's Torgeir Bergrem occupied the gold medal position after the first round.

As we geared up for round two, the Americans and Canadians sat backstage being overly loud as always. The American coach was particularly vocal. A small, noisy man, he busily slapped his boys on the back and shouted motivational slogans: 'You got this

Kyle! Stay in the zone Chris! Red, don't worry about nothing, we're all with ya!'

By contrast, Hamish and I sat in silence. I needed to get my head together. I would need to realign my focus.

Going into my second run, all I could think about was avoiding humiliation. I didn't want to fall again, make a fool of myself and face the prospect of coming last in an Olympic final without scoring a point. I had two runs and knew one would be the backside triple and one the front. It was a no-brainer. I had to hit the backside again. It was a trick I had been landing confidently for more than five years and the chances of falling twice in a row were slim. Red Gerard went before me, got over-ambitious and fell. With two wipeouts one after the other, that meant his medal prospects were finished. I headed up to the drop full of fear.

That fear proved to be exactly what I needed. It triggered an internal reaction and sent me into the state of sensing rather than thinking. The run-in was sweet, and as I launched into the air, it all just came. Muscles did their thing reflexively, nothing was forced, everything flowed. I held on to the grab, stomped the landing and then reality flooded back with the noise of the crowd ringing in my ears. I moved over to the scoreboard area and waited for the cameras, this time with an awesome feeling. They scored me at 82.5. At last, I was off the bottom, moving above the likes of Gerard and McMorris into eighth place.

With some points on the board, I felt much better, but even then I didn't feel a shot at the medal was an option. I had to go up there and give it a rip. Destiny would take its course. I distracted myself in the usual ways, talking shit with Hamish and Rowan, bantering to fend off the onset of panic.

By the time the third round came along, the field had narrowed. Seb Toutant (Canada) and Kyle Mack (USA) topped the leader board by some way, but below them existed all kinds of possible outcomes. The Swede Niklas Mattsson fractured his wrist and had to pull out. Of the remaining nine riders, top qualifier Carlos Garcia Knight endured a tough morning with two wipeouts in two jumps, ruling him out of the running. I felt for the kid but was sure he still had a huge future ahead of him. The same was true for Redmond Gerard. McMorris, one of the pre-Games favourites, was in a similar situation. He had landed one jump, but it was sketchy as hell and scored poorly. Even if he stomped a quad on his last run, he was done for. The same was true for Schärer. Torgeir Bergrem had jumped out of his skin in the first round, then flopped in the second. He, along with several other riders, had to pull something out of the bag on the last jump to be in contention. Max Parrot, Chris Corning, Jonas Boesiger and I were all in this category. Essentially that meant there were four of us in with a shout for the bronze and even an outside chance of something more if Toutant or Mack stuffed up their last attempt.

Gerard went first and fell again. It had been a disappointing competition for the slopestyle gold medallist, but like Knight he was young and clearly had a glittering career in front of him. I was second up, knowing as I headed to the drop that I would have to chuck the frontside. As we ascended, Hamish got in my ear and whispered, 'Don't go too fast, just go a little bit slower. An extra couple of metres before pointing it.'

Again, as I stood at the top, looking out over the stadium and the crowds below, the fear gripped me. I knew I was unreliable on this jump. I had chucked some good ones in practice but also plenty of bad ones. It really would surprise no one, me included, if I screwed it up. I got a buzzing, ringing feeling throughout my body. My palms were sweaty. I shook my hands to relieve the tension and snorted long, deep breaths up through my nose. I got my fist-bumps from Hamish and Rowan, guys that had been with me for years, guys who knew me and my abilities better than I did.

'Billy Morgan to drop!' the official said and then … 'Drop in!'

I launch myself, my mind clears and I feel that I'm at a decent height, without being too big. I roll into the first cork and my hands reach out of their own accord and pull a double grab. The grab feels really solid. 'Fuck,' I think. 'I could be on with this.' I sail past the marker lines in the landing area, see the ground, get my feet down and instantly know I'm a little bit too far forward. I'm close to going over the front of the board, but just about hold it, stand up and find myself in a lovely, solid position to ride out the rest of the landing. I swerve to a stop and have a moment to myself.

What the hell? Did that really just happen?

My senses returned. The crowd were screaming their delight. I punched the air. It was really, really good. Probably the best frontside triple I had ever done and what a time to do it. The double grab was a big hit with the judges, who scored me 85.50 points, even higher than my favoured backside triple. That gave me a combined total of 168 and shot me straight up into 3rd place, only 0.75 behind Mack in the silver medal spot.

I celebrated with some British fans on the sidelines, then began to make my way out, relieved that I had put on a decent show. Immediately, an official jogged over. 'You can't leave!' he said, excitedly.

'What do you mean?' I asked.

Having never been in this position before, I didn't know that standard practice in the Olympics is for riders in medal positions to wait by the scoreboard, while the other athletes took their final jumps. The idea was that your reactions could be caught on camera for the TV audience. I wasn't sure how I felt about that. It was great to be placed for the bronze, but with Max Parrot and other big hitters still to take their last-round attempts, I was sure someone would displace me. I didn't particularly want a moment of personal disappointment exposed to the world.

From around the side of the scaffold, I caught Hamish's eye. He was smiling, arms out wide like a Brit abroad. I stood there waiting for the next rider to do his thing, wondering whether Hamish would have to go for facial physiotherapy after using his mouth muscles in such an uncharacteristic way. Rowan was standing next to him with his arms aloft.

Schärer went after me and landed a backside 12, but it was a bit tame by Olympic final standards. He was a fair way behind me anyway and his third-round jump didn't make much headway. From there, a bizarre chain of events unfolded.

It was as if I was watching in slow motion as Chris Corning, the crazy Yank, dropped in and tried a quad. Maybe it was tactics of desperation as he had a lot of ground to make up. He wasn't far off landing it either, but lack of room made the last phase sketchy and he fell. He walked past me, with the cameras on us. It was a gutsy move on his part, but it had backfired.

'Fair play, mate,' I told him as he went past me. 'You couldn't have done any more.'

'Thanks, man,' he said.

If he had just got over his board a bit more and landed it, he would have overtaken me, probably above Mack and maybe even Seb Toots too. Big risk, big reward, but it didn't pay off.

From there, three riders still remained who could take my place, all of them top-quality snowboarders. The Norwegian Torgeir Bergrem was first up, and he fell too. That left Jonas Boesiger from Switzerland and Max Parrot. Boesiger was a way behind and needed a score in the 90s to overhaul my position, which would have entailed something pretty special. He went big and long and tried a backside 1660 but it didn't work out for him and he ended up on his arse. So that was it, three down, one to go. Me and the superstar that is Quebec's Max Parrot. Him or me for a medal.

In truth, my expectations weren't high. I had hope, but I didn't expect. Max had 85 points on the board from the first round, then had fallen in the second. He only needed a score of 83 on this final jump to match me. That's a good score but reasonably routine for someone like Max. Anything higher than that and I was toast.

The thing is, Max was a proper big dog. The dude had five X Games golds to his name. He had been shredding around on snowboards since he was three years old and his father had been a professional skier. He was exactly the sort of guy who wins Olympic snowsports medals. Little scallywags from Southampton? Not so much.

Max was bound to pull out something spectacular, I was sure of it. It wouldn't have been a huge surprise if he chucked something unreal and won gold. That's the way it works with the true elite. Cometh the hour, cometh the man. Do it when it matters. And Max was most definitely elite. The pressure of the situation would bring out the best in him, I knew it would.

Like a nominee at the Oscars, I kept my face straight for the cameras, but prepared to do my best charitable smile when the inevitable happened and I had to congratulate Max on live TV for beating me: 'Well done, man, you really deserve it, great jump, well done.' Big grin.

Max launched himself into the air and then into a fiendishly complicated gyroscopic trick known as a cab triple underflip 1800. A triple flip with 720 degrees of lateral rotation before landing in a switch stance. That's a crazily difficult thing to execute properly and perhaps even harder to land than a quad. But Max being Max, he sailed through each twist and turn as if it were the most natural thing in the world. As he headed down towards the landing area it was like he already had a medal around his neck.

'Oooohhhh,' said the crowd. I was stunned. It was an awesome trick, performed by one of the sport's giants, but Max couldn't manage to hold the compression on the landing and fell. He actually fell. Just like that, it was over. All of them had fallen – Parrot, Corning, Bergrem – one by one. It was unreal.

There was lots of celebration around me, lots of backslapping and cheering, but I felt a bit distanced from it somehow. I looked over at my friends and team-mates in the crowd going crazy. These people had been like a surrogate family during my years on the tour. I just wanted to be over there with them but wasn't allowed. It was a strange feeling as I leaned over the fence, trying to hug everyone – Rowan, Jamie, Jack, Aimee, Alison, Murray – elation mixed with restriction. The biggest moment of my life and I had to hold back.

What have I got to do now? I thought. *What's the protocol for this? Will there be interviews and photos?*

The organisers had constructed a mini podium on the mountain, just for the big air crowd. Kyle Mack and Seb Toots were both draped in their national flags by then, but no one from the British set-up had one. There was a lot of frantic running around and eventually someone borrowed one from a supporter in the crowd. Mack and Toutant were going crazy, running about, high-fiving spectators, whooping and cheering. I just walked about smiling, feeling a bit silly, wearing the flag like a cape. I had won an Olympic medal but the people I wanted to celebrate with, the people who meant something to me, weren't around me at that point. This public display felt a bit artificial, like a performance for the TV viewers.

Once they set up the mini ceremony, I got to see Hamish and Lesley, my team-mates who had come to support me, and

Ed Leigh and Tim Warwood, both old-school snowboarders and now BBC commentators. That was when the emotion truly began to kick in. I got a lump in my throat as I saw how much it meant to everyone. For some of these guys, my medal (along with Jenny's four years earlier) was the culmination of several decades of work.

This couple of jumps I had just chucked would be remembered as a landmark of sorts. I took a few moments from the chaos to grab my kit bag and check my phone.

Predictably my notifications were going crazy. Ashley had sent me a video of a group of about 100 of my friends and family in a pub in Southampton, pints flying and going absolutely mad at the result. Among them was Dad, his one good fist in the air, utterly ecstatic. It had been so long since I had seen him like that, and at that moment, I felt like exploding. That's when it really got to me, what this was. It suddenly became real. I was the first British male to win an Olympic medal on snow. The sheer joy on Dad's face made me cry.

I quickly ran around the back of the scaffold and called Mum, who couldn't believe what was happening. It was 4am in England by that point but the excitement had kept her up. She was so choked up she could barely speak.

They presented us with our medals and for a couple of hours everything was so hectic, one interview after another, journalists from all over the world. From the point when Max Parrot fell and I knew I had won bronze, it was about six hours before I was able to get out of the spotlight.

Unsurprisingly, as soon as the pandemonium abated, I went straight to the freestyle after-party bar organised by Red Bull, where I got completely smashed in about 45 minutes. Guys were holding me down and pouring unidentified booze down my throat. I had no idea what I was drinking.

A couple of interested strangers, a man and a woman, wandered over to see what was happening. 'What's going on here?' one of them asked.

'Our mate won a medal!' someone replied.

'At the Olympics? Oh, that's amazing! Well done.'

I was on the floor and the man reached down to shake my hand. 'Congratulations!' he said. He sounded German. 'An Olympic medal is an incredible achievement.'

I looked up at him with my eyes in different orbits. Everything around me swayed and blurred. 'It's a brown medal!' was all I could think to reply.

Part Five

AND THEN?

'Never think of the future.
It comes soon enough.'

– Albert Einstein

33.

The Plan to Have No Plan

I WAS in such a state that I had to be pushed back to the Olympic Village in a discarded shopping trolley. I believe the party went on for some time without me. When I awoke the next morning with a thundering hangover, I received a phone call from the British team administrators and braced myself, thinking I was going to be admonished for celebrating too wildly.

'I know we're going out on a limb here,' they asked, 'but do you want to be the flag bearer at the closing ceremony?'

They had intended to use Lizzy Yarnold, the skeleton rider who won a gold in South Korea to add to the one she won in Sochi four years before, but she had returned to the UK early for personal reasons. In what felt like an incredible honour and maybe a personal moment of closure, I led the British team on our final lap around that mad stadium in Pyeongchang. Shoulders back, chest out, Union Jack fluttering overhead. A couple of months later, they brought the bulldozers in and knocked the place down.

People think that once you've done something like that, life will never be the same, and that might actually be true in some ways. On the flight home from South Korea, I found I had been upgraded to first class, free of charge. I had never flown first class before and slept so well.

When we landed at Heathrow, an old lady approached me as we were waiting to disembark and asked to see my medal. I handed it to her so she could have a good look, then people began to leave the plane. I grabbed my bag and headed for the exit, waved at the old girl and went on my way.

'Young man,' she called. 'Young man!' I turned just before reaching the exit to see her waving the medal in the air. 'You forgot this,' she said.

I thanked her sheepishly and made for the door. There followed a whirlwind period of media and interviews. I left the airport and went straight into a sort of press tour. I was interviewed on *The One Show* on BBC TV, appeared on *This Morning* and did some other TV and radio bits. Magazines and newspapers got in on the act, too.

We were invited to the Tunnel Club at Manchester City. Essentially it was several days of being quite jet-lagged and shunted around from one appointment to the next. It didn't seem real, and, in a way, I suppose it wasn't.

I went back home, saw Mum, Dad and Sammi-Jo, had my 29th birthday and realised I had made a subconscious decision. I hadn't given it any real thought at all, but just knew that I wouldn't participate in the snowboard tour that year. The desire to get back on that treadmill just wasn't there.

'Are you retiring then?' people kept asking.

'Dunno. But I definitely need a break from it.'

'So what's your plan?'

That was always a tough question and my stock answer became, 'My plan is to have no plan.'

Over the next year and a half, I tried a bunch of different things but kept myself clear of high-pressure snowboarding environments. Of course, I carried on riding. I'll always do that as long as I'm physically capable, but at the time this book was being written, the temptation to get back involved in World Cup meets and qualifiers had proved an easy one to resist.

I did some nice promotional stuff through Adam and my sponsors. Thanks to Visa I was a guest at the football World Cup in Russia in 2018, where I got to watch a few matches for free. I've never been a massive football fan but enjoyed the scope and scale of the event. I got hooked up with Jacamo, the clothing brand, to appear in a TV and poster campaign for them, which was pretty fun, and I got a gig working as a stuntman on a film in Romania, another cool experience. Other than that, there's been talk of appearing on *Dancing on Ice*, or *I'm a Celebrity, Get Me Out of Here!*, which could be fun if they come off. We'll see.

Without the constant pressure of practising and competing, I started rock climbing, which I really enjoy. I'm able to go cycling more and try different things that I missed during my decade on the circuit. Now, when I take my board up to the mountains, I just enjoy cutting about and doing what I want. I'm surrounded by people who have been boarding for 15–20 years. It's in their bones and their guts; they're ride or die snowboarders, but they don't necessarily hype about it or get overexcited. They just love it for what it is. I find myself far more in tune with that vibe these days. The motivation to keep pushing it, to always try new and ever harder tricks, has faded within me.

Six months after Pyeongchang I found myself watching an FIS World Cup event online. There were no regrets, no feelings of jealousy or competitiveness towards the guys on the screen. All I could think was 'Thank God I don't have to do that.' I've seen it with plenty of other guys, who don't think they've got anywhere else to go. They've reached their peak. They're clearly on their way down the other side but they carry on and you think 'You're just petering out now.' What's the point?

In a sport that relies so heavily on instinct, the stark truth is that muscle memory deteriorates from 24 years old. By South Korea I was nearly six years past my prime and to sustain things I would have to practise so much harder than the youngsters to progress.

Somehow though, I'll need to keep that beast at bay. The need for the buzz, for stoke. Lots of sportsmen struggle with life after they leave their sport. That drive and passion can easily morph into anxiety or stress if it isn't channelled. I think I would like to help the next generation of kids. Hamish and Lesley had a pathway open for me to slide into the Park and Pipe staff, but the successes of athletes such as myself and Jenny wrought other changes.

Rather than stick with the winning set-up established and maintained by Hamish and Lesley, after South Korea the authorities decided to restructure. Park and Pipe has been absorbed under a new umbrella called 'GB Snowsports'. Along with the name, the intention seems to have changed. A new director was brought in from cycling and, as a result of this transition, the immediate opportunity for me to coach disappeared, but I would still like to get involved when I can.

Despite Jenny and myself doing our thing on the world stage, it doesn't mean it will be easy to replicate for future generations. There's a shallow cohort of up-and-coming kids in the UK. That's the reality as usual, but too many facilities have been allowed to dwindle. Sheffield ski village, where Woodsy Woods started, closed after a fire in 2012. Wycombe summit, which used to be one of Europe's largest artificial slopes and where I entered my first comp with Steve Fox, closed in 2005. There are many more. Even those still standing are often in a state of disrepair, while snowdomes are few and far between.

At the moment, the UK is producing less than one athlete every two years who has the potential to make an Olympic podium. The sport continues to move on globally and, unless the UK improves its facilities, we'll be left behind once again. Once we get out there on the world stage, as all our skiers and ski jumpers found for so many years, we're competing against kids who snowboard in their PE lessons at school. Kids for whom snowboarding is like playing football. Kids who live near or even on world-class facilities and world-class mountains. Red Gerard, the breakthrough rider from the Pyeongchang slopestyle, actually grew up with a snowpark in his back garden. Imagine that.

That's what we're up against. But I still like to think, with my track record and the way I somehow managed to conquer those barriers, that I have something to offer.

I'm always being asked whether I'll be at the next Olympics, in 2022. I'll be nearly 33 when those Games take place. Here's the thing: I might be there, but not as a rider. There would be athletes there virtually half my age.

So, the plan that steadily emerged from having no plan is that Sammi and I bought my family home from my dad. He's going to move into a bungalow or somewhere more suited. People say it's strange that I'm buying the house I grew up in, but I always think of this as 'home'. I like it here and so does Sammi-Jo. My son, Cole, was born on 23 August 2020. I'll probably have another kid, and perhaps even get married one day.

It looks like the time might come soon for me to set up a zip wire in the garden and get my kids out climbing trees, or get them to ride crazy water wheels in the middle of nowhere. Maybe that's how all this business works. Moments, intertwining lives; that whole cycle will start again.

34.

Where Will Snowboarding Go?

JUST BECAUSE I'm not competing any more, it doesn't mean I've detached myself altogether. I love snowboarding deeply. It has been my life. It made my life and it will remain my life, in so many ways.

Through experience I've come to appreciate how freesports athletes are redefining what's possible. Lesley McKenna was right all along. It's like a form of evolution. Very few people believed that the quad was possible. Then a week after I kicked that door in, Max Parrot did one too. Now there's four or five guys that have landed them.

Even then, with the natural human tendency towards progression, the environment has to be shaped to make it possible. If you take halfpipe as an example, the level of progression in pipe in the last 12 years, in terms of amplitude and technicality, has been phenomenal. But the halfpipe itself, as a piece of equipment, has doubled in size.

Big air jumps, at least the ones where the gnarliest tricks happen, are going the same way. Some people say it's unsafe and not in the true spirit of the sport, but this is always how freesports have been. People push boundaries, and when they reach limits, they find new ways to push boundaries. Whether it's the competitive element driving it or YouTube and sponsorship, it's all the same internal drivers. The old generation always criticises the new, it seems. Maybe one day, when young riders are chucking quintuple or sextuple corks, I'll be writing angry internet posts about how soulless and lacking in finesse they are. Maybe, but I doubt it.

Of course, snowboarding progression is also limited by what's financially viable. Even at the X Games and the Olympics it's difficult to create the platform for it to happen. You have to compromise, look for venues to host events that might be cheaper, maybe in developing countries with slower economies, hence South Korea.

In the West it costs £300k–£400k just to set up a big air competition. Do it somewhere urban like central London and you can double that. Do it on the side of a hill in Colorado and you can halve it. But it's the inner-city events that generate the most money.

In the future, there'll still be the opportunity for the brands to push progression, like Red Bull did in setting up a jump for me in Italy, but it's hard to see how quad corks can make it to inner-city World Cup-type events. It's just not physically possible or economically viable to set up big enough jumps in those spaces. So, it could be, in terms of tour competitions, that we've already reached a limit. Time will tell.

Ultimately, it all comes down to investment. If the spectators buy into it, the brands buy into it, the Olympics buy into it and those organisations will pay what needs to be paid to create the right circumstances. Maybe then we'll see guys in the Olympics doing incredible tricks that have never been done before.

The American Chris Corning keeps trying quads on relatively small jumps as he did in South Korea, but the psychological position you've got to get yourself into for that would destroy most people. He has to measure his airtime to the last metre.

Land one metre too far and he's looking at serious injury. The thing is with Chris that he was even doing that sort of thing in training, with no prize money or audience. That's just who he is. Once I was a bit like that too, but now? Not any more. Not really.

These days, what I've found I enjoy is riding with people who have no expectations. Red Bull sent me and Scotty Penman out to India in 2020, to ride in the Himalayas with the locals. Those kids were really just there for the stoke. We're talking boards that were 20 years old, bindings held together with shoelaces, the works, but they were super excited to see me throw a single backflip. That was awesome, riding with people who are discovering all this, who have no cynicism or preconceptions and just enjoy it. There's real beauty in that.

For all those who obsess about progression, I do wonder why they continually fall into the trap of trying to bottle it into one thing. If you're a rider, don't ask where snowboarding is going, ask where you're going. Don't ask how it might change, ask how you might. People talk about snowboarding like it's some giant living in the hills, independent and scary, growing and reshaping itself. It isn't. Snowboarding is comprised of the people who do it. I'm snowboarding. You're snowboarding. We're snowboarding. It's going where we're going. End of.

My one regret as I look back is that my career for the last ten years has entailed so much flying, driving and general fuel consumption. It's something I've become so aware of as I've got older. I know I've had a massive carbon footprint. That really bothers me and I'm determined to reduce that now. As a result, I don't eat red meat and I grow my own vegetables. It's a small step in the right direction but the individual can't fix the problem alone.

The effects of CO_2 emissions are visible everywhere in our sport. The last time I went to Saas-Fe, the glacier looked so brown and miserable. Dachstein in Austria has had to close to snowboarders because of shrinkage. I was at Hintertux at the end of the season in 2019. There used to be snow all the way down to the bottom station, but now only the top gondola is open because the glacier has retreated right up. You could see crevasses and rocks, the bare bones of the pistes, with a lot of dark grey replacing all that precious white.

It's something we all need to think about, instead of arguing over art or sport. Environmental organisation Protect Our Winters, led by the legend Jeremy Jones, predicts there will be a 40–80 per cent reduction in the amount of snow in the Alps by 2050. Alpine glaciers lost half their volume between 1850 and 1975. That's a 125-year period. However, another 25 per cent was lost between 1975 and 2000.

That has to be the most important issue for all of us. Skiers, snowboarders, casual or pro, it doesn't matter. Immediate changes are needed. If we carry on like this, there'll be no glaciers and no snowsports left.

When I look back now on my time in competition snowboarding, my main takeaway is the knowledge that I inspired a lot of people to give the sport a try, especially kids from the UK, from towns with no background in snowsports. That's mega.

Perhaps it's an age thing, but now I'm semi-retired and more of a 'free rider', my view on what snowboarding is, is shifting. I do agree that perhaps my really big stuff broadened the gap between kids in snowparks and what the pros are doing. Those kids in India, for example, who were so amazed by a backflip, would look at the top guys on TV and see a level that for them just isn't reachable. That does seem a shame.

Sometimes, in my quiet moments, 31 years old, holding Cole in my arms, I wonder about my contribution in adding to that gap, whether it was really the right thing to do. If I'm honest, there are even moments when I see what the critics meant. Not that I think they were right, but at least I think now I understand where they were coming from, and, from that understanding, comes a sense of peace. I did what I did for my own reasons, to forge a path, to make a life, and I can recognise and accept all aspects of that, positive and negative. I'll take that with me into the future, whatever that might be.

Through snowboarding, I've *dropped in*.

Billy Morgan Career Highlights

2008: 6th in big air at British championships in Laax.

2009: 1st in big air at British championship in Laax.

2010: Joined British snowboarding team.

2011: World's first triple backside rodeo in Breckenridge, Colorado.

2012: 1st in LG London Freeze Festival big air.

2013: Backside triple cork 1440 in Breckenridge, Colorado. 1st in big air at Mile High in Australia. Finished season ranked 2nd in FIS slopestyle world ranking list.

2014: Finalist in Sochi Winter Olympics slopestyle. 1st in Spring Battle in Austria.

2015: World's first quad cork in Livigno, Italy.

2016: Bronze medal in X Games Big Air, Oslo. 1st in Spring Battle in Austria.

2018: Bronze medal in big air, Pyeongchang Winter Olympics.